Peace and Justice at the
Criminal Court

Peace and Justice at the International Criminal Court

A Court of Last Resort

Errol P. Mendes

University of Ottawa, Canada

Edward Elgar

Cheltenham, UK • Northampton, MA, USA

Published by
Edward Elgar Publishing Limited
The Lypiatts
15 Lansdown Road
Cheltenham
Glos GL50 2JA
UK

Edward Elgar Publishing, Inc.
William Pratt House
9 Dewey Court
Northampton
Massachusetts 01060
USA

A catalogue record for this book
is available from the British Library

Library of Congress Control Number: 2009941245

Mixed Sources
Product group from well-managed
forests and other controlled sources
www.fsc.org Cert no. SA-COC-1565
© 1996 Forest Stewardship Council

ISBN 978 1 84844 835 3 (cased)

Printed and bound by MPG Books Group, UK

Contents

Preface

There are times when those who work in the Academy or in public service who focus on justice and human rights may have doubts that human progress is possible given the horrors that the world has witnessed in the last century and the first decade of the 21st Century. This was certainly the case for this author after close to two decades of academic and professional work in the fields of international human rights, justice and law. Then came along the opportunity to experience first hand the work of those in the international arena who devote, not only their professional lives, but also much of their personal lives to building a global institution the primary function of which is to promote peace and justice among our human family. The institution was the International Criminal Court the historic establishment of which is the culmination of centuries of humanity's desire to promote the idea that sustainable peace is only possible in the absence of impunity, as the first chapter of this work will discuss.

It was at the end of 2008 that I readily accepted an invitation to be a Visiting Professional at the International Criminal Court in The Hague during the spring and summer of 2009. I opted for a position in the Legal Advisory Section of the Office of the Prosecutor. This choice was deliberate because I wished to understand how the early investigations and prosecutions were being shaped by the Office of the Prosecutor and, in particular, by the Chief Prosecutor, Luis Moreno-Ocampo.

The experience was immensely enriching as it made me realize that theoretical perspectives of the relationship between the search for peace and the thirst for justice in the intense conflict zones of our world must be tempered with the actual facts on the ground and the reality that the truth lies somewhere between extreme positions on whether peace trumps justice or justice trumps peace.

As the discussion on the conflict in Northern Uganda reveals in Chapter 3 of this book, the solution may be neither a peaceful settlement nor justice fulfilled, but instead may lie only a military endgame. In the spring and summer of 2009, I also learned that the interplay between desired prosecutorial strategies and ultimate judicial outcomes is hugely complex and rarely predicable, given the great challenges of a permanent international criminal tribunal in gathering evidence, producing and protecting witnesses, creating or building upon new modes of criminal liability while attempting to reconcile civil and common law methods of prosecution and judicial decision making.

Given the enormous complexity of the historic challenge laid before the International Criminal Court to combat impunity for the most serious crimes known to humanity and to promote the cause of international justice, there is fertile ground for the armchair critics to throw unexamined barbs at the Court and its officials. The impact of such critiques could undermine the critical support from the international community needed for the future strengthening of the Court and could even imperil its legitimacy. For this reason, this work has attempted to examine the main critics and present contrary perspectives based on what was experienced first hand while at the Court. In particular, the criticism that the Court has imperiled peace in Sudan in its drive to impose accountability on high officials, including the President, has the potential to cause, in my view, unjustified undermining of the Court. This is the focus of Chapter 2.

However, it is also acknowledged that those who are immersed in the daily challenges and complexities involved in the work of the Court should not lightly cast aside legitimate critiques of the Court or its officials. There is no global institution that is perfect. Certainly, given the fact that this historic global institution is in its infancy, it would be unreasonable for there not to be room for improvement and mistakes to be rectified. It also became clear that the global fight against impunity as regards the most serious of international crimes cannot be fought alone by the Court. The co-combatants must be the entire international community and global civil society along with regional and multilateral organizations. To leave this global fight only to the International Court is to program it for failure, as Chapter 4 of this work discusses.

The genesis of the work therefore comes from the linking of decades of theoretical perspectives with the exigencies of real world facts and practical applications of international humanitarian and criminal laws constitutionalized in the Rome Statute of the International Criminal Court. The result is a work that denies that there is a zero sum game between peace and justice. That type of analysis is the preserve of the armchair critic. Nevertheless, the final chapter of this work identifies the potential threats to the future of the Court and how they can be dealt with.

It is up to the international community together with regional and multilateral organizations to help the International Criminal Court become an instrument for both peace and justice. Adapting the wisdom of Martin Luther King – a denial of justice anywhere is a threat to peace and justice everywhere.

Professor Errol P. Mendes
Ottawa, December 21, 2009

Acknowledgments

This work would not have been possible without the support, advice, friendship and mentorship of an outstanding group of individuals dedicated to the cause of international justice, sustainable peace and the fight against impunity. These individuals include Phillipe Kirsch, who was instrumental in establishing the Rome Statute of the ICC and became the first President of the International Criminal Court, Luis Moreno-Ocampo, Chief Prosecutor of the International Criminal Court, Hans Bevers and Rod Rastan, Legal Advisors, Office of the Prosecutor of the International Criminal Court, Olivia Swaak-Goldman, International Cooperation Advisor, Office of the Prosecutor, Pierrick Davidal, Sudan Information Analyst, Office of the Prosecutor, Silvana Arbia, Registrar of the International Criminal Court and Richard Goldstone, former Chief Prosecutor, International Criminal Tribunal for the Former Yugoslavia.

In addition, mention must be made of the wonderful Australian couple, Greg and Glenda Lewin, who shared their house, their friends and generous hospitality while in The Hague and reinforced my belief in the inherent goodness and kinship of humanity regardless of country or race.

I would also like to thank my excellent research assistant, Michelle Lutfy, a most promising international law and international relations student, for assisting with the research and editing of the book. Likewise, I would also like to acknowledge the professionalism of Tara Gorvine, the Acquisitions Editor of Edward Elgar Publishing Inc. who helped greatly with the shaping of the contents of this book.

Finally, the greatest acknowledgment goes to my family and in particular my spouse, Sharon Lefroy, without whose support and patience this book would not have materialized, nor indeed would I have had the ability to take time off from family obligations to match theory with practice.

1 The Court as offspring of centuries of peace with justice

1. JUSTICE MAY BE BRED IN THE BONES OF HUMANKIND BUT PROGRESS IS SLOW

The International Criminal Court, which came into operation on July 1, 2002, is the offspring of more than five centuries of humanity struggling to link peace with justice. For that reason it is absurd to pit the Court at the centre of a peace versus justice dilemma.

This first chapter will discuss how the lessons of history demonstrate the link between the fight against impunity and the prevention of the most serious international crimes. However, as Chapter 4 will discuss, the concept of prevention discussed in this work does not involve the traditional concepts of specific and general deterrence, but offers up the alternative view of prevention as the creation of a global moral and legal culture that promotes the outlawing of impunity and the accordance of pariah status for those who fall outside this evolving global culture.

Even before the modern era of nations and positive domestic and international laws, we have seen in the slow progress of humankind a persistent view that even in the bloodlust of war, there had to be limits to what constitutes a legitimate war and what men in arms could do to both combatants and those not in the furor of battle. The concepts of justice in or for war termed '*ius in bello*' and '*ius ad bello*' can be traced to ancient Greek and Roman philosophers and to the teachings in the Old Testament and transformed again in the natural law teachings of Saint Augustine regarding what constitutes a '*just war*'.[1]

In this evolution of principles of just war or justice in war, through the pre-modern era, the progress of human justice seemed to demand that those who engaged in the violence of war or armed conflict had to observe evolving common standards of humanity, if any semblance of a return to peace was to endure after the violent combat ended and in the interests of a sustainable peace. One of the earliest recorded trials and punishments in Europe meted out by a local tribunal constituted by representatives of the Holy Roman Empire for crimes committed during the occupation of the town of Breisach was that of Peter von Hagenbach who was executed on conviction of war crimes in 1474. The trial and punishment, while significant, may also have been used to cover the responsibility of von Hagenbach's superior, the Duke of Burgundy, whose orders he was following.

In the context of more recent history, it should not be forgotten that the International Criminal Court (ICC) is a creation of international law, which itself is a product of the desire of humanity to link the desire for peace and security with universal concepts of justice.

One of the earliest architects of international law, Hugo Grotius, in the early part of the 17th Century linked the right of states to use violence only for defensive purposes and the notion that those who waged war with illegal or wrongful intent would have to be held accountable for their actions. At the earliest stages of the formulation of international law, Grotius was already focusing on the need for justice to accompany the ending of war:[2]

> Furthermore, according to the principles which in general terms we have elsewhere set forth, those persons are bound to make restitution who have brought about the war, either by the exercise of their power, or through their advice. Their accountability concerns all those things, of course, which ordinarily follow in the train of war; and even unusual things, if they have ordered or advised any such thing, or have failed to prevent it when they might have done so.

> Thus also generals are responsible for the things which have been done while they were in command; and all the soldiers that have participated in some common act, as the burning of a city, are responsible for the total damage. In the case of separate acts each is responsible for the loss of which he was the sole cause, or at any rate, was one of the causes. . .

The driving force of a major part of international law right up to the early part of the 20th Century was to develop processes such as bilateral and multilateral treaty negotiations and organizations to limit the illegal use of force by states and ensure that judicial mechanisms could settle disputes that could trigger wars and other violent conflicts. It is not an accident of history that the scene of much of these developments seems to end up at the European countries of the Netherlands and Switzerland, and in particular the cities of The Hague, the present site of the International Criminal Court, and Geneva, the city that gives its name to the laws of war.

The Swiss architects of the modern laws on war crimes and crimes against humanity, Gustave Moynier and Henri Dunant, saw the horrifying impact of battles on the dying and the wounded during the Napoleonic wars, especially at the battle of Solferino. They pressed for rules to limit the brutality of the battlefield and for basic rules of humanity for the wounded and the non-combatants. After founding what eventually became the International Committee of the Red Cross, the two Swiss humanitarians were successful in getting the Swiss government to convene negotiations on the laws of war that would eventually become the Geneva Conventions of 1864. The purposes of these earliest international rules that put limits on what was permissible in situations of war included the humane treatment of sick, wounded or out-of-combat soldiers and allowing unimpeded access to medical aid provided by neutral organizations such as the Red Cross. Moynier sought to have a convention drafted for an international criminal court to prosecute breaches of the Geneva Conventions, but was not successful. That would have to wait for another century and more events to happen to trigger the establishment of a permanent court.[3]

In the 19th Century, President Abraham Lincoln commissioned international law jurist Francis Lieber to draft the military code for the Union Army regarding rules of war concerning prisoners of war, the wounded and civilians under occupation.[4] If ever there was a leader who realized that justice both *ad bello* and *in bello* was required to promote a sustainable peace after the conflict 'with malice to none and charity for all' it was President Lincoln.

The Hague Conventions of 1899 and 1907 were a turning point in the move to the establishment of the positive laws of armed conflict in the form of an international treaty. The Conventions drew and expanded on the earlier Geneva Conventions and the Lieber Code to create the first substantial body of the laws of war and armed conflict. Acknowledging the growing plight of civilians in such conflicts, the Hague Conventions established some of the first major provisions dealing with the protection of civilians in regulations annexed to the Conventions, while stating in the preamble 'the inhabitants and the belligerents remain under the protection and rule of the principles of the law of nations, as they result from the usages established among civilized peoples, from the laws of humanity, and the dictates of the public conscience'. This famous statement in the preamble to the Hague Conventions, known as the Martens Clause, recognizes the possibility of a common human understanding of what is required by the public conscience of nations during armed conflicts,[5] the satisfaction of which is a *sine qua non* of any notion of sustainable peace in the aftermath of war.

The major weakness of the Hague Conventions, however, was that they imposed obligations only on states and did not pretend to extend to imposing criminal accountabilities on individual transgressors of the provisions of the Conventions. However, the Hague Conventions did establish in the modern era that a body of international law called humanitarian law dealing with the laws of war and crimes of war would be a common standard for all nations. The future would foretell that repudiation of such common standards of humanity would result in the bloodiest century of modern history.

At these earliest attempts to codify the common standards of humanity in armed conflict, there was an acknowledgment that a lack of accountability for violations of these common standards would hinder the prospect of a durable peace. In the view of one writer, the failure of the 1899 and the 1907 Hague Peace Conferences to achieve peace with justice brought on the horrors of World War I.[6]

In 1915, the World War I Allies had announced that the Turkish slaughter of the Armenian population was a new crime against humanity and civilization, for which all members of the Ottoman government and their agents would be held responsible.[7]

However, the Allies did not follow through on the need to enforce the newly established norm of crime against humanity and the threatened prosecutions of the Turkish government representatives in the 1920 Treaty of Sèvres did not materialize as Turkey did not ratify the Treaty. Instead, the subsequent Treaty of Lausanne extended amnesties to the perpetrators of the newly established crimes against humanity.[8]

This act of impunity by the Turkish government in the face of the newly established norm of crimes against humanity was noted by a future leader who would go on to instigate a global military conflict and commit the greatest mass slaughter in human history, namely Adolf Hitler. In justifying his decision to invade Poland on August 22, 1939, and send millions of men, women and children to their death 'mercilessly and without compassion' in that country in order to create more '*Lebensraum*', the greater living space for the German people, he uttered a sentence that should link indelibly the concepts of peace and justice in humanity's conscience:

Who, after all, speaks today of the annihilation of the Armenians?[9]

Sadly, in the words of the German philosopher Hegel, one of the few things that the international community learns from history is that it does not learn from history. The inability to follow through on those charged with war crimes, including the emerging concept of responsibility for wars of aggression, was repeated at the end of World War I when the victorious Allies proposed to try Kaiser Wilhelm II for 'a supreme offence against international morality and the sanctity of treaties', but failed to follow through after the Netherlands refused to extradite him. The Kaiser had taken refuge there. However, the 1919 Treaty of Versailles did recognize the right of the Allies to try German military personnel for war crimes.

Yet again, the political will seemed to be lacking and few trials of German soldiers occurred, with minimal sentences handed down.[10] The failure to establish an effective justice process in the aftermath of the first global war could well have emboldened the leaders of the future Third Reich to instigate their slaughter of millions of civilians. The lesson of the early 20th Century seems to indicate that the failure to follow through on justice imperils the prospect of peace in the future.

In the aftermath of the slaughter and genocidal horrors of World War II, the victorious Allies finally seemed to realize the importance of linking justice with the prospect of sustainable peace in the future. Some of the Allied leaders, including Churchill and the influential U.S. Treasury Secretary Henry Morgenthau, had initially persuaded President Roosevelt to commit the antithesis of justice, namely the swift execution of the core Nazi leadership. However, there was a realization that a sustainable peace in Europe demanded an accounting by the Nazi leaders for their horrible crimes before an international tribunal of law. The U.S. Secretary of War Henry Stimson argued against this form of victors' vengeance pointing out the links between peace and justice:[11]

> We should always have in mind the necessity of punishing effectively enough to bring home to the German people the wrongdoing done in their name, and thus prevent similar conduct in the future, without depriving them of the hope of a future respected German community. (Those are the two alternatives.) Remember, this punishment is for the purpose of prevention and not for vengeance. An element in prevention is to secure in the person punished, the conviction of guilt. The trial and punishment should be as prompt as possible and in all cases care should be taken against making martyrs of the individuals punished.

There was renewed determination in the Moscow Declaration of 1943 by the Allies that those who had initiated the war and had committed war crimes had to stand trial regardless of where those crimes were committed.

In preparing the groundwork for the Nuremberg Trials of the Nazi war criminals, the London Conference of August 1945 led by the four main Allied powers incorporated the Hague Conventions, the stillborn Kellogg–Briand Pact that proposed the norm of crime against peace and the crimes against humanity concept crystallized in the context of the Armenian genocide. The Tokyo Tribunal that would try the Japanese war criminals also incorporated these earlier attempts to link justice with the peace in the aftermath of the war in the Asia Pacific.

The Agreement for the Prosecution and Punishment of Major War Criminals and the Charter of the International Military Tribunal were adopted on August 8, 1945. The Agreement and Charter for the Tribunal established the criminal liability of those charged before the Nuremberg Trials. The details of such criminal liability would foreshadow the definition of serious international crimes that would be listed as being within the jurisdiction of the future ICC: conspiracy to commit crimes against peace; planning, initiating and waging wars of aggression; war crimes and crimes against humanity. Again, foreshadowing the *modus operandi* of the ICC, the focus of the indictments was not aimed at lower level German military personnel, but at twenty-four individuals who gave birth to the title of their trial, namely the Trial of the Major War Criminals. After a long and historic hearing that lasted almost a year, the Tribunal handed down twelve death sentences and convicted nineteen other major Nazi leaders. The trials of thousands of Nazi officials of lesser rank continued in Germany and elsewhere, reaching their zenith in the abduction, trial and conviction of Adolf Eichmann in Israel on December 11, 1961.

While the Nuremberg trials were criticized for being a form of victor's retribution or vengeance, the demands and foundations of justice recognized by human civilization over the centuries required that there be an accounting for the atrocities committed by the major Nazi leaders. Indeed, the particular criminal liability of crimes against humanity was a recognition that past criminal atrocities, such as the Armenian genocide, could not go unpunished if future similar actions were to be deterred. The fact that the impunity of those who had orchestrated the Armenian genocide was used by Adolf Hitler to justify the Holocaust is conclusive proof of this requirement for an accounting for crimes against humanity.

The Nuremberg Trials were followed widely in Germany and throughout the world. While Germans might have been more comfortable with a German court trying the top leadership of the National Socialist regime, the imperatives of a sustainable peace in Europe required that the population face the horror that was committed in their name and for them to willingly cooperate in the post-war effort to purge the country of the Nazi philosophy that had led to the most gruesome atrocities that humanity had ever experienced.

One basis of criminal liability was still waiting to be established, namely the crime of genocide. Although the Nuremberg prosecutor used the term 'genocide' to charge the major Nazi war criminals, this ground of criminal liability was yet to be established. The origins of that criminal liability had been proposed since the 1930s with the tireless work of Polish lawyer Rafael Lemkin. He was so appalled by the horror of the Armenian genocide, the Iraq Arameans in the 1930s and finally the Second World War Holocaust, that he began a life's work to establish the crime of attempts to wipe out in whole or in part an entire group of people, which he termed genocide. His campaign was finally successful when, on December 9, 1948, the U.N. General Assembly passed the Convention on the Prevention and Punishment of the Crime of Genocide. The Convention entered into force on January 12, 1951. The historic definition of genocide in Article II of the Genocide Convention would reverberate down the years and we find the same definition substantially unchanged in Article 6 of the Rome Statute of the ICC.

While the Genocide Convention called for the establishment of a permanent international crime of genocide, it lacked the essential feature of enforcement through an independent tribunal which could attach criminal liability on individuals in the manner that future ad hoc international criminal tribunals and the ICC could accomplish. Instead the Genocide Convention provided only that prosecution of this most serious of international crimes would proceed either at the national or the international level before a penal tribunal the jurisdiction of which Contracting Parties had agreed to. There had been a proposal to establish a Court to hear allegations of genocide in earlier drafts of the Genocide Convention but, as with those who opposed the creation of the ICC, some of the members of the international community argued that the time was not ripe for such an institution.

2.   THE CAMPAIGN FOR JUSTICE, BEFORE AND AFTER THE COLD WAR

The fleshing out of the details of any such future tribunal would be left to the International Law Commission which had also just been established. In the 1950s both the International Law Commission and the U.N. General Assembly were the prime movers on the establishment of draft codes of international crimes and started work on the drafting of the statute of an international criminal court. However, the Cold War placed severe ideological barriers to progress on both fronts and the impacts of the condoning of such international crimes were felt by the peoples of East Timor and many other fronts where the Cold War raged.

The history of the Cold War is replete with the evidence that justice is not a dispensable option to a sustainable peace either in a country, a region or indeed for the entire international community.

From the genocides in Cambodia and East Timor to the slaughter of civilians in Indonesia, South and Central America and in the Soviet Union, the prevalence of impunity for serious international crimes extended around the world and to both sides of the Cold War. The failure of the U.N. Security Council and its permanent members to either prevent or stop an unfolding of genocides and mass slaughter, such as the one that killed up to a third of the population in East Timor, would register in the minds of many of the drafters and supporters of the ICC Statute in Rome in 1999.

One casualty of the Cold War was the efforts by the ILC to draft and establish a permanent international criminal court. The ILC had submitted drafts of the statute of such a court along with a draft code of offenses. However, the U.N. and its member states had moved the international justice agenda to the side in the face of opposing ideological camps.[12]

With the end of the Cold War, it is an irony of international justice history that it was the fear of the exploding global narcotics trafficking, rather than exploding impunity, that triggered the move by the international community and the international human rights movement to establish the ICC. In 1989, the two Caribbean states of Trinidad and Tobago were successful in getting the U.N. General Assembly to pass a resolution requesting that the ILC take up again the task of considering the establishment of an international criminal court that could deal with drug trafficking along with its ongoing work on a draft code of international crimes.

By 1994 the ILC had completed the task of developing the main procedural and organizational structure of the court, but would not complete the task of drafting the 'Code of Crimes Against Peace and Security of Mankind' until 1996. These documents would become the foundations of both the ad hoc Tribunals for Yugoslavia and Rwanda and later for the ICC.

The history and legacy of the ad hoc Tribunals for Yugoslavia are in many respects the emergence of both a local and a global thirst for justice in the aftermath of the demise of the Cold War and the guilt arising out of the failure of the United Nations and the major powers in the Security Council to live up to the promise of 'never again'.

Yugoslavia, a country of historically warring ethnic groups, was one of the first casualties of the failure of the U.S. and other major powers to establish a new global order of peace and security with the fall of the Soviet Union. With the death of Marshal Tito, aspiring Serbian leaders would ignore the basic standards of humanity and use the disintegration of the multiethnic state to gain territorial and political power at any cost.

In the immediate aftermath of the declaration of independence by Bosnia in March of 1992, President Slobodan Milošević of the Federal Republic of Yugoslavia (FRY) and his army together with the Bosnian Serbs, led by the soon to be indicted war criminals Radovan Karadžić and General Ratko Mladić, initiated a savagery unmatched since World War II. The atrocities reached their zenith in the siege of Sarajevo and the massacre at Srbrenica that shocked the conscience of the world, but saw little action from the U.N. Security Council or the assembled economic and military might of Europe.

The United Nations Commission of Experts' report on the war crimes in Bosnia revealed the horrific details of what would soon be judged in individual cases to be war crimes, crimes against humanity and, as regards Milošević, the ultimate crime of genocide. He would die before judgment was passed on his crimes.[13] Over 200,000 people would perish before the Dayton Peace Accord ended the war.

The U.N. Commission of Experts on Bosnia warned that preventing such crimes is as much a moral cause as a military cause which demands that the international community ensure such horrors do not reoccur and strongly proposed the establishment of an international tribunal to hold the main perpetrators of these crimes accountable:[14]

> The United Nations experience in Bosnia was one of the most difficult and painful in our history. It is with the deepest regret and remorse that we have reviewed our own actions and the decisions in the face of the assault on Srebrenica. Through error, misjudgment and an inability to recognize the scope of evil confronting us, we failed to do our part to help save the people of Srebrenica from the Serb campaign of mass murder. . . .. Srebrenica crystallized a truth understood only too late by the United Nations and the world at large: that Bosnia was as much a moral cause as a military conflict. The tragedy of Srebrenica will haunt our history forever.

> In the end the only meaningful and lasting amends we can make to the citizens of Bosnia and Herzegovina who put their faith in the international community is to do our utmost not to allow such horrors to recur. When the international community makes a solemn promise to safeguard and protect innocent civilians from massacre, then it must be willing to back its promise with the necessary means.

The U.N. Secretary General, Kofi Annan, agreed with the Commission Report, and in November of 1999 apologized for the U.N.'s failing in Bosnia. The Security Council decided on February 22, 1993, to agree with the recommendations of the Commission and called for the establishment of a criminal tribunal to prosecute 'persons responsible for the serious violations of international humanitarian law committed in the territory of the former Yugoslavia since 1991'.[15]

In a subsequent Security Council Resolution, the Statute of the International Tribunal for the Former Yugoslavia (ICTY) was adopted on May 8, 1993.[16] The Statute of the ICTY was to apply the customary international law rules of humanitarian law and its territorial jurisdiction would be limited to the former Yugoslavia. The Court could prosecute for international crimes that started in 1991. There was an unspoken consensus in the Security Council and the international community that without the main organizers and perpetrators of the conflict in the disintegrating Yugoslavia being held to account, the prospect for an enduring stability in the Balkans would be greatly diminished.

Sadly the consensus to hold to account those responsible for the gravest of international crimes only after the international community had so abjectly failed to stop it in the first place would be repeated in Rwanda. The report of the Independent Inquiry into the actions of the United Nations during the 1994 genocide in Rwanda produced similar views stating categorically that 'The United Nations failed the people of Rwanda during the genocide in 1994'.[17]

The report urged far more effective genocide prevention strategies, which included the obligation under the Genocide Convention to 'prevent and punish' genocide. Given these two independent reports, it is hard to fathom those who argue that in the interests of peace, whether temporary or not, those who perpetrate the worst crimes known to humanity should not be held accountable.

Rwanda itself requested the Security Council to establish the second ad hoc international criminal tribunal for the genocide by the previous Hutu government and its militias. In November of 1994, the Security Council acceded to the request and created the Rwanda Tribunal for the prosecution of genocide and other serious violations of international humanitarian law committed in Rwanda and neighboring countries in 1994.[18]

The legacy of both Tribunals, but more substantially the ICTY, is of very progressive approaches to the interpretation of international humanitarian law and human rights law that have transcended the principles from the Nuremberg Trials. The most important of the progressive interpretations of the law by the ICTY on the gravest of international crimes by both Tribunals is that crimes against humanity can be committed outside international conflicts, that war crimes can be committed during internal conflicts and that those who have organized, perpetrated and aided and abetted these crimes can and will be held accountable. While some have argued that the tribunals appeared to be motivated by the guilt of the international community for failing to stop the mass slaughter in the Balkans and Rwanda, both were regarded as essential to the restoration of peace and security.

The U.N. Security Council in setting up the ICTY stated that, even with the ongoing crimes constituting a threat to international peace and security, the Tribunal would assist in putting an end to such criminality and 'contribute to the restoration and maintenance of peace and security'.[19]

The ICTY itself made the link between peace and justice in the following manner:[20]

The key objective of the ICTY is to try those individuals most responsible for appalling acts such as murder, torture, rape, enslavement, destruction of property and other crimes listed in the Tribunal's Statute. By bringing perpetrators to trial, the ICTY aims to deter future crimes and render justice to thousands of victims and their families, thus contributing to a lasting peace in the former Yugoslavia.

Likewise, the Security Council in establishing the Rwanda Tribunal asserted that prosecuting those responsible for serious violations of international humanitarian law would 'contribute to the process of national reconciliation'.[21] The official site of the Rwanda Tribunal also claimed that the Tribunal would 'contribute to the process of national reconciliation in Rwanda and to the maintenance of peace in the region'.[22]

The Security Council linkage of the violation of humanitarian law norms with a threat to the peace to establish the Tribunals under its powerful Chapter VII powers was also laying the ground for further global initiatives to establish more effective international responses to such violations.[23] That more effective global response would come in the determination by a majority of the world's states to establish a permanent international criminal court in the summer of 1998.

However, it was clear that the two Tribunals were designed only for designated territories and specific allegations of gross impunity, and could not be a substitute for a permanent criminal court given ongoing allegations of gross impunity around the world. Some of the experts who have studied the establishment and legacy of the ICTY and ICTR are convinced that the ICC would not have been created without the two previous ad hoc Tribunals. In particular there is a claim that an extraordinary transformation in world opinion occurred largely as a result of the ICTY's operations.[24] There is also a claim that the ICC has learned from both the successes and the failures of the ad hoc Tribunals in terms of both procedure and substantive legal issues, including the definition of the crimes codified in the Rome Statute of the ICC.[25]

The legacy of the ICTY and ICTR ad hoc Tribunals also provides a history lesson. Prosecutions of those most responsible for serious crimes can lead to their marginalization, which itself could be a critical factor in peace negotiations and ultimate stability in the situation of conflict. Human Rights Watch has given a compelling account of how the indictment of Radovan Karadžić by the ICTY in the context of the Bosnian conflict led to his marginalization and prevented him from being a participant (and perhaps a spoiler) in the Dayton peace talks that ended the Bosnian conflict.[26]

Likewise, the arrest warrant for Charles Taylor, the sitting Liberian President, at the start of the peace talks was also viewed as being conducive to the negotiations to end the conflict by 'delegitimizing' Taylor domestically and internationally. This may well have led to forcing him to leave office and the country a few months later.[27]

Perhaps the lasting legacy of the ICTY and the ICTR, like the Nuremberg trials, is the creation of a detailed historical record through the evidence presented at fair and neutral trials. As in the case of the Nuremberg trials, the evidence of the atrocities committed in the former Yugoslavia and Rwanda can act as a bulwark against revisionism used by future unscrupulous leaders who deny past serious crimes and assert imagined humiliations to revive inter-communal conflict and human rights abuses.[28]

The success, partial or otherwise, of the ICTY and the ICTR have spawned other non-permanent hybrid international tribunals that seek justice with the peace that was established, sometimes long after the conflict has ended.

The Special Court for Sierra Leone was a hybrid tribunal set up jointly by the Government of the country and the U.N. under Security Council Resolution 1315. It was given a mandate to prosecute those with the greatest responsibility for serious violations, not only of international humanitarian law, but also of the law of Sierra Leone committed by various rebels and the army in the territory of the country since November 30, 1996.

As with other conflict situations in Africa, the civilian population of Sierra Leone suffered some of the most savage atrocities that humanity has witnessed during the eleven-year civil war that started in 1991, much of it driven by the push to control the highly profitable trade in what has come to be known as 'blood diamonds'. Thousands of civilians were abducted and used as slave labour in the mining of diamonds, with accompanying widespread mutilation of limbs as an instrument of terror. Thousands more were killed in militia attacks, some burned alive in their homes after extensive looting of civilian property. There was also widespread enslavement of children under 15 as child soldiers and approximately 275,000 women and girls were victims of mass and systemic sexual violence and forced to become 'bush wives' of the militia members.

The Trial and Appeals Chamber judges of the Sierra Leone Special Court are jointly appointed by the government of Sierra Leone and the U.N., with the international judges forming the majority in both chambers. While this hybrid tribunal has attempted to integrate the country's judiciary into the work of the tribunal, it is still regarded in international law as an international court independent from the domestic legal system of Sierra Leone. This tribunal has moved with relative speed and managed to prosecute two cases successfully before it completed its mandate. One case, completed on June 20, 2007, resulted in three accused from the Armed Forces Revolutionary Council receiving forty-five to fifty year sentences. The other case, completed on August 2, 2007, involved two accused individuals from the Civil Defense Forces receiving sentences of fifteen and twenty years. The Court also had to deal with the Charles Taylor prosecution, the first former African Head of State to be indicted for serious violations of the relevant laws described above. For security reasons, his prosecution was moved to The Hague although still under the jurisdiction of the Special Court for Sierra Leone. Although the hearing of evidence started late on January 7, 2008, the case for the prosecution has ended already after hearing the evidence of ninety-one witnesses. The remaining prosecution case concerns a fugitive, Johnny Paul Koroma, but the Special Court has not closed the possibility of pursuing other individuals connected with the commercial links to the blood diamonds that was the catalyst for the atrocities committed in the country.

The other ad hoc hybrid tribunals set up by the Government of Cambodia and the U.N. and the East Timor mixed panels have so far proved much less effective. As regards the Cambodia tribunal, the refusal of the Cambodian government and especially its authoritarian Prime Minister, Hun Sen, with his own checkered past, to accept a truly independent international tribunal has led to a weak hybrid tribunal composed of a tribunal under Cambodian law controlled to a large extent by Cambodian judges and prosecutors, with international judges and prosecutors attempting to ensure international credibility. The Cambodian tribunal is part of special chambers of the Cambodian court system called the Extraordinary Chambers in the Courts of Cambodia. The Cambodian National Assembly approved the law establishing the Extraordinary Chambers on January 2, 2001. The subject matter jurisdiction covers genocide, crimes against humanity, grave breaches of the Geneva Conventions and various violations of the 1954 Hague Convention and the 1961 Vienna Convention on Diplomatic Relations. However homicide, torture and religious persecution are to be prosecuted under Cambodian law. The prosecutions are limited to the most senior leaders of the Democratic Kampuchea who are most responsible for the genocide and atrocities committed during the 1975–79 period.[29] After thirty years, no one has been convicted of some of the worst atrocities since the Holocaust in World War II because of the decades of attempts to block accountability for the crimes committed by both China and the United States.

The Tribunal began on February 17, 2009, its first trial being that of Kaing Gech Eav (Duch) one of the Khmer Rouge leaders most responsible for the deaths of up to two million people. Duch, the commander of the infamous torture and execution Centre S21 in Phnom Penh, is one of five former Khmer Rouge leaders currently facing prosecution before the Extraordinary Chambers. However, serious allegations of political interference, low professional standards and corruption have dogged the Court since its establishment in 2001.[30] The case for a permanent international tribunal free of political interference, such as the ICC, is best made by the challenges facing the Cambodian hybrid tribunal.

The East Timor situation is just as troubling as that of Cambodia. After the killing and destruction by Indonesian-led forces and militias that followed the U.N. sponsored referendum in 1999, the U.N. Transitional Administration of East Timor (UNTAET) established in 2000 special mixed international/East Timorese judicial panels within the Dili District Court to prosecute those who allegedly committed serious criminal offenses that constituted also violations of international humanitarian law. There is great concern about the viability and effectiveness of these panels, even though approximately twenty-one individuals have been convicted with sentences ranging from four to thirty-four years' imprisonment. The criticism includes the postponement of scheduled hearings due to the unavailability of the judges and some appeals not being heard because the judges have not been appointed. Given the failings of this particular experiment in hybrid tribunals, many civil society groups are calling for a U.N. sponsored independent criminal tribunal.[31]

The demands of justice require not only true independence of any international or hybrid criminal tribunal to prosecute the most serious of international crimes, but also the external guarantees that ensure the tribunal can meet its mandate of ensuring that such crimes do not go unpunished and to act as a catalyst for peace in the future.

All these ad hoc international criminal tribunals will end. The ICTY and the ICTR are scheduled to wind up all of their judicial activities by 2010, although circumstances may allow some trials to continue until 2011. None of the others are permanent. When they all end there will be a vacuum which could only be filled by a permanent international criminal tribunal like the ICC or a new mandate from the regional human rights courts that would focus primarily on the most serious international crimes listed in the Rome Statute. If the ICC did not exist it would have to be invented as it will likely be the 'only game in town'.

3.   THE BIRTH OF THE INTERNATIONAL CRIMINAL COURT

While the ad hoc Tribunals were being established and started operations, the U.N. General Assembly renewed its work to establish a permanent criminal tribunal that would not be limited to a defined territory. An Ad Hoc Committee of the Assembly would start with the draft statute of such a permanent court produced by the International Law Commission (ILC). However, the political nature of the Ad Hoc Committee soon manifested itself and some members even questioned the viability of such a permanent court. As the work went on, it became clear that the ILC's desire to have a permanent court that would have primacy over national courts in the case of grave international crimes would give way to the Ad Hoc Committee's desire to give primacy to national courts to prosecute such crimes, and that a permanent court would only have 'complementarity' jurisdiction if the national courts were unable or unwilling to genuinely prosecute such crimes.[32] This would become a crucial provision of the ICC that should be a major counter argument to those who would suggest that the ICC promotes a western and colonial approach to international humanitarian law and human rights.

In a similar fashion, and with a similar lasting legacy, the Ad Hoc Committee insisted that the permanent court's jurisdiction would be limited by a detailed statute that would define the crimes that would be the subject of prosecution by the ICC. In addition the Committee insisted on a listing of general principles of law and other substantive and procedural parameters that the ICC would have to operate within. The fear and uncertainty about too much judicial discretion was a motivating force for this U.N. Committee.

In contrast to the much less defined parameters of the ad hoc Tribunals for the FRY and Rwanda, these detailed provisions, insisted on by the Ad Hoc Committee and later agreed upon at the Rome Conference that established the ICC, would have, in the view of this author, the effect of 'constitutionalizing' the law relating to the most grave of international crimes together with the applicable general principles of law, including human rights norms. Following the bureaucratic nature of the U.N., the General Assembly decided in 1996 to submit the work of the Ad Hoc Committee to lengthy sessions of a 'Preparatory Committee' that involved member states, NGOs and International Organizations in multi-week sessions that ultimately produced a final draft called the 'Zutphen draft' to the Rome Diplomatic Conference in 1998.[33]

What took place at the Diplomatic Conference in Rome that started on June 15, 1998, is a testament to the success of the global human rights and humanitarian movements linking up with a progressive group of nations called the 'like-minded caucus' to produce a milestone in human progress, namely the establishment of the ICC. However, among the 160 state delegations and the hundreds of NGOs at the Rome Conference, an historic battle was shaping up between those states that wanted state sovereignty to trump the imperatives of fighting impunity, and those that wanted the world to see a new stage in the development of the rule of law in global affairs.

The former group, led by the United States with strong support by China, India and Israel, wanted the permanent court to be subject to a Security Council veto on prosecutions. In addition these countries wanted the elimination of the power of an independent prosecutor of the new court being able to start an investigation on his own initiative called the *'proprio motu'* jurisdiction. The like-minded caucus of states led by Canada, backed by an army of civil society groups and NGOs, refused to concede on these issues. Special mention must be made of the very powerful and effective lobbying strategies of the Coalition for the International Criminal Court (CICC) which is led and convened by Executive Director William Pace. Presently comprising approximately 2,500 organizations around the world, including the leading human rights organizations such as Amnesty International and Human Rights Watch, the CICC since 1955 has been the main force of global civil society in lobbying for the establishment of the Court. With the establishment of the Rome Statute, the CICC has worked tirelessly to strengthen international cooperation with the Court and ensure its effectiveness and independence, while promoting stronger national laws that advance the complementarity nature of the Rome Statute. The CICC has been involved in every stage of the development of the Court from working in the preparatory Committee leading to the Rome Statute to active participation in the annual Assembly of States Parties meetings.

The like-minded group of states led by Canada together with their civil society partners won the day, in no small measure due to the great diplomatic skill of Canadian diplomat Phillipe Kirsch who was elected president of the Rome Conference's Committee of the Whole. His Committee had the daunting task of dealing with and brokering solutions regarding the most contentious issues. On July 17, 1998, the Statute of the International Criminal Court was adopted at the Rome Conference with 120 states voting in favour, twenty-one abstentions and without a formal roll call; only the United States, China and Israel declared that they were opposed to the adoption of the ICC Statute. The Rome Conference also called upon the U.N. General Assembly to initiate another Preparatory Commission to draft the Elements of Crime and the Rules of Procedure and Evidence which would give further definitions to the crimes listed in the ICC Statute.

Negotiations at the Rome Conference had tried hard to get the U.S. on side. Before the Rome Conference, the Clinton Administration supported a permanent international criminal court if the right protections for its military personnel were built into the Statute of the court. Indeed the U.S. had been the catalyst for the establishment of the ad hoc Tribunals for the FRY and Rwanda. Some of the leading U.S. experts had convincingly argued that the lessons learned from these Tribunals, despite their lack of resources, had shown how crucial criminal indictments and arrest warrants could combat impunity by isolating individuals responsible for these crimes and strengthening the hands of domestic rivals and trigger international political will to take aggressive action to bring about the end of the conflict.[34] Such views had been confirmed by the removal of President Slobodan Milošević, the leader of the FRY, who had triggered the mass slaughter in the Balkans on June 28, 2001, to stand trial for genocide, crimes against humanity and war crimes to the ICTY in The Hague. This was an historic first time that a former Head of State had been brought before an international criminal tribunal.

There is irony in the fact that the U.S. had pressured strongly for an ICC that would be controlled by the U.N. Security Council including eliminating the power of an independent prosecutor to start an investigation *proprio motu*. The U.N. Security Council was the same body that the U.S. ignored in the decision to take military action in Kosovo to end the slaughter there. To dispel criticisms of its contrary positions, the U.S. justified its position at the Rome Conference by asserting that, as the lone superpower, it would have the greatest burden of intervening in humanitarian crises and this would potentially open its military personnel to investigation by an independent prosecutor of the ICC and the jurisdiction of the Court.[35] The like-minded caucus of states and the NGOs that led the opposition to this U.S. position has suggested that the U.S. position was dictated more by the U.S. Pentagon rather than the State Department and arose from the mistrust of the U.S. military of the decision of the International Court of Justice (ICJ) in *Nicaragua v. United States*[36] which resulted in the withdrawal of compulsory jurisdiction of the ICJ.

When the actual provisions of the ICC Statute are examined, it is clear that the U.S. had little to be concerned about. Some would argue that most of the Pentagon's concerns had been addressed in the detailed provisions of the Statute. This included the fundamental principle of complementarity which required the primacy of national courts' jurisdiction over the crimes listed in the Statute. Only if the U.S. courts were unable or unwilling to prosecute any alleged offenses listed in the ICC Statute would the jurisdiction of the Court be triggered. Likewise, the Rome Conference had decided to curtail the ability of the Chief Prosecutor to overreach his *proprio motu* powers of investigation by imposing the supervision of the Trial Chamber of the Court over these independent powers of the Chief Prosecutor. The omission of the U.S. from the majority of states supporting the introduction of a global order against impunity was a sad historic event. This was the same superpower which had shown the greatest leadership in the Nuremberg and Tokyo War Crimes Tribunals, the Universal

Declaration of Human Rights and the establishment of the two ad hoc Tribunals for the FRY and Rwanda. But the challenge for the ICC was just beginning with the election of George W. Bush and his Administration who would be a ferocious opponent of the newly established ICC.[37]

The Statute came into force on July 1, 2002 when it received its sixtieth ratification. The pace of ratifications was substantially faster than had been expected. This result was even more significant than at first may be apparent. While even states, including the U.S. and Israel, that had opposed the Statute signed on just before the deadline of December 31, 2000, those wishing to ratify after signing had to take very significant legislative and administrative steps in their own jurisdictions to comply with the obligations of being parties to the ICC Statute.

In a relatively very short space of time, many of these states passed legislation to ensure their own criminal laws were compatible with the ICC Statute, especially as regards the crimes of genocide, crimes against humanity and war crimes, and to allow their courts the ability to exercise universal jurisdiction over these crimes. Likewise, the ratifying states also had to provide for the necessary legislative and administrative mechanisms for cooperation with the ICC over the investigation, arrest and transfer of alleged criminals targeted by the Chief Prosecutor of the ICC. As of June 1, 2008, 108 states, a majority of states in the world, had signed and ratified the Rome Statute of the ICC.

These rapid legislative and administrative changes in many of the 110 states that have presently ratified the Statute could by themselves foster sustainable peace in their respective territories without the Court ever having started an investigation in any of these countries. However, there is great concern that of the present 110 States Parties, only thirty-nine have implemented the legislation necessary to implement the Rome Statute.

Greater numbers of States Parties implementing the Rome Statute will be needed to cement the argument that the ICC is an institution that promotes peace with justice as opposed to justice against peace. As of March 1, 2010, 110 states, a majority of the world had signed and ratified the Rome Statue of the ICC.

The Assembly of States Parties is therefore a type of both legislative and oversight body of the ICC. Made up of all the ratifying states, the Assembly sessions are also open to NGOs and observer states. In addition to electing the above key positions in the Court and approving the budget of the ICC, the Assembly also provides oversight and guidance to the administration of the Court. A growing controversial role for the Assembly is also to consider referrals from the Court regarding non-cooperation by states. This role may well become the greatest challenge for the Assembly as the Court begins to urge States Parties to do more in ensuring that the arrest warrants issued by the Court are executed, especially as regards the arrest warrant issued against the President of Sudan, Omar al-Bashir.

In the same period in which the States Parties were building the Court's basic rules and infrastructure, the U.S. Bush Administration was focused on undermining the Court. The Bush Administration first indicated on May 6, 2002 that it would not become a party to the Rome Statute, thereby 'unsigning' from the majority recognition of the need for a global rule of law against gross impunity for genocide, crimes against humanity and war crimes. This unprecedented unsigning of its international legal obligations was followed by the Bush Administration pressuring states receiving military and financial aid to sign bilateral agreements that would make US military officials and civilians immune from being subject to the jurisdiction of the ICC. The Bush Administration officials were proceeding under the view that Article 98(2) of the Rome Statute permitted states to impede surrender of an accused if it would require a violation of their legal obligations to another State.

Just over 100 states succumbed to such geopolitical blackmail by the Bush Administration by 2006, while fifty-four countries stood on their principles in the same period and refused to bend to the ideological campaign against the ICC by the Bush Administration. Some of the poorest countries in Africa, including Benin, Mali, Tanzania and Losotho, lost critically needed foreign aid funds for refusing to go along with the demand for Article 98(2) agreements.

Only a handful of the ratifying states succumbed to this pressure, with key U.S. allies such as Canada, Mexico and most Western European states leading the opposition to this attack on the ICC. The petulant attempts by the Bush Administration continued with threats to veto U.N. Security Council resolutions on peacekeeping if the jurisdiction of the ICC over such operations was not ousted. The attempts to undermine the ICC reached absurd heights when former President Bush on August 2, 2002 signed the American Service Members' Protection Act which was nicknamed the 'Hague Invasion Act'. This astonishing work of former Bush officials led by the senior State Department official and later U.S. Ambassador to the U.N., John Bolton, prohibited U.S. government agencies from cooperating with the ICC and included the authorization of the use of force to free any American national who was detained or imprisoned by the ICC.[38]

The fact that large numbers of the world's states were able to resist the attempts by the former Bush Administration to undermine the newly born ICC is a testament to the will of humanity not to retreat in the evolution of a global rule of law against gross impunity. Leading experts have asserted that the establishment of the Court is one of the most important developments in international law. It could contribute not only to the restoration of peace and reconciliation in specific situations but, in the words of Professor William Schabas, contributes to the evolution of a more peaceful global society:[39]

> The Influence of the Rome Statute will extend deep into domestic criminal law, enriching the jurisprudence of national courts and challenging prosecutors and judges to display greater zeal in the repression of serious violations of human rights. National courts have shown, in recent years, a growing enthusiasm for the use of international law materials in the application of their own laws. A phenomenon of judicial globalization is afoot. The Statute itself, and eventually the case law of the International Criminal Court, will no doubt contribute in this area.

4. THE STATUTE OF THE COURT; BALANCING NATIONAL SOVEREIGNTY, PEACE AND JUSTICE

The desire to balance national sovereignty with justice led the drafters of the ICC Statute at Rome to impose a much more detailed set of provisions on the crimes within the jurisdiction of the court and the rules of evidence and procedure in comparison to the ad hoc Tribunals for Yugoslavia and Rwanda. This was partly a reaction to criticism that the ad hoc Tribunals had too much liberty to interpret and even modify the provisions relating to jurisdiction, procedure and evidence under which they operated. The imposition of such detailed rules upon the ICC was the subject of much heated discussion at the Rome Diplomatic Conference.[40]

The provision in the ICC Statute that allows states almost complete leeway to pursue national reconciliation and peace through their own investigative, judicial and other similar institutions is the principle of complementarity.

The very definition of this concept can be found in the preamble to the Rome Statute. That preamble states that 'the International Criminal Court established under this Statute shall be complementary to national criminal jurisdictions'. This concept that the ICC does NOT take supremacy to national courts is repeated in the very first Article of the Rome Statute. So while the preamble to the Rome Statute speaks with such eloquence about the common desire of humankind not to let the most serious of crimes go unpunished and that such crimes threaten the peace, security and wellbeing of the world, it also accepts that territorial integrity or political independence is a fundamental part of the purposes and principles of the United Nations. These principles must be balanced against the fight against impunity for the most serious crimes that in the 20th Century have shocked the conscience of humanity. What the preamble is stating in a circuitous fashion is that without a permanent institution dedicated to justice against impunity the chances of a sustainable peace without mass atrocities as witnessed in the last century is greatly diminished.

Despite this primacy of national sovereignty and courts over the jurisdiction of the ICC, the U.S. negotiators at the Rome Conference were not convinced that their military personnel could still avoid being hauled before the ICC. Such a fear would almost be a fantastical admission that the much lauded American justice system is not to be regarded as legitimate. This is because the ICC statute balances national sovereignty and justice carefully by stating in Article 17 that the Court can still have jurisdiction where the state is unwilling or unable genuinely to carry out its own investigation or prosecution. This safeguard for justice ensures that impunity cannot hide behind illusory or non-existent national judicial institutions.

National sovereignty and the ability to conduct genuine domestic investigative and judicial proceedings in civil conflicts are further reinforced by the detailed provisions on the ICC's jurisdiction over subject matter, territory and persons, the parameters around the independence of the Chief Prosecutor, the oversight of the Pre-Trial Chamber and the role of the U.N. Security Council.

Turning to the jurisdiction of the Court over subject matter, the ICC Statute in Article 5 also balances national sovereignty over justice by limiting the Court's jurisdiction to only the most serious crimes of concern to the international community as a whole. These are of such grave character that in many cases peace efforts have either failed or never been undertaken because the perpetrators have initiated the crimes as a sustained strategy to obtain or keep power. The crimes listed in Article 5 are (a) The crime of genocide, (b) Crimes against humanity, (c) War Crimes; and (d) the as yet undefined crime of aggression. The first three crimes are defined further in great detail in Articles 6 to 8 of the Statute and further elaborated in the Elements of Crime as drafted by the Assembly of States Parties. The Rome Conference resolved the contentious issue of the crime of aggression, demanded by the nations which had been colonized in the past, by leaving it to the Assembly of States Parties to define it, starting within seven years of the establishment of the Court.

What we see in the provisions of the ICC Statute is the constitutionalization of the whole body of international criminal law that by itself also incorporates the body of customary and treaty based humanitarian law and international human rights law. While the ad hoc Tribunals had also prosecuted and interpreted customary international law on crimes against humanity, the ICC Statute consolidated over a century's worth of jurisprudence and customary law on the most serious of international crimes into a constitutionalized definition of these crimes, but also expanded their scope to cover gender crimes including various forms of sexual violence, the criminalization of the enslavement of child soldiers and attacking U.N. peacekeepers.

One writer, Sadat, has claimed that while the Rome Statute of the ICC takes the form of a treaty, it has the status of a constitution. This view of the ICC Statute challenges the 'Westphalian model' of international law that is premised on the unwritten nature of that law, which is that international law can only be prescribed by the consensual acts of states or other law making bodies. This theory claims that the ICC Statute represents a 'constitutional moment' in the development of international law, but acknowledges that, while the Rome Treaty was revolutionary, it was not an easy achievement given the opposition by powerful states such as the U.S., and that as a matter of law, institutional structure and process, many of the prerogatives of sovereignty remain.[41] The foundation of this view of the constitutional nature of the ICC Statute is that the U.N. Charter is a form of 'constitution' for the international community, which cannot be ignored by non-party states. The creation of the ICC is therefore part of the development of the U.N. system, as it has been created through the efforts of U.N. bodies including the Rome Conference.[42]

The codification of the customary international humanitarian laws into the ICC Statute will, according to the view of the 'constitutionalists', of whom this author is one, lead to the judicial chambers of the ICC interpreting the Rome Statute as they would a constitutional document. With the progress of cases heard by the ICC Chambers, over time the constitutional approach may lead to the expansion of the definition of crimes beyond that presently provided in customary international humanitarian or human rights law.

Not surprisingly there are strong critics of this constitutional view of the ICC Statute, especially among American jurists. Another writer, Gallant, suggests that the ICC is more a result of evolutionary prescriptive norms from various sources of international law, including the U.N. and the Assembly of States Parties of the ICC. Behind such opposition to the view of the ICC as a form of constitution for international criminal law is the refusal to accept that such a momentous event could have occurred without the consent of nine of the world's most powerful and populous countries, including the U.S., China and India.[43]

It should be noted, however, that the U.S. did sign the Rome Statute, but later the Bush Administration took the unprecedented step of 'unsigning' from the ICC Statute. There is also growing evidence that the new Obama Administration will lessen American reluctance to join the ICC

Statute, but will face difficulty in getting the challenging two-thirds majority of the U.S. Senate in order to ratify the accession of the U.S. to the ICC Statute.[44] This will be discussed more fully in the final chapter of this book.

The constitutional view of the ICC Statute may also be at odds with the specific provision of Article 10, which states that '[n]othing in this Part shall be interpreted as limiting or prejudicing in any way existing or developing rules of international law for purposes other than this Statute'. While this provision would seem to prevent codification of previous customary international criminal law in the Rome Statute, its main purpose is to allow for new developments that may not have been foreseen at the Rome Diplomatic Conference, such as the outlawing of new weapons, or even existing nuclear weapons, not listed in Article 8 of the Statute.

As far as the actual provisions in the Statute and the Elements of Crimes are concerned, there is little doubt that the Trial and Appeal Chambers of the ICC will treat them as a constitutionalized version of prior customary and treaty laws relating to the most serious international crimes. The practical effect of this constitutionalization could lead to the Chambers of the ICC giving wider interpretations of prior customary and treaty law, the way that judiciaries around the world give liberal interpretations of entrenched constitutions to make them relevant to societal developments.

The definition of the crime in Article 7 and expanded further in the Elements of Crime includes progressive interpretations of the ICTY Tribunal that extended the definition to 'gender crimes'. These gender crimes can also constitute war crimes under Article 8 of the ICC Statute. By entrenching such prior jurisprudence of the ad hoc Tribunals, the ICC Statute has become a constitutional document for this and other international crimes. The ICC Statute now spells out that the crime includes not only the variations of murder, torture, enslavement and deportations or forcible transfer of populations, but also detailed provisions relating to 'gender crimes'. These include rape, sexual slavery, enforced prostitution, forced pregnancy, enforced sterilization, or any other form of sexual violence of comparable gravity.

As regards the definition of war crimes, here also the Statute takes into account the jurisprudence of the ad hoc Tribunals and also codifies over a century of international treaty and customary laws dating back to ancient notions of '*ius in bello*' and the early codifications in the Hague Conventions of 1899. The three main categories that are extensively defined in the Statute and the Elements of Crime are (a) grave breaches of the Geneva Conventions of 1949, (b) other serious violations of the laws and customs applicable in international armed conflict, within the established framework of international law and followed by a very long list of such violations, and (c) in the case of armed conflict not of an international character, serious violations of Article 3 of the Geneva Conventions of 1949 that focus on non-combatants including those who have laid down their arms or are *hors de combat* by sickness, wounds or detentions or any other cause.

One major aspect of the overlap between the constitutionalized provisions relating to international and internal conflicts is that the ICC Statute builds on the jurisprudence of the ad hoc Tribunals by issuing a warning of potential criminal prosecution to those who think that national sovereignty preserves impunity for war crimes. The ICC Statute thereby could well act as a proactive instrument of sustainable peace in the troubled parts of the world, as will be discussed in greater detail in Chapter 4.

The provisions in Article 6 of the ICC Statute on the crime of genocide also draw on the provisions of the Genocide Convention and the jurisprudence of the ad hoc Tribunals. Regarded as the most serious of the international crimes and its legacy of the Holocaust, the definition includes the requirement of specific intent or *dolus specialis* to destroy, in whole or in part, a national ethnical, racial or religious group. The five specific acts that must be committed with the specific intent are killing members of the group, causing serious bodily or mental harm to the members of the group, deliberately inflicting on the group conditions of life calculated to bring about its physical destruction in whole or in part, imposing measures intended to prevent births within the group and forcibly transferring children of the group to another group. The Elements of Crimes elaborates that these acts must be part of a manifest pattern of similar conduct, implying that the acts requiring specific intent must be part of a general plan or policy.

As will be seen in the next chapter, with the investigation by an independent U.N. Commission into the Darfur atrocities and subsequently by the Chief Prosecutor's investigation and prosecution of the President of Sudan al-Bashir, some perpetrators may escape the charge of genocide due to this requirement of specific intent for the successful prosecution of genocide. Leaders may well be intimately involved in the mass slaughter of civilians and may be at the top of a command structure that carries out what could well be regarded as a genocide, but unless the specific intent to destroy in whole or a substantial or significant part of the group can be convincingly demonstrated before the Court, some of these most senior officials may well escape the charge of genocide. The Statute drafters decided not to alter this requirement of specific intent for the crime of genocide arising out of the wording of Article II of the Genocide Convention and the jurisprudence of the ad hoc Tribunals. However, even if those who organize genocidal atrocities escape the charge of genocide, they will most likely be prosecuted successfully under the charge of crimes against humanity and possibly war crimes.

As evidenced in the case of Slobodan Milošević, when there is potentially sufficient evidence to accuse a leader of a nation or militia with the 'crime of crimes' charge of genocide under the ICC Statute, it is the beginning of a process of isolation by most of the international community of this individual and removing him from the conflict situation to face justice and thereby further the process of sustainable peace. Sometimes, just the charge of genocide accomplishes this situation even if, as again in the case of Milošević, the individual escapes judgment by passing away, or in the case of President al-Bashir a preliminary failure to prove specific intent.

Turning to subject matter jurisdiction, again we see a balancing of national sovereignty with justice, and the allotment of the primary place of peace and security and therefore global politics not to the Court but to the U.N. Security Council. This fact is often forgotten by the critics who accuse the Court of ignoring the place of peace in the pursuit of justice. These critics frequently ignore that the jurisdiction of the Court can substantially only be triggered primarily by States Parties and the U.N. Security Council which are thereby given the primary role to pursue non-judicial means to sustainable peace processes. The Prosecutor's independent ability to start an investigation *proprio motu* has been demonstrated not to be the main foundation of the ICC's caseload, as will be discussed below.

Under Article 13 of the ICC Statute, the Court can only exercise jurisdiction over the defined crimes listed in three situations. Firstly, where a 'situation' regarding a specific conflict is referred to the Prosecutor by a State Party. Secondly, where the U.N. Security Council acting under its Chapter VII powers relating to threats to international peace and security refers a situation to the ICC Prosecutor. Finally, as regards the jurisdiction hotly contested by the U.S. at the Rome Diplomatic Conference, the Prosecutor can initiate an investigation on his own authority *proprio motu* in respect of the listed crimes.

All the cases that have so far gone to trial comprise the first two heads of jurisdiction. None of the ongoing investigations carried on under the *proprio motu* powers of the Prosecutor are the main situations that have triggered the so-called peace versus justice debate surrounding the role of the Court and its mandate under the Rome Statute. Instead, as will be discussed in the following two chapters, much of the peace versus justice critique of the ICC surrounds a referral of the situation in Darfur, Sudan, by the U.N. Security Council and the referral by Uganda as regards the actions of the Lord's Resistance Army in Northern Uganda.

This form of jurisdiction of the ICC was the result of the strong coalition between the like-minded group of states, led by Canada and the NGOs at the Rome Diplomatic Conference that managed to stave off the attempt by the U.S. and other states that wanted a Tribunal dominated substantially by the Security Council. These opponents of the *proprio motu* jurisdictions feared there could be political prosecutions started by a Prosecutor who would not be accountable to anyone. The final version of the ICC Statute would have proved this fear to be groundless as this power of the Prosecutor to see any investigation come to fruition, including issuing any arrest warrant, or to have confirmation of the charges once the alleged perpetrator is arrested is subject to the approval of a Pre-Trial Chamber. This insertion of a powerful oversight judicial tribunal, although very much in keeping with the civil law traditions around the world, must also be seen as a crucial part of alleviating concerns that national sovereignty would be subject to an unaccountable or overzealous Prosecutor.

Some of the African states which have ratified the Rome Statute, are endorsing the African Union opposition to the arrest warrants of al-Bashir and are contemplating non-cooperation seem to be forgetting their obligations under Article 12(1) that States Parties do not have a choice as to whether to accept the jurisdiction of the Court; they are legally obliged to do so. They are also legally obliged to cooperate with the Court.[45]

The complementarity principle adds further dimensions and complexity to the jurisdiction of the Court and the powers of the prosecutor to investigate or prosecute a situation. The ability of the prosecutor to investigate or prosecute a case is subject to a fundamental rule of admissibility that all relevant national court or state institutions are 'unwilling or unable genuinely' to investigate or prosecute the same case. In other words the Court is only a global criminal court of last resort and can only seek jurisdiction if there is evidence that the national authorities are attempting to shield the accused from any accountability for their grave criminal actions.[46] This was in contrast to the ad hoc Tribunals of the ICTY and the ICTR which had primacy over the national courts.[47]

The concern to balance national sovereignty with the fight against impunity was most evident in the negotiations leading up to the Rome Statute of the ICC. There was a consensus by states that the Court should only have jurisdiction if either there was an absence of national institutions willing and able to prosecute the most serious of international crimes or any such institutions were unwilling to do so or were even disposed to shield the perpetrator of the crimes. The result of the long and arduous negotiation was to give the Court jurisdiction under Article 17 of the ICC Statute only where there was compelling evidence that demonstrated the following: a) unwillingness to pursue the prosecution of the serious crimes, b) that any such proceedings were intended to shield the alleged perpetrator from responsibility, c) were unjustifiably delayed, d) were not conducted independently or impartially and, finally e) were conducted in a manner inconsistent with an intent to bring the person concerned to justice.

It should be kept in mind that while these criteria of unwillingness or inability to genuinely prosecute may seem to put the ICC in a position to sit in judgment of national judicial systems, in reality it would become obvious to the entire world that a national system would be failing these criteria if those who were alleged to have committed the most serious crimes known to humanity were able to escape the most basic forms of accountability known to most jurisdictions in the world.

In most cases, a national judicial system would fail the criteria when, as we shall see in the case of Sudan, those under indictments by the Court are not only immune from prosecutions, but given promotions or are summarily released after a brief detention. Article 17 of the ICC Statute that defines the parameters of complementarity also offers another likely situation of the Court taking jurisdiction where the state is unable to obtain the accused or the necessary evidence and testimony or otherwise unable to carry out the proceedings because there has been a total or substantial collapse or unavailability of the national judicial system.

As will be discussed in subsequent chapters, the ICC has commenced investigations and prosecutions in four African countries. What seems to have been forgotten by the critics, who accuse the Court of bias towards Africa, is that in three of the countries involved the situation was referred to the Court by the governments of the countries themselves. The Court accepted jurisdiction in the situations in Northern Uganda, the Democratic Republic of Congo and the Central African Republic on the basis of referral by the governments of these countries. The situation in Darfur was, as the next chapter will reveal, referred to the ICC by the U.N. Security Council. This record of the Court's prosecutorial strategy so far reinforced the fact that the ICC is a court of last resort. It is a logical conclusion that the referring African countries would not have referred their country situations to the Court if it was felt that their prosecutorial and judicial systems were able and capable of prosecuting and judging those accused of serious international crimes within their jurisdictions. For example, it is hard to rebut the presumption that the Democratic Republic of Congo had determined that its own prosecutorial and judicial systems were not able and capable of prosecuting and trying the Congolese militia leader Lubanga Dyilo who stands accused of serious crimes under the ICC Statute.

As an added layer of protection of national sovereignty, not only must the Prosecutor of the Court decide that there is no national judicial system that is willing and genuinely able to prosecute the alleged serious crimes, he or she must also convince a Pre-Trial Chamber of the Court that there is sufficient evidence to support the Prosecutor's decision on complementarity.

In such situations, confirmed by both the investigations by the Prosecutor and the decision of the Pre-Trial Chamber, there is less likelihood for a situation to be a choice between peace and justice. The fact of the total breakdown or inability of any form of impartial judicial system or the manipulation of the judicial system by the perpetrators or their allies in a state where there is violent conflict would be a strong indicator that the prospect of negotiations leading to a sustainable peace would be very slim.

Impunity is most rampant around the world when it occurs at the highest levels of government, and especially when it involves the Head of State, and when such impunity exists in the middle of violent conflict, it is the situation that often gives rise to the gravest of violations of humanitarian law standards as codified under the ICC Statute.

When such impunity occurs, there is a very slim chance of any prospect of a durable peace. The drafters of the ICTY and the ICTR had understood this fact and had provided that '[t]he official position of any accused person, whether as Head of State or Government or as a responsible Government official, shall not relieve such person of criminal responsibility nor mitigate punishment'.[48] Such provisions were a legacy of the Nuremberg Charter, which also removed any immunity from the core Nazi leaders in Germany and, as discussed, was a method of preventing the exacting of vengeance against these leaders in the cause of using trial and punishment as prevention and a foundation for a durable peace in Europe.

These reasons for not affording immunity to heads of state and high government officials found their way into the ICC Statute, which asserts in Article 27 the legacy of the Nuremberg trials in the following words:

1. This Statute shall apply equally to all persons without any distinction based on official capacity. In particular, official capacity as a Head of State or Government, a member of a Government or a government official shall in no case exempt a person from criminal responsibility under this statute, nor shall it, in and of itself, constitute a ground for reduction of sentence.
2. Immunities or special procedural rules which may attach to the official capacity of a person whether under national or international law, shall not bar the Court from exercising its jurisdiction over such a person.

The reason why this provision is of such importance is that, until the Nuremberg Charter,[49] traditional notions of state sovereignty and under international law, sovereign immunity were an ironclad defense, especially for Heads of State, while other officials asserted various forms of immunities when they acted in accordance with superior orders. These concepts of international law were major obstacles to the fight against impunity for grave international crimes. Under traditional customary international law, until the Nuremberg Charter the Head of State was seen as the personification of the sovereign state and so was entitled to absolute immunity, while other high state officials were considered to have functional immunities.[50] The International Court of Justice has ruled that as regards national courts exercising universal jurisdiction, customary rules still afford various levels of sovereign immunity to Heads of State and high foreign officials.[51]

There is a strong argument to be made that making Heads of State and high government officials accountable and punishable for serious international crimes is critical for preventing such crimes and promoting the foundations of a durable peace in troubled societies. The legacies of the two ad hoc Tribunals are especially important in this respect. The indictments by the ICTY of the Yugoslav President, Slobodan Milošević, together with the first President of the Bosnian Serbs, Radovan Karadžić, and General Ratko Mladić of the Bosnian Serb army, were crucial to the ending of the conflict in this troubled region. Holding them accountable for the most serious of international crimes under Article 7 of the ICTY Statute was crucial to demonstrate that they were the architects of a policy and program of genocide and ethnic cleansing at the highest levels of government.

Likewise, the prosecution and conviction for participating in genocide and crimes against humanity against Jean Kambanda, the former Prime Minister of Rwanda, by the ICTR was also deemed critical to the national reconciliation process in the aftermath of the genocide in that country. Kambanda had also acted at the highest levels of government and through the media to plan and incite the genocide against the Tutsi population and moderates in the Hutu hierarchy.[52]

The ad hoc Tribunals regarded and indeed the ICC can also regard the involvement of Heads of State and high government officials in the most serious international crimes as aggravating factors in determining punishments.[53]

Making Heads of State and high government officials accountable for involvement in the most serious international crimes is indispensable to the prevention of future conflicts and the deterrence of such crimes. Indeed the legal duty of all states to cooperate in bringing these individuals to justice has reached the level of *obligatio erga omnes*, a universal duty on every state in the world.[54]

Those who are supporting the impunity of at least one Head of State and high government officials indicted by the ICC should bear this mind, as the next chapter will discuss in the context of the ICC arrest warrants in Sudan.

In the debate over whether justice is reconcilable with the pursuit of peace in the mandate and present work of the ICC, one provision of the ICC Statute catches the attention of those who claim that the Court is able to avoid upsetting any negotiations for peaceful settlement of violent conflicts. Article 53(1) of the ICC Statute states that if the Prosecutor is satisfied that there is a reasonable basis to initiate an investigation and believes that the case is within the jurisdiction of the Court and is or would be admissible under Article 17 of the Statute, he or she must determine whether, taking into account the gravity of the crime and the interests of the victims, 'there are nonetheless substantial reasons to believe that an investigation would not serve the interests of justice'. Article 53(2) then addresses the initiation of a prosecution after an investigation has produced sufficient evidence to proceed with the investigations. The provision states that upon investigation, the Prosecutor may conclude that there is not sufficient basis to proceed because it 'it is not in the interests of justice, taking into account all the circumstances, including the gravity of the crime, the interests of the victims and the age or infirmity of the alleged perpetrators, and his or her role in the alleged crime'. These provisions could present the most challenging and complex aspects of the ICC mandate and could throw the debate over the respective roles of peace and justice at the ICC into the forefront of headlines around the world. This is especially the case if heads of state who are supposed to be the guarantors of peace in their country are the target of any investigation and prosecution. As shall be discussed in the next chapter, this debate was triggered with full fury in the context of the arrest warrant for the President of Sudan, Omar al-Bashir.

Surprisingly, there is no clear explanation in the ICC Statute itself as to what the objective of the phrase 'interests of justice' was intended to be, even though the phrase appears in key areas of the Statute and the Rules of Procedure and Evidence of the Court. However, as shall be discussed, the mandate of the Prosecutor under the ICC Statute and the very purpose of the establishment of the Court, as evidenced in the preamble to the Statute, can provide the most significant guidance.

In the structure of the mandate and operations of the Office of the Prosecutor, the interests of justice consideration can occur only after determinations on both jurisdiction and admissibility. These are very heavy thresholds that the Prosecutor must cross before he or she can find a reason not to proceed in the interests of justice. The ICC Statute is focused on investigating and prosecuting the most serious crimes of concern to the international community. For any situation to be admissible, not only do the alleged crimes have to be those within the jurisdiction of the Court, but they also have to be of 'sufficient gravity to justify further action' under Article 17(1)d of the ICC Statute. The Office of the Prosecutor has asserted that in determining whether any situation is of sufficient gravity, he or she will consider the scale of the crimes, the nature of the crimes, the manner of their commission and their impact.

Therefore, even before considering whether there are substantial reasons to believe that it is not in the interests of justice to initiate an investigation or commence a prosecution, there has already been a decision that evidence indicating the gravity of the alleged crimes against humanity, war crimes or genocide is actually or potentially very high, is admissible under the criteria laid down in the Statute and that there are sufficient grounds to proceed with the investigation or prosecution. This means that the reference to 'The Gravity of the Crime' as one of the explicit factors to be considered in determining the interests of justice must lead to a strong presumption against any extraneous factor, such as potential peace negotiations, being taken into account in determining when it is in the interests of justice NOT to proceed with an investigation or prosecution. This strong presumption is even stronger if there is any demand not to proceed with a prosecution in the interests of justice. The preliminary investigation will have produced sufficient evidence of the gravity of the crimes that would make it very difficult to put aside such evidence and forget about it in the interests of justice.

This conclusion is reinforced by the objectives and purpose of the ICC Statute itself as stated in the Preamble. Paragraph four of the Statute's Preamble confirms the intention of the States Parties to put an end to impunity for the perpetrators of the most serious crimes of concern to the international community and thus to contribute to their prevention. Likewise the last paragraph confirms the resolve of the States Parties to guarantee lasting respect for and the enforcement of international justice. These are surely overwhelming aspects of the interests of justice in addition to the obligatory standards imposed on the mandate and operations of the Prosecutor. Such a conclusion can sometimes be regarded as clashing with the potential for peaceful settlement of violent conflicts where the most serious of international crimes are alleged to have been committed. Nevertheless, the ICC Statute imposes a regime of law and the rule of law, not one which is subject to the shifting winds of politics and political expediency. It is for these reasons that the Prosecutor has not yet made a decision to investigate or not proceed with a prosecution after determining that it would not be in the interests of justice.[55]

As will be discussed in the next chapter, there is also a grave danger that those who are alleged to have committed the most serious of international crimes could use the prospect of interminable peace negotiations to escape any form of investigation and prosecution, thereby creating a form of impunity by interminable peace negotiations which may never succeed. This has become most contentious in the context of the investigations and prosecutions in Darfur, Sudan, and Northern Uganda, as the next two chapters will discuss. In both cases, the alleged perpetrators seemed to develop a strategy of interminable negotiations, which may well have been programmed in advance for failure.

Another explicit factor that the Prosecutor is to take into account under Article 53 in determining whether the interests of justice should prevail over any investigation or prosecution is the interests of victims.

The taking into account of the interests and participation of victims, who under the Rome Statute are able to present their views and concerns to the Court, has been regarded as one of the most unique and historic features of the ICC, unparalleled in the history of international criminal tribunals.

Taking into account the interests of victims will often require taking into account conflicting perspectives of victims. While undoubtedly some will argue strenuously for investigations and prosecutions for the most serious international crimes based on compelling evidence to go ahead, the views of other victims could well diverge. The Prosecutor has faced these divergent views of victims in virtually all the investigations and prosecutions to date, and no doubt will do so in all future ones. Because investigations and subsequent prosecutions will often involve the world's most dangerous places, the interests of victims will also focus on the safety, physical and psychological wellbeing, dignity and privacy of victims who are also likely to be witnesses as required by Article 68(1) and Article 54(1)b of the ICC Statute. Indeed the Registry of the ICC has established a Victims and Witnesses Unit that focuses on ongoing risk assessments for victims and witnesses. Ultimately to properly assess the interests of victims and victim witnesses, the Prosecutor has to conduct extensive consultations with a wide range of individuals, groups and other stakeholders beyond the identified group of victims.[56]

The Office of the Prosecutor has followed this approach in the situation in Northern Uganda which will be discussed in a following chapter and has made more than twenty-five missions to the region to gather the various views and interests of victims and has established extensive protective measures for victims and potential witnesses. However, this has not led to the Prosecutor deciding to terminate any investigations or prosecutions as regards the indicted alleged perpetrators in Northern Uganda in the interests of justice.[57]

As will be clear from a following chapter, even though many victims may have wished to have the investigations and prosecutions stopped in the hope of a peace agreement, it was again clear that the main perpetrators were using that hope to implement a form of impunity under the façade of seeking peace.

Finally, the Prosecutor is also entitled to take into account the particular circumstances of the accused as described in Article 53(2)c. The interests of justice will not be served in this regard if, for example, the accused is terminally ill or is even a suspect who has been himself the victim of serious crimes or human rights violations. The continuation of any investigation or prosecution in such a case would not be in accord with the objective of the Court as enunciated in the Preamble to achieve lasting respect for and the enforcement of international justice.[58]

Article 53 does not provide an exhaustive list of considerations for the Prosecutor to consider what may be in the interests of justice in determining whether to begin an investigation or prosecution, but it is subject to the parameters described above. Given the high thresholds of jurisdiction and admissibility, there is the strongest of presumptions in favour of seeking accountability for the most serious of crimes. This is not to downplay the importance of other forms of accountability pursued by other groups and individuals. The Office of the Prosecutor has endorsed and supported other forms of genuine and effective strategies to combat impunity. These include the vital role to be played by domestic prosecutions for individuals lower down the hierarchy of organizations that have planned and implemented the serious crimes and traditional justice mechanisms such as Truth Commissions and reparation programs. These alternative forms of seeking redress for acts of impunity are exceedingly valuable forms of complementary mechanisms for the ICC to ensure that what is termed the 'impunity gap' are addressed.[59]

These interpretations of the interests of justice based on the objectives of the ICC Statute and the mandate and operations of the Office of the Prosecutor have not stopped critics of the Court, who allege that in some situations the ICC has acted to subvert ongoing peace processes. As the following chapters will discuss, this has reached a zenith in the case of the prosecutions and arrest warrants in Northern Uganda and Sudan.

Former Secretary General Kofi Annan stated that 'justice, peace and democracy are not mutually exclusive objectives, but rather mutually reinforcing imperatives'. He stated this in the context of a report on recommendations requested by the U.N. Security Council at a meeting in January of 2006 on post-conflict national reconciliation and the role of the United Nations. He argued that approaches focusing only on one or another institution, or ignoring civil society or victims, will not be effective.[60]

In keeping with these views of the U.N. Secretary General, justice versus peace cannot be seen as a zero sum game. Indeed both are partners in the process of establishing a sustainable peace in the troubled regions of our world. If peace and justice are indeed such partners, then there has to be an institutional division of labour in terms of which organizations and institutions promote justice and which ones promote peace.

The mandate of the ICC is to combat impunity for the most serious of crimes known to humanity. In very exceptional circumstances it can desist from doing so in the interests of justice, as discussed above. The concept of the interests of justice cannot be taken to encapsulate the entire gamut of issues relating to peace and security in conflict zones. To do so would turn the ICC from a judicial body to a global political body and, as discussed throughout this chapter, severely hinder the justice role played by the Court in preventing future conflicts and promoting sustainable peace through that function. Indeed the Statute of the ICC recognizes this institutional division of labour on justice and peace.

The Office of the Prosecutor and the Court are bound by the mandates given to them by the ICC Statute. These mandates are focused on the law relating to the fight against impunity and the need to ensure that serious crimes do not go unpunished. The agenda for peace given to the ICC is that stipulated in its Preamble, that if such crimes do go unpunished it threatens the peace, security and wellbeing of the world. The statement by Adolf Hitler on the forgotten Armenian genocide is conclusive proof of this peace agenda of the ICC.

This does not mean that the ICC will not be involved in situations that call for attention to be paid to the larger political context and the potential for peace through political negotiations. That larger context is not, however, the role given to the ICC by its Statute. Instead the Statute offers that role to the U.N. Security Council.

There is the ability under the ICC Statute for the U.N. Security Council to 'trump' the law and justice role of the Court by deferring any investigation or prosecution by the ICC where it considers it necessary for the maintenance of international peace and security. Article 16 of the Statute states that 'no investigation or prosecution may be commenced or proceeded with under this Statute for a period of 12 months after the Security Council, in a resolution under Chapter VII of the Charter of the United Nations, has requested the Court to that effect'. That request may be renewed by the Council under the same conditions. Finally, it should be noted that under Article 53 a decision by the Prosecutor not to investigate or prosecute made in the context of the interests of justice will only be effective if confirmed by the Pre-Trial Chamber which may also on its own initiative review the same decision by the Prosecutor. The

Prosecutor may also reconsider his decisions in this area based on new facts or information.

5.   THE FIRST STEPS IN THE FIGHT AGAINST IMPUNITY BY THE ICC; COMBATING NOT JUST IMPUNITY, BUT UNFOUNDED ALLEGATIONS OF BIAS TOWARDS AFRICA

The greatest clarity on how the provisions of this historic ICC Statute can contribute to combating impunity for the most serious of crimes will be demonstrated over time by the actual investigations, prosecutions and decisions by the Court in the first few years of its existence since July 1, 2002. While details of such actions as regards the situations in Northern Uganda and Sudan will be discussed and analysed in the following two chapters, this chapter will conclude with an overview of the main investigations and prosecutions carried out by the Court in the first six years of its existence.

In these first few years of the Court's existence, there has been trenchant criticism of the ICC that substantially all of its investigations and prosecutions have been in Africa, prompting allegations that the ICC is a western Court that is biased towards the southern hemisphere and reckless as to the potential for peaceful settlement of conflicts, especially in the ongoing violent conflicts in Africa. As will be discussed, these critiques are themselves substantially ignorant of the facts that have given rise to the first investigations and prosecutions by the ICC.

There have indeed been twelve arrest warrants issued against twelve Africans accused of perpetrating the most serious of crimes under the ICC Statute under four situations addressed by the Court. What those who accuse the ICC of bias towards Africa consistently do not acknowledge is that, of the twelve arrest warrants and prosecutions, three of the situations that gave rise to these warrants and prosecutions were referred to by the African governments of Uganda, the Democratic Republic of Congo (DRC) and the Central African Republic.

What should also be a blow to the critics who allege that the ICC has a bias towards Africa is that the very first *proprio motu* investigation in an African country being sought by the Prosecutor has the full blessing of the African government. On November 7, 2009, the Prosecutor announced that he will be requesting the authorization of the Pre-Trial Chamber under Article 15 of the ICC Statute to open an investigation into the post-election violence in Kenya. The post-election violence in Kenya is discussed in Chapter 4. At a meeting in the same week the Kenyan government, through the statements of President Mwai Kibaki and Prime Minister Raila Odinga, promised their full cooperation with the investigation. The Prosecutor also indicated that any trials of those most responsible for the crimes could take place either in Kenya itself or in Arusha, Tanzania.[61]

In the case of Uganda, as will be extensively discussed in Chapter 3, it was not the ICC that went looking for an African situation to investigate and to prosecute Africans; it was an African Head of State who sought out the ICC frustrated with the inability to end the violent conflict in the north of his country and perhaps seeing the ICC as a way out of a brutal and endless conflict. The facts, which will be discussed in greater detail in Chapter 3, are in brief, the following.

In 1987, a messianic figure, Joseph Kony, established a brutal militia called the Lord's Resistance Army (LRA) seeking to overthrow the government of President Yoweri Museveni and establish a Christian national government based on the Ten Commandments. The LRA went on a rampage in Northern Uganda which resulted in the LRA torturing, mutilating and killing thousands of civilians, and abducted approximately 20,000 children forcing them into the most horrible conditions of enslavement as child soldiers and sex slaves, ordering them often to mutilate and kill their own parents and relatives.

After failing to eliminate them militarily and after several failed attempts to negotiate a peaceful settlement, President Museveni became the first Head of State to refer the situation to the ICC. While some have alleged this African Head of State may have done so to further his own political and military goals, it is beyond any logic based on facts to assert that the ICC went looking to impose a Western view of international justice on Uganda and its people. However, it did not stop the critics. As Chapter 3 will discuss, after the ICC handed down arrest warrants for Joseph Kony and four of the top LRA leaders, there was strong criticism from both inside and outside Africa that the ICC was interfering in the domestic attempts at justice and traditional methods of peaceful reconciliation as regards the savagery of the LRA. What these critics have often omitted is that it was Uganda that referred the situation to the ICC. These critics also seem to ignore mounting evidence, as discussed in Chapter 3, of the track record of Joseph Kony and the LRA in pretending to offer peace while preparing and rearming for the continuation of some of the most brutal savagery seen in the African continent.

The DRC is perhaps the most active and complex African situation facing the mandate and operations of the ICC, potentially leading to the major part of its caseload in the first six years. All the present arrest warrants and prosecutions in the DRC are again the result of a referral by the government of that country, and again put paid to the unfounded critique that the ICC went looking to impose western forms of international justice in such a major African country.

The roots of the present situations, referred to the ICC by the government of the DRC, go back to the attempt by rebels backed by Uganda and Rwanda to attack the DRC government in 1998 with the aim of overthrowing it. While beaten back on several occasions, they mutated into a savage band of opposing militias, many with the backing of the five neighboring countries of Uganda, Rwanda, Namibia, Angola and Zimbabwe, some of which sent in their own troops. In 1999, all six countries and the main militias signed the Lusaka Peace Accords supposedly including a ceasefire and a framework for peaceful settlement of disputes. The U.N. Security Council established at that time the largest peacekeeping force in the world, MONUC, to assist with the implementation of the Peace Accords, and later in July of 2003, under a Chapter VII mandate authorizing the use of force, increased its size to approximately 10,800 peacekeepers. Sadly, as with many such conflicts where the massive mineral wealth and power of the Congo is at stake, the ceasefire was broken on countless occasions and the militias renewed their atrocities against the civilian populations. It is important to note that often it is not justice that is the adversary of peace, but the greed to control the resources of a country and the power that comes with it that on countless occasions ends the prospect of peace.

The ICC Prosecutor had begun investigations in the Ituri district of eastern Congo in July of 2003, under his *proprio motu* powers, in a part of the Congo where some of the worst atrocities against civilians were taking place. However, to again demonstrate the working partnership of the ICC with African governments, on March 3, 2004, President Joseph Kabila referred to the ICC situations that could constitute serious crimes, not only in the Ituri District, but also throughout the DRC. The Prosecutor willingly accepted the referral because it was a guarantee of cooperation from the government of the DRC in what is probably the most difficult of environments to conduct complex investigations and ensure a successful prosecution.

After eighteen months of investigations in the DRC, on January 12, 2006, the Prosecutor sought a sealed warrant against Thomas Lubanga Dyilo, a brutal Congolese warlord. He was charged with the crimes of enlisting and conscripting children under the age of 15, as well as using them in violent combat. While there has been criticism of the limited charges against this alleged perpetrator whom others have accused also of sexual violence and systemic rape constituting war crimes and crimes against humanity, the ICC has defended its position on the grounds that the content of the charges was triggered by the possible imminent release of Lubanga by the DRC authorities.

On February 10, 2006, the ICC Pre-Trial Chamber issued a sealed arrest warrant against him and he was surrendered by the DRC on March 17, 2006. It should be noted that this was the first arrest warrant ever executed by an African government on behalf of the Court, again demonstrating not a conflict between African peace process and justice, but a partnership between the ICC and an African government. After several delays due to non-disclosure of evidence by the Office of the Prosecutor that almost derailed the prosecution of Lubanga, the ICC began its historic first trial of an indicted criminal on January 23, 2009. The trial is regarded as substantially important in the development of international criminal law as it is the first case in which the use of child soldiers will be prosecuted as constituting an international crime.[62]

Pursuant to the referral of all potential situations of serious crimes in the DRC, on August 28, 2008, the Pre-Trial Chamber unsealed an arrest warrant against another Congolese warlord, Bosco Ntaganda, alleging he was the perpetrator of war crimes of enlistment and conscription of children under the age of 15 and, like Lubanga, using them actively in hostilities in the Ituri region of eastern Congo. Indeed, the Pre-Trial Chamber disclosed that Bosco Ntaganda was the Deputy Chief of General Staff for Military Operations of the militia led by Lubanga Dyilo.

Bosco Ntaganda remains at large, because on his indictment he switched sides and joined the government forces to try to eliminate other militias in another troubled part of the DRC, namely North Kivu. The DRC government is claiming that it will not now execute the arrest warrant until there has been the 'pacification' of the province of North Kivu.[63] The BBC is also reporting that Bosco Ntaganda may also be playing a leading role in the U.N. peacekeeping force, MONUC, which is engaged together with Congolese forces in military operations against Hutu rebel forces in eastern Congo. Officials from both the DRC military and MONUC have denied the claim, but according to the BBC a high ranking Congolese military official confirmed that the indicted alleged war criminal is involved in the joint operations.[64]

There are occasions when it is not justice which is the adversary of peace, but governments' manipulation of both peace and justice in order to pursue their own self-interested political agendas.

Approximately a year earlier, on October 17, 2007, the DRC executed an ICC arrest warrant against Germain Katanga, another Congolese warlord, and surrendered him to the Court in The Hague. He is charged with crimes against humanity and war crimes allegedly committed in 2003 in the town of Bogoro in the Ituri District of the DRC. Like the indictment against Lubanga, these include willful killings, conscripting child soldiers and using them to take part in active hostilities, and systemic rape and sexual slavery.

Following the arrest of Katanga, on February 6, 2008, an ICC arrest warrant was executed by the DRC government against Mathieu Ngudjolo Chui, another leader of the same militia that had also been led by Katanga. He was surrendered to the ICC the following day. Again there is some irony that at the time of his arrest Chui was in military training with the DRC military in the capital, Kinshasa, following his appointment as a colonel in the DRC army in 2006.[65] Chui is charged with the same crimes as Katanga, and the ICC trial will allege that the two jointly committed through other persons a substantial number of war crimes and crimes against humanity, including willful killings, rape and sexual slavery pursuant to the list of crimes in Articles 7 and 8 of the Rome Statute. At the time of writing the Trial Chamber of the ICC will be opening up the trial of the two warlords in September 2009.

Governmental duplicity may be a bigger adversary to peace than any form of international justice pursued by the ICC. Human Rights Watch is alleging that the militia of both indicted Congolese warlords had received financial and military backing from high-ranking officials in the DRC government and also in Uganda, which had supported the same militia group, and that Katanga had been personally involved in meetings in which such support was discussed. Claiming that the indicted militia leaders did not act alone, Human Rights Watch is requesting the Prosecutor of the ICC to investigate the links between the indicted men and high-ranking officials, not only in the DRC, but also in Uganda and Rwanda.[66]

The Central African Republic (CAR) is the final one of three African countries that have made the decision that there is no conflict between peace and justice by referring the situation in the CAR to the ICC. There is again the complexity of ascertaining the true intentions of referring governments in this situation also.

The CAR was successful in having a democratically elected government in 1993 led by President Ange-Felix Patassé. But after considerable unrest in the government, the Army Chief of Staff, François Bozizé, overthrew the government in a military coup in March of 2003. He was subsequently elected in 2005. Former President Patassé had enlisted the help of troops and militias from the DRC and mercenaries from Chad and Libya to help prevent his ouster, and then used them to stage a counter coup against the man who had ousted him. Criminal proceedings in the CAR were started against Patassé for the most brutal of crimes committed against civilians, including those committed under his control by militias from the DRC.

As if to demonstrate that the ICC can in practice be the court of last resort in the fight against impunity for the most serious of international crimes, the highest court in the CAR admitted that the national judicial system could not effectively investigate and prosecute crimes committed by the various militias and troops and advised the referral to the ICC. The government of the CAR agreed and referred the situation to the ICC on December 22, 2004. Pursuant to this referral by the third African country to the ICC, the Prosecutor began investigating serious crimes committed in the country since July 1, 2002, the effective date of the operation of the ICC. The Prosecutor announced he would focus on the use of systemic sexual violence and other war crimes to terrorize the population and will also review the ongoing violence near the border with Chad and Sudan.[67]

Pursuant to these investigations the Prosecutor sought a sealed arrest warrant for DRC militia leader Jean-Pierre Bemba and, following confirmation by the Pre-Trial Chamber, on May 24, 2008, Belgian authorities executed a sealed arrest warrant against Bemba and surrendered him to the Court in The Hague on July 3, 2008. Bemba stands accused jointly or through another person of three counts of crimes against humanity, rape and torture, as well as five counts of war crimes that also include rape and torture and outrages against personal dignity allegedly committed in the CAR. These acts of inhumane savagery were allegedly committed to prevent the coup against President Patassé. One of the main lines of defense put forward by Bemba's defense team is that his forces were under the command and control of the Patassé government. This has been rejected by the ICC Prosecutor. According to an ICC Prosecutor, Bemba's troops were instructed to traumatize and terrorize the local population and went from house to house, pillaging and raping mothers, wives and daughters to eliminate any resistance to the Patassé government.[68] One report describes how a woman was repeatedly raped as she lay on the corpse of her dead husband and then there was an attempt to cut her throat in front of her children.[69] Another report of a representative of a victim described how a district official had been raped for four hours in front of his wife and children before the troops raped them also.[70]

The Pre-Trial confirmation of the charges has been delayed by the request of the Chamber on March 3, 2009, to submit an amended document containing the charges, as the evidence submitted by the Prosecutor appeared to establish a different crime, namely criminal liability as a commander or superior under Article 28(a) of the Statute, without predetermination of the criminal responsibility of Bemba. On June 15, 2009, the Pre-Trial Chamber confirmed some of the charges brought by the Prosecutor against Jean-Pierre Bemba for crimes committed in the CAR from on or about October 26, 2002 to March 15, 2003. The Court found there was sufficient evidence to try Bemba on charges that he was criminally responsible as a person effectively acting as a military commander within the meaning of Article 28(a) for two counts of crimes against humanity involving murder and rape and three counts of war crimes also involving murder and rape and pillaging.

However, the Pre-Trial Chamber rejected the Prosecutor's charges alleging that Bemba was criminally responsible jointly through another person or through other persons on five counts of war crimes and three counts of crimes against humanity. The Pre-Trial Chamber seemed to be signaling that it would not be easily convinced that charges can be sustained on the complex modes of liability involving indirect perpetration and co-perpetration, derived from some of the most complex areas of German criminal law. The Prosecutor is appealing the decision of the Pre-Trial Chamber.

There is additional significance to the indictment against Bemba as he previously held one of the highest posts in an African country before the arrest warrant for President al-Bashir of Sudan. Bemba served as the Vice-President of the DRC, second only to President Kabila after the Lusaka Peace Accords ended the 1998 war in the DRC that involved five neighboring countries and was termed Africa's world war. After his ouster by Kabila, in the wake of his militias' combating the DRC army in the capital, Kinshasa, Bemba went into exile in Europe which facilitated his arrest in Belgium. In another sign that justice has to contend with potential duplicity and opaque political objectives of even those governments that refer situations to the ICC, at the end of 2008 the current CAR government led by President François Bozizé entered into talks with rebel and opposition leaders who included Patassé, the instigator of the crimes against humanity and war crimes in the CAR.[71]

On September 30, 2009, the Prosecutor of the ICC announced the decision to investigate and potentially prosecute the Kenyan officials most responsible for the post-election violence in that country. The events leading up to this decision are discussed further in Chapter 4. Apart from this announcement, the only situation that was not referred by an African country that has resulted in an active prosecution by the ICC is the historic decision by the U.N. Security Council on March 31, 2005, to refer the situation in the Darfur region of Sudan to the ICC. Sudan is not a party to the ICC Statute, and therefore the only way in which the situation in Darfur could be brought before the ICC was a referral by the U.N. Security Council, as discussed above. As will be discussed in the following chapter, an independent commission of the U.N. had already investigated the humanitarian and human rights crisis in Darfur and had identified over fifty individuals linked to the Sudanese government and the Janjaweed militias controlled by Khartoum which the Commission suspected of committing crimes against humanity and war crimes. The same Commission had recommended a further judicial investigation into the situation in

Darfur by the ICC and that the suspects be investigated and potentially prosecuted in the ICC.

The events leading up to this historic Security Council referral will be discussed in detail in the following chapter. What should be noted at this point is that the decision of the most powerful members of the world to allow the ICC to investigate allegations of crimes against humanity, war crimes and possible genocide in Darfur was the end result of a sudden end to a stand off in the Security Council. Both China and the U.S. threatened to use the veto on any possible referral under the Rome Statute. Earlier in March of 2005, France had stated its intention to submit a resolution calling for a referral of the situation in Darfur to the ICC. The U.S. put up strong resistance, and instead proposed the setting up of yet another ad hoc U.N.–African Union Tribunal in Tanzania to investigate the allegation of serious international crimes in Darfur. This proposal drew little support from the members of the Council, who argued that only the ICC had the investigative staff ready to begin the work.[72] The sometimes irrational and ideological opposition by the Bush Administration to the ICC and the possible referral of the Darfur situation to the ICC led one opinion writer in the *New York Times* to accuse that U.S. Administration of 'not knowing' what it disliked more – genocide or the International Criminal Court, which seeks to punish it'.[73]

Ultimately China, afraid of the accusation by the international community that it was complicit in the Sudanese government's actions in Darfur due to its important oil and gas interests in Sudan and mindful that its own human rights reputation was extremely fragile just a few years before the 2008 Beijing Olympics, decided to abstain. The U.S. was also forced to abstain and allowed the Security Council resolution referring the Darfur situation to the ICC. In part, this abstention was due to the fact that both the U.S. Congress and President Bush's own Secretary of State, Colin Powell, had recently used the word 'genocide' to describe what the U.N. itself called the world's worst humanitarian crisis.

However, along with China and other recalcitrant Security Council members, the U.S. not only insisted that the ICC receive no additional funding for the heavy burden it had just received from the Security Council, but astonishingly the Security Council also determined to exempt 'States not Party to the Rome Statute' from compliance. Given the high probability that the ICC might well find the highest officials in Sudan guilty of the crime of genocide, in effect the former Bush Administration along with their 'partners in crime' in the Security Council seemed to assert that this highest body of the U.N. could exempt member states from their obligations under one of the most universally accepted legal obligations they had, namely the prevention and punishment of the crime of genocide under the Genocide Convention of 1948. The much too heavy price for the abstention of China and the U.S. under the former Bush Administration may well reveal itself in future attempts to ensure the most serious of crimes known to humanity do not go unpunished. If the Security Council is able to exempt member states from their '*erga omnes*' legal obligations, then the international community faces the prospect that there are no universal legal obligations that apply to all nations! This would make a mockery of the promise of 'never again'.

As will be discussed in the following chapter, the investigations by the ICC Prosecutor pursuant to the U.N. Security Council referral led on May 2, 2007, to the confirmation of arrest warrants by the Pre-Trial Chamber of the ICC against Ahmad Harun, a former Sudanese State Minister of the Interior, a key figure in the planning and implementation of the humanitarian crisis in Darfur, and Ali Kushayb, a Janjaweed militia leader. They were charged with dozens of counts of crimes against humanity and war crimes in Darfur.

Pursuing his investigations into the situation in Darfur, on July 14, 2007, the ICC Prosecutor sought an arrest warrant against President Omar al-Bashir on charges of genocide, crimes against humanity and war crimes. On March 4, 2009, the Pre-Trial Chamber confirmed five counts of crimes against humanity and two counts of war crimes against al-Bashir, but refused to confirm the charge of genocide as the Prosecutor had failed to provide evidence of the specific intent to commit genocide. A more detailed discussion of this historic decision by the Pre-Trial Chamber to issue an arrest warrant to a sitting Head of State will follow in the next chapter. The Prosecutor has appealed the Chamber's finding on genocide, given that there was a strong dissent by one of the three judges on whether there was sufficient evidence to demonstrate on a permissible lesser burden of proof that al-Bashir should stand trial for the crime of genocide. The Pre-Trial Chamber has allowed the appeal to the Appeals Chamber of the ICC on this ground, as will also be discussed in the next chapter.

In a development which could demonstrate that the ICC does not have a propensity for bias against the Khartoum government, the ICC Prosecutor also announced that after a more recent investigation, he expected to provide to the Pre-Trial Chamber evidence that will indict several rebel leaders in Darfur in connection with an attack on the eastern Darfur town of Haskanita that killed ten African Union peacekeepers in September of 2007. On May 18, 2009, the Pre-Trial Chamber set the date of October 12, 2009 for confirmation of the charges against Bahr Idriss Abu Garda, one of the rebel leaders, who is suspected of having committed three war crimes during the attack against the U.N. peacekeeping mission in September 2007. To the surprise of many, especially President al-Bashir and his two indicted officials, Abu Garda appeared voluntarily for the initial appearance before the Chamber on a summons rather than an arrest warrant, as he accepted the jurisdiction of the Court and wished to prove his innocence. On October 19, 2009, Abu Garda appeared voluntarily before the Pre-Trial Chamber for the confirmation of charges hearing. He is the first suspect to have appeared, and to have appeared voluntarily in the context of the situation in Darfur. The offer of voluntary appearance for the initial appearances before the Pre-Trial Chamber had also been made to al-Bashir, Harun and Kushayb. The Pre-Trial Chamber was also reviewing in November of 2008 the Prosecutor's application for the issuance of arrest warrants or alternatively summonses for two other individuals who allegedly also participated in the attacks on the Haskanita peacekeepers.

The accusations that the ICC Prosecutor and Court have shown bias in selecting Sudan to focus its investigations and prosecutions are clearly without any substance, given that it had no choice in following the legal framework of the ICC Statute once the U.N. Security Council had referred the situation to the Court and its Prosecutor.

As we shall see in the following chapter, any potential threat to a sustainable peace in not just Darfur, but the entire country of Sudan, has been threatened not by the ICC and its justice mandate, but by the Machiavellian and duplicitous tactics of President al-Bashir and his top officials. They have engaged in deliberately destabilizing and then destroying minorities in his country in order to control the resources and the power in this tragedy filled country.

What is significant in the unraveling of the artificial peace versus justice critique against the ICC and its Prosecutor is the fact that while the latter was given the potentially powerful *proprio motu* power to initiate investigations leading to potential prosecutions, it has not been the primary source of the caseload of the ICC. The Chief Prosecutor, Luis Moreno-Ocampo, has instead adopted the policy of inviting and welcoming voluntary referrals by any state, including any African state, as the first step in the triggering of the jurisdiction of the Court. It was this policy that respected the national sovereignty of all states, including the African states that the ICC stands accused of being biased against, that led to the three situations in Northern Uganda, the DRC and the Central African Republic being the major focus of the Court. This policy was also adopted because it increased the likelihood of critical cooperation and support issues that were needed between the countries involved and the Court. It is Africa itself which cries out for the fight against impunity as a precondition for sustainable peace on this troubled continent. It is a fitting testament to the vision that justice is bred in the bones of humankind and that this sense of universal justice looks to the ICC as the 'Court of Last Resort'.

NOTES

1. Benjamin N. Schiff, *Building the International Criminal Court* (Cambridge University Press, 2008) at 15–16.
2. Hugo Grotius, *De Jure Belli Ac Pacis Libri Tres* (1625) book III, chapter X, at para. IV, trans. in Benjamin B. Ferencz, *Enforcing International Law* (Oceana Publications, 1985) at 137.
3. Christopher Keith Hall, 'The First Proposal for a Permanent International Criminal Court' (1998) 332 *Int'l Rev. Red Cross* 57.
4. U.S. Army, 'Instructions for the Government of Armies of the United States in the Field' (General Orders No. 100, 1863).
5. For the history and significance of the Martens Clause, see T. Meron, 'The Martens Clause, principles of humanity, and dictates of public conscience' (2000) 94:1 *Am. J. Int'l L.* 78.
6. Hilarie McCoubrey, *International Humanitarian Law*, 2nd ed. (Ashgate, 1998) at 27–28.
7. *Supra* note 1 at 20–21.
8. William A. Schabas, *An Introduction to the International Criminal Court*, 2nd ed. (Cambridge University Press, 2004) at 4.
9. See the Armenian National Institute's website devoted to the historical record of the Armenian genocide, available at the following url: http://www.armenian-genocide.org/hitler.html.
10. *Treaty of Peace between the Allied and Associated Powers and Germany*, 28 June 1919, T.S. 4, Art 227. Schabas, *supra* note 8 at 4, asserts that there were few actual trials held in Germany and minimal sentences were handed down. They were perceived as a failure of this early attempt to establish an international criminal justice process.
11. G.J. Bass, *Staying the Hand of Vengeance: The Politics of War Crimes Tribunals* (Princeton University Press, 2001) at 157.
12. Schabas, *supra* note 8 at 8.
13. See the Final Report of the Commission of Experts established pursuant to Security Council Resolution 780, (1992) and Add.2 Annexes II, IX, IX(A), IX(B), 27 May 1994, UN Doc. s/1994/674. See also B. Ajbola, 'Human Rights in the Federation of Bosnia-Herzegovina' (1997) 12:2 *Conn. J. Int'l L.*189–196; D. Kresock, 'Ethnic Cleansing in the Balkans: The Legal Foundations of Foreign Intervention' (1994) 27 *Cornell Int'l L.J.* 203–239; T. Meron, 'Rape as a Crime under International Humanitarian Law' (1993) 87:3 *Am. J. Int'l L.* 424.
14. Report of the Secretary-General pursuant to General Assembly resolution 53/35, *The Fall of Srebrenica*, UN GAOR, 54th Sess., UN Doc. A/54/549 (15 December 1999).
15. UN Security Council Resolution 808 (1993).
16. UN Security Council Resolution 827 (1993).
17. See the Report of The Independent Inquiry into the Actions of the United Nations during the 1994 Genocide in Rwanda, UN Doc. S/1999/1257 (15 December 1999) available at the following url: http://www.un.org/News/dh/latest/rwanda.htm.
18. UN Security Council Resolution 955 (1994).
19. UN Security Council Resolutions 808 & 827 (1993).
20. ICTY official Website located at the following url: http://www.icty.org/sections/AbouttheICTY.
21. UN Security Council Resolution 995 (1994).
22. ICTR official website located at the following url: http://69.94.11.53/default.htm.
23. Theodor Meron, 'War Crimes in Yugoslavia and the Development of International Law' (1994) 88 *Am. J. Int'l L.* 78 at 79.
24. See for example, Leila Nadia Sadat, 'The Legacy of the ICTY: The International Criminal Court' (2003) 37:4 *New Eng. L. Rev.* 1073.
25. *Ibid.* at 1074–1078. See also Yoram Dinstein, 'Case Analysis: Crimes Against Humanity After Tadić' (2000) 13:2 *Leiden J. Int'l L.* at 373–393.

26. 'Selling Justice Short, Why Accountability Matters for Peace', *Human Rights Watch* (7 July 2009) at 25–27.
27. *Ibid.* at 20–25.
28. *Ibid.* at 117–122.
29. See Suzannah Linton, 'Cambodia, East Timor and Sierra Leone: Experiments in International Justice' (2001) 12:2 *Crim. L.F.* 185 at 190.
30. 'Cambodia: First Trial to Test Tribunal's Credibility; Court's Independence Remains a Concern as Khmer Rouge Trials Begin', *Human Rights Watch* (14 February 2009).
31. '"Special Panels" in East Timor', *Human Rights First,* available at the following url: http://www.humanrightsfirst.org/cah/ij/w_context/w_cont_06.aspx.
32. For a detailed discussion of the origins of some of the key provisions of the ICC Statute during the negotiations, see Adriaan Bos, 'From the International Law Commission to the Rome Conference (1984–1998)' in A. Cassese, Paola Gaeta and John R.W.D. Jones, eds., *The Rome Statute of the International Criminal Court: A Commentary* (Oxford University Press, 2002) at 35–64.
33. *Report of the Preparatory Committee on the Establishment of an International Criminal Court*, Addendum, UN Doc. A/Conf.183/Add.1.
34. M. Scharf, 'The Politics behind the US Opposition to the ICC' (1999) 5 *New Eng. Int'l & Comp. L. Ann.* Pt V.
35. *Ibid.*
36. *Case Concerning Military and Paramilitary Activities in and Against Nicaragua (Nicaragua v. United States of America)* [1984] I.C.J. Rep. 392.
37. Scharf, *supra* note 34 at 3.
38. For an outstanding portrayal and analysis of the vitriolic and ideological attacks against the establishment of the Court by the Bush Administration led by the then U.S. State Department Official and later U.N. Ambassador John Bolton, see Erna Paris, *The Sun Climbs Slowly, Justice in the Age of Imperial America* (Alfred Knopf Canada, 2008) at 52–85.
39. Schabas, *supra* note 8 at 24.
40. There is a rich literature on the negotiations at the Rome Diplomatic Conference; see for example R. Lee, *The International Criminal Court: The Making of the Rome Statute; Issues, Negotiations and Results* (Kluwer Law International, 1999); Phillippe Kirsch & John T. Homes, 'The Birth of the International Criminal Court: The 1998 Rome Conference' (1998) 36 *Can. Y.B. Int'l Law* 3.
41. Sadat, *supra* note 24.
42. Leila N. Sadat & S. Richard Carden, 'The New International Criminal Court: An Uneasy Revolution' (2000) 88 *Geo L.J.* 381.
43. Kenneth S. Gallant, 'Jurisdiction to Adjudicate and Jurisdiction to Prescribe in International Criminal Courts' (2003) 48 *Vill. L. Rev.* 763.
44. See Nicholas Kralev, 'U.S. warms to Global Court' *Washington Times* (30 April 2009).
45. ICC Statute Article 86.
46. ICC Statute Article 17 (1) a–d.
47. ICTY Statute Article 9; ICTR Statute Article 8.
48. ICTY Statute Article 7(2) and ICTR Statute Article 6(2).
49. Article 7 of the Nuremberg Charter stated that 'the official position of defendants, whether as Heads of State or responsible officials in Government Departments, shall not be considered as freeing them from responsibility or mitigating punishment'.
50. E. Lauterpacht & C.J. Greenwood, *International Law Reports,* vol. 128 (Cambridge University Press, 2006) at 143.
51. *Case Concerning the Arrest Warrant of 11 April 2000 (Democratic Republic of the Congo v. Belgium)* [2002] I.C.J. Rep. 3.
52. *The Prosecutor v. Jean Kambanda, Judgment and Sentence*, ICTR 97-23-s (4 September 1998) (International Criminal Tribunal for Rwanda, Trial Chamber).
53. As occurred in the judgment of the ICTR in the case of *The Prosecutor v. Jean-Paul*

Akayesu, ICTR 96-4-T (2 September 1998) (International Criminal Tribunal for Rwanda, Trial Chamber).

54. Yusuf Aksar, *Implementing International Humanitarian Law, From Ad Hoc Tribunals to a Permanent International Criminal Court* (Routledge: Taylor & Francis, 2004) at 96.
55. Office of the Prosecutor, 'The Interests of Justice' *International Criminal Court Policy Paper* (4 September 2007) at 4.
56. *Ibid.* at 5–6.
57. *Ibid.*
58. *Ibid.* at 7.
59. *Ibid.* at 7–8.
60. See an account of this meeting at the website of 'Responsibility to Protect' United Nations Documents, titled 'Security Council – Stresses Importance, Urgency of Restoring Rule of Law in Post-Conflict Societies' (10 June 2004) available at the following url: http://www.responsibilitytoprotect.org.
61. See the website of the ICC for the announcement of the first *proprio motu* investigation titled 'Kenyan authorities committed to cooperate as ICC Prosecutor informs them that in December he will request ICC Judges to open an investigation into post-election violence', available at the following url: http://www.icc-cpi.int/NR/rdonlyres/10C0F90F-1AC5-4832-8E08-E3E4D28829F1/281179/UpdatedsheetKenya_3_2.pdf.
62. IWPR Staff in The Hague, 'Lubanga Trial a Landmark Case' *Global Policy Forum* (23 January 2009) available at the following url: http://globalpolicy.org/component/content/article/164/28631.html.
63. Kinshasa, Radio Okapi, 9 May 2009.
64. 'Congo ex-rebel working with UN' *BBC Report* (29 April 2009).
65. Human Rights Watch, 'ICC/DRC: New War Crimes Suspect Arrested' *Global Policy Forum* (7 February 2008) available at the following url: http://www.globalpolicy.org/component/content/article/164-icc/28629.html.
66. *Ibid.*
67. *Ibid.*
68. Reed Stevenson, 'Congo's Bemba Accused at Hague of Ordering Rape' *Global Policy Forum* (12 January 2009).
69. Mike Thompson, BBC News, 'Warlord Trial Gives Victims Hope' *Global Policy Forum* (8 December 2008).
70. Stevenson*, supra* note 68.
71. *Ibid.*
72. Evelyn Leopold, AlertNet, 'France pushes for UN Vote on Sudan; US May Veto' *Global Policy Forum* (24 March 2005).
73. Adam Wolfe, Power and Interest News Report, 'Trying Times in Darfur and the Establishment of International Criminal Law' *Global Policy Form* (4 March 2005).

2 Is it peace or justice that ends the alleged first genocide of the 21st Century?

1. RETALIATION AGAINST THE WRIT OF JUSTICE

On July 8, 2008, in the killing fields of Darfur, an estimated 200 Arab Janjaweed fighters on horseback and 40 heavily armed vehicles ambushed U.N. peacekeepers in the under-resourced UNAMID mission, killing seven peacekeepers with twenty-two others wounded (seven critically) during a confrontation that lasted more than two hours. The peacekeepers were killed as they were on a military patrol investigating the killing of two rebel soldiers in North Darfur. The casualties included five Rwandan soldiers and two police officers from the same country, together with one soldier from Ghana and one from Uganda. U.N. Secretary General Ban Ki-Moon condemned the attack as an unacceptable act of extreme violence in the strongest possible terms.[1]

BBC Reporter Laura Trevelyan reported that some U.N. officials suspected the ambush was orchestrated by the Sudanese government with its Janjaweed proxies in retaliation for a possible imminent indictment of a high level Sudanese official, perhaps even President al-Bashir. The Janjaweed's hostility could be linked to the fear that the UNAMID force could be used to arrest those indicted by the International Criminal Court (ICC).[2]

The BBC report was, in part, confirmed when prosecutors at the Court ruled that they would present evidence that supported charges of war crimes, crimes against humanity and genocide against President Omar al-Al-Bashir himself. On July 14, 2008, the Chief Prosecutor, Luis Moreno-Ocampo, presented the evidence to the Pre-Trial Chamber of the ICC seeking an arrest warrant that would be issued against the President for genocide, crimes against humanity and war crimes claiming that he was personally responsible for the displacement, killings and rapes in Darfur over the past five years. The Chief Prosecutor in his application for a warrant for the arrest of the Sudanese President seemed determined to present the most controversial grounds for indicting a sitting Head of

State, namely the charge of genocide. This would be controversial as it was almost a rebuttal of the findings of the international legal experts on the International Commission of Inquiry set up by the United Nations, which concluded a situation of genocide in Darfur did not exist. The most controversial part of the Chief Prosecutor's presentation of the evidence claimed that '[t]he evidence establishes reasonable grounds to believe that al-Bashir intends to destroy in substantial part the Fur, the Masalit and Zaghawa ethnic groups as such'.[3]

As would be learned later, the Trial Chamber of the Court on March 4, 2009, with one dissenting judge, would agree with the learned international law jurists who had previously decided that the hell that al-Bashir had visited upon the African tribes of Darfur did not amount to genocide.

2. PUTTING PEACE AND ALLEGATIONS OF GENOCIDE, CRIMES AGAINST HUMANITY AND WAR CRIMES IN SUDAN INTO CONTEXT

One day before the Universal Declaration of Human Rights was adopted in 1948, the General Assembly of the U.N. adopted a Convention which, although not as celebrated as the Universal Declaration, is deemed by the most eminent jurists to bind both signatories and non-signatories alike because of its most fundamental principles on human rights.[4] The treaty is the Convention on the Prevention and Punishment of the Crime of Genocide, adopted by the United Nations General Assembly on December 9, 1948.[5]

The Genocide Convention came into force on January 12, 1951. Like many international human rights treaties, it is again rife with reservations, even by the United States.[6] The Genocide Convention was intended to go beyond the principles of the Nuremberg Charter which established the war crimes tribunal at Nuremberg. That Charter required a link between 'crimes against humanity' and the international conflict of the Second World War. The critical provisions of the Genocide Convention made it clear that genocide could be committed during an international conflict, an intra-state conflict and during peacetime, and that individuals could be held criminally responsible for the crime of genocide.

Article I
The Contracting Parties confirm that genocide, whether committed in time of peace or war, is a crime under international law which they undertake to prevent and punish.

Article II

In the present Convention, genocide means any of the following acts committed with intent to destroy, in whole or in part, a national, ethnical, racial or religious group, as such:

  (a) Killing members of the group;
  (b) Causing serious bodily or mental harm to members of the group;
  (c) Deliberately inflicting on the group conditions of life calculated to bring about its physical destruction in whole or in part;
  (d) Imposing measures intended to prevent births within the group;
  (e) Forcibly transferring children of the group to another group.

Article III

The following acts shall be punishable:

  (a) Genocide;
  (b) Conspiracy to commit genocide;
  (c) Direct and public incitement to commit genocide;
  (d) Attempts to commit genocide;
  (e) Complicity in genocide.

Article IV

Persons committing genocide or any of the other acts enumerated in Article III shall be punished, whether they are constitutionally responsible rulers, public officials or private individuals.

These provisions of the Genocide Convention and the Geneva Conventions reach beyond the traditional ambit of international law that focuses on juridical relations between states. It imposes individual responsibility for the most atrocious of human rights abuses, even where such abuse is done in the interests of the state. Thus the Convention should have been one of modern history's greatest instruments for breaking down the tendency of nation states to hide behind the principle of non-interference in the domestic affairs of sovereign states in the face of mass slaughter of civilians. The fact that the shield of sovereignty continued to be used by those who intended to commit this most heinous of crimes despite the lessons of the Holocaust is the most abhorrent legacies of the second half of the 20th Century and the first decade of the 21st.

On April 2, 2004, Jan Egland, the U.N. Under Secretary for Humanitarian Affairs, pleaded with the Security Council to not remain passive while more villages in Darfur were destroyed, more people massacred, more women and girls brutally raped and tens of thousands more being displaced and seeking refuge in little more than concentration camps where they faced starvation and worse. He was preceded by the courageous advocacy by Mukesh Kapila, the top U.N. humanitarian crisis expert in Sudan, who urgently reported to the U.N. Secretariat in 2003 and 2004 of the large scale ethnic cleansing and killings organized by the Khartoum government and the Janjaweed in Darfur. These reports were based on extensive interviews by Kapila and his staff of victims and refugees in Darfur. Kapila urged the U.N. Secretariat to press for an internationally policed ceasefire in Darfur. Both Egland and Kapila were rebuffed by the Security Council and the U.N. Secretariat. Both U.N. bodies seemed to want to regard Darfur as a humanitarian crisis requiring more food aid and blankets rather than yet again ensuring against failure of the sacred promise of 'never again'. Soon both Egland and Kapila understood the reason for the inaction was that both the Secretariat and key members of the Security Council were keen not to let anything be in the way of what they considered a successful outcome of the peace process in the south of Sudan.[7] This peace process will be detailed and analyzed later in this chapter.

On May 25, 2004, Secretary General Kofi Annan, in a major speech at the U.N. on Africa Day, congratulated the establishment of the Peace and Security Council of the African Union in Addis Ababa, Ethiopia, and the good progress in the peace process in the south of Sudan. However, he pleaded with the international community not to ignore the suffering of the people of Darfur. On the same day, the President of the Security Council, Munir Akram of Pakistan, issued a presidential statement outlining grave concern over the deteriorating human rights situation in Darfur and called for humanitarian access, respect for a previously agreed ceasefire and for the Janjaweed to be disarmed. The Council did not even endeavor to turn the statement into a resolution of the Council, and so it became destined to be of as little impact as the mountains of presidential statements from the Council that had been ignored in other crises around the world. In June of 2005, the Security Council in Resolution 1547, which dealt primarily with the emerging north–south peace accords at Naivasha, Kenya, also called on the parties to use their influence to bring an immediate halt to the fighting in Darfur. What is interesting is that this meager reference to Darfur was inserted at the insistence of the French, who refused to buckle to the wishes of Britain and the United States that even such a passing reference to the unfolding genocide would interfere with the peace process and the establishment of a peace-keeping force in the south.[8]

When Jan Egland and Secretary General Kofi Annan visited Darfur in July of 2004, their treatment by al-Bashir, Salah Gosh, his intelligence chief and other Khartoum officials demonstrated the contempt that the al-Bashir regime had for the U.N. bolstered by their Russian and Chinese allies in the Security Council. On a visit to a displaced persons' camp that had contained more than 3,000 starving refugees, the U.N. visitors found a camp that had been emptied of its wretched inhabitants by the Khartoum regime to prevent the world's media from witnessing the results of their evil work. Shortly after Annan's return, on July 30, 2004, the Security

Council, unable to resist the growing global civil society anger at its inaction, passed Resolution 1556 under its more robust Chapter VII mandate. The Resolution deemed the carnage in Darfur a threat to international peace and security. In addition, the Security Council demanded that Sudan disband and disarm the Janjaweed and try those involved in gross human rights abuses within thirty days. The Council threatened sanctions if Khartoum did not implement the resolution within the deadline. Finally, the resolution confirmed the presence of a small African Union monitoring force, called AMIS, the African Mission in Sudan.[9]

The stunning inaction that followed what should be the commands of the most powerful international body on the planet demonstrates the priority of national interests over critical humanitarian and human rights concerns of key players in that body. Sudan was counting on China and Russia to protect it from any real sanctions at the U.N. China had abstained from Resolution 1556. This is not surprising as it was the main supplier of military equipment used by the Sudanese armed forces and perhaps even the Janjaweed against the rebel groups and the civilian populations in Darfur. Secondly, by the time of the passing of the Resolution, Sudan was providing China with more than two-thirds of China's overseas oil production. The evolution of this Chinese dependency will be described later in this chapter. The hunger for Sudanese oil for the factories, trucks and cars of China was fuelling the mass slaughter and rape of the anguished masses in Darfur. BBC reports have demonstrated that China has even broken the U.N. arms embargo against Sudan by supplying fighter aircraft and servicing them in Darfur so that they can be used against defenseless civilians, including many children, in Darfur.[10] Part of the incentive on the Chinese to engage in this illegal activity could be to have an oil exploration block that extends into Darfur, ethnically cleansed for Chinese companies to explore in peace. These reports have also documented hard evidence that Chinese military trucks equipped with lethal firepower have crossed into Darfur and are being used against defenseless civilians.[11]

It is little wonder that Resolution 1556 was ignored by al-Bashir. His Janjaweed militia proxies were not disarmed. Indeed the Sudanese forces ramped up their collaborative killing spree with the Arab militias in the aftermath of the Resolution. After the thirty day deadline had passed, the Security Council met again, and on September 18, 2004 issued another futile Resolution, 1564. Only 'grave concerns' at the 'climate of impunity' was asserted by the Security Council this time. Wanting to maintain some remnant of credibility, the Resolution also warned Sudan that the Council would consider additional sanctions, including against the oil production or targeted at government members. The only concrete outcome was the establishment of an International Commission of Inquiry (ICI) to inquire into the extent of the human rights abuses in Darfur and ascertain whether it constituted genocide. One U.S. official experienced with the workings of the Security Council is quoted as stating:[12]

> It's a mistake to assume that the Security Council will be the leader on any issue. It doesn't work that way and the system has been broken most of the time. Each time we tried to bring up Darfur, even sanctions in general, China blocked it. Russia and China would not even turn up for meetings to discuss sanctions. We wanted to see oil sanctions immediately, which we think would have sent a strong message to the government to get serious. Everything gets watered down and a one page resolution becomes seven pages. We couldn't even mention the word sanctions, we had to call them measures

To no one's surprise, Resolution 1564 produced no tangible result, as did a further resolution months later. Resolution 1574 did nothing to deal with the defiance of the Khartoum government regarding the disbanding of the Janjaweed and only weakly suggested appropriate further action if Sudan kept on thumbing its nose at the world, with of course, the hypocrisy of the Russians and Chinese to back them up.

Even before the investigation by the ICI, parts of the U.S. Administration had already examined whether the carnage in Darfur amounted to genocide or something less. The U.S. Ambassador for war crimes, Pierre Richard Prosper, had informed Congress in June of 2004 that there were 'indicators of genocide'. At the request of Secretary of State Colin Powell, a State Department team had conducted extensive field research of over a thousand Darfur refugees in Chad. The team reported back after weeks on the ground that the situation there was the worst human rights crisis in the world, documenting the evidence that hundreds of villages had been destroyed in the process of the most massive ethnic cleansing of African Muslim tribes in modern history. The team detailed systemic use of rape as a weapon of war and the herding of well over a million into internally displaced camps and approximately 200,000 refugees fleeing to Chad.

On the release of the report, Colin Powell, testifying on September 9, 2004, before the Senate Foreign Relations Committee, seemed to have triggered the full force of the Genocide Convention. He was testifying before a Congress that had demanded that the U.S. Administration start calling the carnage in Darfur a genocide and for multilateral or unilateral sanctions that could help end the ethnic cleansing. After consulting Prosper on the legal definitions of genocide, Powell summoned up the courage and stated to the Congress that genocide was being committed. Using the evidence produced by the State Department team, he affirmed that there existed the critical element of intent by the Sudanese government in collaboration with the Janjaweed to 'destroy in whole or in part' the peoples of Darfur, according to the terms of the Genocide Convention. The intent could be deduced through the scale of the violence, the use of rape as a weapon of war, the destruction of villages, and the taking of food supplies, livestock and other means of survival. Additionally, the obstruction of humanitarian and medical aid, including food, reinforced the intent required by the Convention to destroy in whole or in part the Darfur tribes. The U.S. report and the Secretary of State did not see any requirement that the Genocide Convention required proof of the intent by the Khartoum government to 'annihilate' the entire peoples of Darfur.

While the confirmation of the criminality of what was happening in Darfur rocketed round the world and made headlines, it was a perfect example of an act full of sound and fury, but signifying almost nothing. No real move to force effective sanctions by the U.S. against the Khartoum government came out of the admission that the promise of 'never again' was yet again being horribly violated. Instead Colin Powell claimed that the U.S. was already doing everything it could to get the Sudanese government to act responsibly. He urged everyone not to get too preoccupied with the designation of the carnage in Darfur as genocide.[13]

What was not being done was to use potentially the most effective measures and sanctions against the Khartoum regime to stop the Darfur slaughter. These could have included progressively tougher unilateral sanctions against the oil production that fed the Sudanese military, targeted economic sanctions against the Khartoum leadership and its assets abroad, providing greater financial and logistical resources for the overstretched A.U. monitoring force and putting much greater pressure on the Security Council to increase the size of that force together with more effective rules of engagement that would allow it to protect civilians against the marauding Janjaweed. Finally, if the Security Council had been prevented by Russia and China from establishing a no-fly zone in Darfur to prevent the Antonov bombers and gunships from devastating the Darfur villages, the U.S. could have contemplated a unilateral no-fly zone together with its allies such as France. There certainly was a precedent for such courageous action based on the no-fly zone enforced by the U.S. and its allies against Saddam Hussein in the Kurdish region in Iraq. Given the enormous territory of Darfur, the logistical nightmare of organizing a military intervention by the U.S. and its allies, and the fact that the world's only superpower was increasingly bogged down in the Iraqi invasion quagmire, armed intervention by the U.S. and its allies may not have been even advisable. However, there was certainly much, much more that was not being done by the U.S., contrary to the words of the Secretary of State.

Instead, Colin Powell asserted that the Genocide Convention obliged only the signatory states to call on the U.N. to take action if a situation fell into the genocide category. But to make sure that the U.S. inaction was not too apparent, Colin Powell was instrumental in getting the U.N. Security Council to establish yet another fact finding body, the ICI, to confirm the situation as genocide under Resolution 1564.

After its own fact finding mission to Darfur, the ICI in its report in January of 2005 surprised some of the leading international jurists around the world, including this author, in concluding that the situation in Darfur was not genocide due to difficulty of finding specific intent on the part of the Government of Sudan and the militias under their control regarding the atrocities in Darfur, although the ICI did find that genocidal acts had occurred.

The Commission summarized its conclusion as follows:

> The Commission concluded that the Government of the Sudan has not pursued a policy of genocide. Arguably, two elements of genocide might be deduced from the gross violations of human rights perpetrated by Government forces and the militias under their control. These two elements are, first, the actus reus consisting of killing, or causing serious bodily or mental harm, or deliberately inflicting conditions of life likely to bring about physical destruction; and, second, on the basis of a subjective standard, the existence of a protected group being targeted by the authors of criminal conduct. However, the crucial element of genocidal intent appears to be missing, at least as far as the central Government authorities are concerned. Generally speaking the policy of attacking, killing and forcibly displacing members of some tribes does not evince a specific intent to annihilate, in whole or in part, a group distinguished on racial, ethnic, national or religious grounds. Rather, it would seem that those who planned and organized attacks on villages pursued the intent to drive the victims from their homes, primarily for purposes of counter-insurgency warfare.

> The Commission does recognize that in some instances individuals, including Government officials, may commit acts with genocidal intent. Whether this was the case in Darfur, however, is a determination that only a competent court can make on a case by case basis.

The most compelling critique of the ICI's findings was that the strategy of the government was to use the proxy militias to substantially carry out the killings and ethnic cleansing and, as such, it found that genocidal acts may have been committed which only a competent court could decide whether the acts could fulfill the definition of the crime under the Genocide Convention. In such a case there was no need to focus only on whether the government had the intent of genocide, but rather whether it was aiding and abetting and complicit in other criminal ways in the genocidal intent of the Janjaweed.

Surprisingly the Commission did not elaborate in any significant way on the intent of the Janjaweed. There was a mountain of evidence that the Janjaweed did have the necessary intent to annihilate or destroy in whole or in part the Darfur tribes. They were aided and abetted in terms of weapons supply and command and control by the Sudanese military forces in committing the actual *reus* or act of genocide. There is ample precedent in international humanitarian law that those who aid and abet international crimes do not have to share the genocidal intent to be found guilty of the international crime. Rather, the intent that has to be proved is the intent to provide such aiding and abetting with the knowledge of the perpetrator's actual intent. As such, the Commission had enough facts to determine joint criminal liability for genocide with the Janjaweed.

Perhaps realizing the consequences of not finding a policy of genocide which would have triggered a positive duty of the international community and the U.N. to commence action under the Genocide Convention, the Commission stated that their ultimate finding of international criminality on the part of the Sudanese government was of equal consequence to a finding of genocide:

> The conclusion that no genocidal policy has been pursued and implemented in Darfur by the Government authorities, directly or through the militias under their control, should not be taken in any way as detracting from the gravity of the crimes perpetrated in that region. International offences such as the crimes against humanity and war crimes that have been committed in Darfur may be no less serious and heinous than genocide.

However, the continuing carnage in Darfur has shown that the finding of crimes against humanity and war crimes on the part of the Sudanese government seemed to have been treated as less serious and heinous than genocide.

The ICI would partly compensate for its refusal to find evidence of genocide on the part of Sudan's leaders by recommending that the situation in Darfur be referred by the Security Council to the International Criminal Court (ICC) that had come into force on July 1, 2002. The ICI also proposed that the names of fifty-one individual perpetrators, including twenty-six officials of the Government of Sudan, members of militia forces, members of rebel groups, and certain foreign army officers acting in their personal capacity be the subject of investigation by the Chief Prosecutor of the ICC for possible indictments.

Few expected that these recommendations would be taken up, given the potential veto of any Security Council reference of the Darfur situation to the ICC by China and Russia. In addition, the U.S. under the George W. Bush administration had become a ferocious opponent of the ICC despite the fact that most of its allies and friendly countries in Europe, Latin America, Africa and Asia had ratified the Statute of the ICC that had established the mandate of the Court. The U.S. opposition in July of 2001 joined by China, Qatar, Libya and ironically Saddam Hussein's Iraq, was based on the fear that the global military actions of the lone superpower could result in American military personnel and contractors being hauled before the ICC. This was reinforced by the neo-conservative decision makers of the Bush Administration that American sovereignty and exceptionalism should not be restrained by any international body. Ideology did not give way to hard facts that there was little to fear by American military personnel or those who regarded American sovereign power as unrestrained. The drafters of the Treaty had tried their best to draw the U.S. into the supporters of the Court by making the ICC only the international criminal court of last resort if domestic legal processes were unable or unwilling to prosecute violations of international criminal law.

To the surprise of many supporters of the ICC, on March 31, 2005, the Security Council passed Resolution 1593 referring the situation in Darfur since July 1, 2002 to the Chief Prosecutor of the ICC. The Security Council based its decision on the determination that the situation in Sudan continued to constitute a threat to international peace and security. This was especially surprising as President Bush's hand-picked U.S. Ambassador to the U.N., John Bolton, was regarded as the most vicious of opponents of the ICC and the U.N. in general. It was later learned that Bolton and the Bush Administration gave in after other key members of the Security Council, including Britain and France, forced the Security Council into a renewal of an exemption against any potential investigation or prosecution of American personnel by the ICC. The U.S. together with China, Algeria and Brazil abstained from voting on the referral of the Darfur situation to the ICC. Secretary of State Condoleezza Rice was quoted as admitting that the U.S. abstention was due not to the sudden change of heart by Mr. Bolton and the Bush Administration, but because of pressure from the U.S. Congress. Secretary Rice also gambled on the fact that China would not want to be seen isolated on the worst human rights crisis in the world, given the fact of Chinese complicity in the conflicts in the south of Sudan.[14]

The U.S. administration may also have been relieved that the ICI had not put the label of genocide on the situation in Darfur. Some have even suspected that the Commission had concluded the situation was one of genocide, but members of the Security Council had pressured the ICI not to come to that conclusion.[15] Perhaps, it would have made no difference. There were some experts, like Pierre-Richard Prosper, a former war crimes prosecutor, who were prepared to argue that if the situation in Darfur had been found to be genocide by the ICI, the duty for states such as the U.S. to prevent and punish under the Genocide Convention would mean very little. It could mean no more than the minimum of diplomatic engagement and a maximum of some type of military action. The primary duty to prevent and punish would fall on the perpetrator itself, Sudan![16]

What did happen, in part as a result of the findings of the ICI, was the attempted reinforcement of the weak A.U. monitoring force in Darfur by the end of 2005. Over 6,000 troops from Rwanda, Nigeria and Senegal were in place, but, given the size of the territory they had to cover, these additional troops were unable to stop the killings. Indeed, the situation sometimes went beyond the hypocritical to the farcical. There were reports that members of the rebel groups and Sudanese military forces used the A.U. bases as housing for their members and were able to access all of the A.U.'s information, movements and intelligence![17]

The Khartoum government responded to the reference to the ICC by its well tried use of the cover of peace negotiations to continue its proxy wars in Darfur. These peace processes were brokered by the African Union at Addis Ababa, Ethiopia and Abuja, Nigeria. The Khartoum government and leaders had demonstrated this tactic in the south of Sudan, and again with purported ceasefires in Darfur in 2003 and 2004 which it had broken almost immediately. Even when these prior ceasefires proved illusory, the African Union opted to send only observers.

On May 2, 2007, the ICC issued arrest warrants for Ahmad Harun, the minister of the interior and head of security in Darfur charged with recruiting, arming and funding the Janjaweed, and a militia leader, Ali Abd al-Rahman alias Ali Kushayb. The latter was called the 'colonel of colonels' by the ICC prosecutors and the Janjaweed militia in Western Darfur comprising several thousand armed men. He was alleged to have personally participated in the attacks, including the execution of thirty-two men and was alleged to have inspected a group of naked women before they were raped by his men.

The ICC prosecutor, Luis Moreno-Ocampo, had asked the Court to issue the warrants after an intensive two year investigation into their roles in the conflict. The charges against them included ninety-two counts of war crimes and crimes against humanity, including torture, rape and murder, committed in four towns and villages between 2003 and 2004.

The Sudanese government immediately refused to hand over the men to the ICC and instead asserted that it did not recognize the jurisdiction of the Court. The Chief Prosecutor insisted that, given the referral by the U.N.'s Security Council of the situation in Sudan to the Court, the Khartoum government was under a legal duty to do so. In response, the Sudanese government claimed that it was able to try all the perpetrators of any offences in Darfur in its own courts and for that reason, because of the complementarity provision in Article 17 of the Rome Statute, the ICC had no jurisdiction. The Khartoum government tried to develop a façade of complementarity by setting up a Special Criminal Court on the Events in Darfur with three permanent seats in different parts of Darfur the jurisdiction of which included crimes under international humanitarian law. As Human Rights Watch has observed, these courts have been ineffective, not convicting any of those most responsible for the atrocities in Darfur. In addition, even though the Sudanese criminal code has been amended to include international crimes, there have been no prosecutions. There have been continuing promises to investigate Kushayb for crimes in Darfur that do not unfold due to lack of political will to combat the continuing state of impunity for past atrocities.[18]

As if to show that the Khartoum government was incapable of any form of complementarity jurisdiction to try the two men, the Sudanese government made Harun the Minister of Humanitarian Affairs, whose jurisdiction included the oversight of the refugee camps in Darfur, the same approximately 2 million people he had terrorized and whose families his government forces and militia proxies had slaughtered. The Khartoum government contributed further to its contempt by making Harun the head of a committee to investigate human rights violations. More troublesome for the fragile peace in South Sudan, on May 8, 2009, al-Bashir named Ahmad Harun a governor of the disputed South Kordofan province, the location of the bitterly fought over oil reserves that lie on the north–south border and which also includes the contested town of Abyei over the administration of which Khartoum and the government of southern Sudan fought. This is not only an act of defiance against the ICC, but also endangers the viability of the peace agreement with the southern rebels.

In a similar contemptuous act towards the ICC, Kushayb, the Janjaweed killer, has been released from prison with the government claiming there is no evidence against him.[19]

The Sudanese government and its allies argue that the arrest warrants may derail the potential for peace in Darfur and potentially in the south of Sudan. In response, the Chief Prosecutor, Luis Moreno-Ocampo, and others have rightly pointed out that with Khartoum making Harun the wolf guarding the terrorized chickens in the refugee camps, there can be no lasting humanitarian or security solution.[20] Likewise, the Sudanese government itself seems to be a lead player in derailing the UNAMID peacekeeping efforts in Darfur and perhaps even the CPA in the south.

There has been the sound of deafening silence from the most powerful governments and institutions of the world to the contempt shown by the Khartoum government to the global rule of law as interpreted by the ICC and backed by the U.N. Security Council.

3.   THE PRESIDENT THREATENS THE PROSPECT OF PEACE IF JUSTICE IS PURSUED

There had been reports that the Khartoum government had threatened that the indictment of the President would badly affect the stability of the whole region. One Sudan analyst, Juliet Flint, suggested that the President could retaliate against aid workers and the UNAMID peacekeepers.[21] Sadly, even with the killing of the UNAMID soldiers from African countries, both the A.U. and the Arab league sprang to the defense of Al-Bashir claiming that any indictment of the Sudanese leader would jeopardize the peace process in Darfur.[22] These supporters of the Sudanese President failed to see that the person they were defending had imperiled the peace the most, if he ever had any intentions of a lasting peace either in Darfur or in the south of Sudan.

In the meanwhile the death and destruction toll in Darfur continued to mount. There is no accurate number for several reasons. First, the Khartoum government has a keen interest in downplaying such figures as merely the result of inter-tribal conflict. Second, even before the carnage of approximately 2,700 villages by the Sudanese army and the Janjaweed, the number of village populations was uncertain. After the ethnic cleansing, the mass burning and burial of bodies by the killers, including the throwing of women and children down wells to poison the water, has further complicated the counting. Finally, the deaths of refugees in camps from famine, conflict-related illness and further marauding by the Janjaweed complicates the counting of the toll of the tragedy of Darfur.

A U.S. State Department analysis has concluded, based on reports by the humanitarian group, Doctors without Borders, and State Department reports from the refugee camps in Darfur and Chad, that the number of dead range from 350,000 to 400,000, with another 3.5 million needing humanitarian assistance and therefore also in danger.[23] As if there are no bounds to the cruelty of the Khartoum regimes, on August 10, 2008, the *New York Times* revealed that Sudan is exporting vast quantities of its own crops to other countries while millions of people in Darfur are in danger of starvation. The Khartoum government is capitalizing on high global food prices, while it receives billions of pounds of free food destined for the starving people in Darfur and elsewhere in Sudan. The Report confirms that this food assistance from the U.N. and Western aid groups is being hijacked every day, and less and less of the aid is reaching those in desperate need, especially children whose malnutrition rates are soaring.[24]

By April of 2009, the joint U.N.–African Union special representative to Darfur, Rodolphe Adada, reported to the U.N. Security Council that violence in Darfur had subsided into a low-intensity conflict rather than an on-going genocide. Rodolphe claimed that around 130–150 people were dying every month, substantially down from the tens of thousands who were killed during the period of most intense hostilities in the 2003–2004 timeframe. However, he added that there was a high risk of escalation.[25]

Susan Rice, the newly appointed U.S. Ambassador to the U.N., who had described the situation in Darfur as an ongoing genocide, took issue with this downplaying of the crisis in Darfur during closed door discussion with the U.N. representative. She was joined by envoys from Britain, France, Austria and Mexico. According to the UNAMID peacekeeping force some 2,000 people had died during the 15 months between January 1, 2008 and March 31, 2009, one-third being civilians. There are several NGOs who also support the view that the throes of genocide continue in the disease ridden, resource starved and overcrowded refugee camps in Darfur.[26]

To the surprise of many Sudanese observers, on August 27, 2009, the U.N. military commander of the UNAMID peacekeeping force, General Martin Agwai, on leaving his post asserted that the six year war in Darfur had ended. He asserted that the region now suffered only low-level disputes and banditry.[27]

One Sudan analyst, Gill Lusk, condemned the assessment as 'unhelpful' as it could lead to the perception that the Darfur problems had been solved. While accepting that the level of fighting had declined, the analyst attributed it to the fact that it is the Khartoum government that 'turns the tap on and off – they can restart the violence whenever they want'.[28]

4. ARE REALISTIC PEACE NEGOTIATIONS EVEN POSSIBLE WITH THE MASTER ARCHITECT OF TWO MASS SLAUGHTERS OF CIVILIANS IN HIS OWN COUNTRY?

The year 1989 was a momentous year in modern world history. The fall of the Berlin Wall and the demise of the Soviet Union seemed, in the words of then President George H. Bush, to usher in a 'new world order' of international peace, security and respect for human rights. In Sudan, however, 1989 ushered in, on June 30, one of modern history's most brutal regimes when Brigadier General Omar Hassan Ahmed al-Bashir staged a military coup and took control of the Khartoum government. The power behind the General and indeed the engineer of the military coup was the radical Islamist group, the National Islamic Front (NIF), led by the Machiavellian and brutal Hassan al-Turabi. It was not the first military coup suffered by this troubled country. Just two years after the country became independent on January 1, 1956, a military coup occurred and its leaders began the harsh attempts to spread Islam to the Christian and animist southern Sudanese. This created the first civil war between southern rebels and northern forces. A brief civilian government that began in October of 1964 did not last long and did not effect a lasting peace with the southern rebels. In 1969, another General, Jafaar al-Nimeiri, staged another coup, this time with the help of military assistance from the Cold War alliance of the Soviet Union. The Arab north's attempt to crush the southern rebels continued. However, when a communist attempt to overthrow Nimeiri failed in 1971 and a Libyan backed attempt also failed in 1976, the General turned towards the West. He concluded the Addis Ababa peace agreement with the southern rebels in 1972. The agreement established a very fragile form of regional autonomy for the south.[29]

In the following decade, the peace agreement would unravel primarily because of the growing influence within the Nimeiri government of 'National Reconciliation' of radical Islamists called the Muslim Brothers led by none other than Hassan al-Turabi. This individual, in a continuing Sudanese form of farce, held the main Justice portfolio of Sudan, the position of Attorney General of Sudan. Turabi and the radical Islamists would ultimately convince Nimeiri to renege on the Addis Ababa peace agreement, in part, because oil had been discovered in the southern part of Sudan by the American oil company Chevron. This presented the prospect of a radical Islamist regime in Africa that would be able to spread its influence far and wide through the revenues from the exploitation of its energy resources.[30]

A southern Sudanese army rebellion in 1983 led to an open civil war with northern forces. Nimeiri formally reneged on the Addis Ababa peace agreement. He followed this betrayal with the imposition of Sharia law and Arabic as the official language on the south. These impositions led to the creation of the first major rebel army in Sudan, the Sudan People's Liberation Movement (SPLM), under the leadership of the charismatic John Garang. Major victories by the SPLM in the south made the Khartoum government realize that another attempt at a peace agreement was necessary, but it was too late for Nimeiri. He was overthrown in April of 1985.

A civil government was subsequently elected, but the elections resulted in a powerful opposition party, the NIF, the party name of the Muslim Brothers led by Hassan al-Turabi. Al-Sadiq al-Mahdi, the leader of the largest party, the Umma, became the Prime Minister. Al-Mahdi was close to concluding another peace agreement with the SPLM.

To many who knew the track record of al-Turabi and his radical followers, it would only be a matter of time before the NIF would engineer another coup to stop any peace agreement with the SPLM and to assume total power in Sudan. The coup would be necessary in order to begin their genocidal plan of action, this time with the NIF's chosen front man called Major General Omar Hassan al-Bashir. As expected, the military coup led by the General occurred on June 30, 1989.

Almost immediately on assuming power, General al-Bashir followed the Islamist agenda of al-Turabi and the NIF. The key part of the agenda was to make sure that southern Sudan and indeed other parts of Sudan, including Darfur, would be dominated by the Arab Islamic elites of Khartoum and the northern Arabs. In pursuance of this agenda, the constitution and the legislature were suspended, political parties and unions were banned, the media gagged and any pre-existing attempts at a peace agreement with the SPLM were abandoned. Sharia, as the law of Sudan, was affirmed and included the permitted execution of apostates and unbelievers, taking children from non-Muslim parents and promoting the concept of jihadist war against the Christian and animist south.

The genocidal plan began with gathering jihadists from Sudan, Libya, Chad and elsewhere to fight against the SPLM, forcing public servants and students into military training and ideological education and finally establishing military conscription. Those opposing the radical Islamists were 'disappeared' or tortured and imprisoned in 'ghost houses', the name for the secret jails of the NIF.

However, given the success of the SPLM in the south, the NIF government initiated a proxy strategy that would subsequently be honed to horrible perfection in Darfur. Tribal militias, especially from the Nuer tribe, were armed in the South and southern Darfur. These militias were incited to begin a proxy war against the SPLM and southern tribes, in particular the Dinka tribe of John Garang. The Sudanese intelligence agencies also began inciting dissension within the ranks of the SPLM itself to create splinter groups. The goal was simple. With the SPLM winning victories against the northern forces, a divide and conquer strategy was the only way to contain the main rebel forces in order to stage other aspects of the genocidal plan. The northern forces together with their proxy militias waged war, not only against the SPLM, but also the civilians that supported them, resulting in mounting civilian casualties.[31]

These genocidal divide and conquer strategies would later be perfected in Darfur. Astonishingly, in 1992, the NIF even turned their guns towards the Nuba tribe, a majority of which were Muslim, but were African in ethnic origin. This demonstrated the racist ideology and intent of the NIF to create an Arab dominated Islamic state in Sudan. It also foreshadowed the terrible fate that awaited the Muslim tribes in Darfur who were also African in origin. Nuba farmers were driven off their land and forced into camps. As if the mass murders of men were not sufficient, the NIF initiated a systemic war plan of rape of Nubian women and stymied food aid from foreign donors that was destined for a starving population. The fate of the people in Darfur was already foretold.[32]

By 1998, the NIF had managed what seemed inconceivable to those who had cried 'never again' at the end of the Second World War. The U.S. Committee for Refugees (USCR) claimed that by 1998 the Sudanese genocide had resulted in more deaths than the combined massacre of civilians in Bosnia, Kosovo, Afghanistan, Chechnya, Somalia, and Algeria. The USCR claimed that approximately two million Sudanese had died directly because of the fifteen year civil war, or from other genocidal initiatives of the NIF such as forced starvation resulting from hindrance of U.N. and other relief agencies delivering critical food supplies, forced displacement and conflict-related diseases in refugee camps.[33] By 1998, some 4.35 million Sudanese were either internally displaced or refugees in neighboring countries, the gravest situation of its kind in the world. This was genocide by any interpretation of the term under the 1948 Genocide Convention.

Not satisfied with their record of civilian massacres, the Khartoum government rained down aerial bombardments on civilians, including children, and colluded in the enslavement of southerners, especially from the Dinka and the Nuer which had rebelled against the Khartoum government.[34] The northern government collaborated with and armed the militia of the Baggara tribe, notorious for their practice of slavery. The Baggara captured men, women and children as slaves for work as domestic and agricultural workers in western and northern Sudan. The NIF government denied involvement in this modern day slavery, claiming the practice was merely intertribal abductions caused by tribal hatreds. In reality, Khartoum's intelligence agencies, led by the head of its intelligence agency, Salah Gosh, had constructed this brutal practice as a cheaper method of conducting the war against the rebel tribes.

In 1998, the U.N. Special Rapporteur on Sudan claimed the method of enslaving the southerners 'indicates a deliberate policy on the part of the government to ignore or even condone this practice of slavery. . .. In most of the cases brought to the attention of the government of the Sudan, the reported perpetrators belong to the Sudanese army and the Popular Defense Forces, which are under the control of the government of the Sudan. Even in the cases involving members of different tribal militias, the slavery occurred within the context of the war and there are the same perpetrators and victims.' The same U.N. Rapporteur concluded that women and the girl children were subject to the most degrading forms of sexual slavery, abuse, torture and rape. In his 1999 report, the Rapporteur detailed how the militia escorted the northern forces' supply train to the south where they were allowed to loot southern villages, rape and abduct women and children, demand ransom and force some to convert to Islam.[35]

The cruelty of the NIF did not stop with their divide and conquer strategy. They also consorted with the most evil of men outside the borders of Sudan in order to obtain foreign assistance in the slaughter of the southern rebels and their civilian supporters. The NIF enlisted the aid of probably the most bizarre and sadistic of killers from the neighboring region of Northern Uganda, the Lord's Resistance Army (LRA) led by a messianic figure, Joseph Kony. This killer, who was subsequently indicted for crimes against humanity by the International Criminal Court, implemented his insane calling to promote the Christian Ten Commandments by abducting thousands of very young children and training them as child soldiers. Girls as young as 10 years were raped by the LRA. The children together with the LRA would subsequently terrorize, mutilate and slaughter their own parents and people. The NIF provided the LRA with weapons and refuge in return for periodic attacks on the SPLM and their civilian supporters in southern Sudan.

A former Canadian Deputy Director of UNICEF, Stephen Lewis, has accused al-Bashir of crimes against humanity for complicity in the atrocities committed by Kony and the LRA. He claims that over a ten year period between 20,000 and 30,000 children were abducted, with a third being killed, another third 'lost forever in the bowels of Sudan and another third escaping back to Uganda'. When the Deputy Director of UNICEF begged al-Bashir to stop the collaboration with the LRA, al-Bashir denied there were any abducted and abused children in Sudan, even though Lewis had interviewed many escapees from Sudan. Lewis gave details to al-Bashir and his foreign minister of the location of the camps in Sudan where the abducted children were held as slaves, including many of the girl children forced into sexual slavery by local Sudanese military commanders. Again the Sudanese President and his foreign minister 'scoffed' at the evidence and walked away. Lewis felt he had met a man who was 'evil incarnate' who was 'knowingly presiding over the deaths and emotional dismemberment of thousands of children'. Lewis reveals that in 1999 and 2000, UNICEF managed to get some of the children out of Sudan, hiding them in transit and threatening to expose the complicity of the Sudanese government to finally get its cooperation.[36]

During this grotesque bloodbath orchestrated by al-Bashir and his NIF regime, the international community held out hope that the Khartoum government could be persuaded to reach a sustainable peace agreement with the southern rebels. There was a failed attempt by the Nigerian government to reach a peace agreement in Abuja in 1992. The NIF regime, fearing that the U.S. could send its troops into Sudan the way it had done in Somalia, proposed in 1997 that the Inter-Governmental Authority on Drought and Desertification (IGAD) attempt another peace process. The process would soon be supported by the U.S., Britain, the European Union and Canada together with the neighboring countries of Eritrea and Ethiopia. The African mediating countries feared that the NIF's brand of radical Islam would spread further into East and Central Africa. It was clear that at many points in the long drawn out IGAD negotiations, the Khartoum government was not interested in the main claims of the southern rebels. These claims included that Sudan could be a united country only if it became a secular and democratic country with its resources, especially the oil resources, to be shared equally between the north and the south. In the absence of such an agreement, the southern negotiators insisted on the right to self-determination through a referendum. Such irreconcilable positions in the IGAD peace process only gave the NIF regime more room and time to buy more destructive weaponry with its newly gained oil revenues and to inflict greater ethnic cleansing in the south.

There is hardly a more despicable crime that a government can commit against its own people than attempting genocide through starvation. Death through forced starvation must be the cruellest form of mankind's inhumanity. The Khartoum government has become expert at this evil. The NIF government initiated the forced starvation by bringing to a grinding halt one of the most extensive humanitarian efforts worldwide organized at the time, to bring food to the millions of starving southerners. In particular the government refused humanitarian relief and food to areas inhabited by the Dinka and Nuer peoples in order to forcibly displace them from the area of potential oilfield development and force them to search for food elsewhere. The pursuit of this goal led to the deaths of over half a million people. The NIF government would repeat this despicable goal in Darfur within a few years to cleanse that region of its African tribes. It was only as late as October 2002, under intense pressure from the international community and to avoid seeming more hypocritical than usual during another round of peace talks, that the Khartoum government would fully permit humanitarian access to the starving southerners.

There is little doubt that history will record that national oil companies from China and Malaysia and an independent Canadian company played a part in the genocide orchestrated by al-Bashir and his NIF regime. In 1999, the Khartoum government transformed into the governing party named the National Congress Party (NCP) after it had expelled al-Turabi a year earlier. His actual and potential ability to be a mischief maker and desire to remain the real power behind the NIF regime proved too much for President al-Bashir. While Islamic nationalism remained the backbone of the NCP, the overwhelming imperative of President al-Bashir was to maintain the control of the country and enjoy the fruits of one of the largest oil discoveries in Africa. It could also be an imperative for him to undermine any peace agreement either with the south of Sudan or in Darfur to ensure that the revenue stream from the oil that keeps him in power does not cease.

There is little doubt that with the first revenues from oil exports in August of 1999 this resource became a major reason for the continuation of the genocide in the south carried on by the NCP government. This new rationale for genocide was buoyed by the ability to purchase weapons, such as the Antonov bombers and attack helicopters from the Russians and Chinese, to slaughter and displace even more civilians from the Nuer and Dinka tribes in the south of Sudan. The long running famine, in part instigated by the Khartoum regime, and epidemics that would leave two million southerners dead and many more enslaved also helped al-Bashir in clearing the oil fields.

In particular, the forced displacement of the Dinka was a key factor in providing a safe operating environment for the Sudanese and foreign oil companies that would produce the revenues to continue the civil war. Adding to the misery of the local tribes, the oil pipeline to the Red Sea necessitated, in the minds of the Sudanese rulers, the displacement and killing of civilians in the Western Upper Nile by government and militia forces. The pipeline and ancillary roads and pumping stations were built with the assistance of thousands of Chinese workers foretelling the growing influence of China in this tragic landscape. Not satisfied with their success, the NIF government also instigated factional fighting between the rebel groups in the oil production area. The western and Asian oil companies started to deny that any gross human rights violations were taking place that were connected to the oil exploration and production. They even denied that there were any forced displacements due to the oil production and established whitewashing investigations to prove it, followed by glossy social responsibility publications for their investors. Such hypocrisy was exposed for what it was by human rights groups, such as Human Rights Watch.

These companies then formed a consortium with the Sudanese national oil company, Sudapet, which was called the Greater Nile Petroleum Operating Company (GNPOC). Arakis Energy and its Sudan assets were taken over by Talisman, one of the largest independent oil companies in Canada. Talisman's technical experience and know how transformed the discovered oilfields of Heglig and Unity into a world class enterprise. Soon the production and revenues not only made it worthwhile to construct the 1,000 mile pipeline to the Red Sea to export the production, but also provided the revenues to purchase the weapons of mass civilian destruction from the Chinese and Russians. Human Rights Watch has detailed how the conflict and displacement increased significantly after Talisman became the operating company in key blocks of the oil fields. In mid-May 1999, the Sudanese government launched a devastating attack on the Dinka population in the area of the oil fields, starting with aerial bombardments, followed by ground troops looting and burning everything, causing the displacement of tens of thousands of people. In the same year, the northern forces began one of their largest efforts at displacement around the oilfields north of Bentiu. The attacks on the Dinka and Nuer civilian populations included Russian purchased Antonov bombers, helicopter gunships and even tanks.

The U.N. Special Rapporteur on Sudan, Gerhaut Baum, confirmed in 2002 to the U.N. Commission on Human Rights that the oil production had seriously contributed to the conflict and the deterioration of the human rights situation including the widespread displacement. There was a growing mountain of evidence, demonstrated by NGOs and southern Sudanese, that the area of the oilfields was the subject of gross human rights abuses by the Khartoum government. Human Rights Watch concluded that, based on its extensive research, the Chinese, Indian and Malaysian state oil companies, together with Talisman prior to its sale to the Indian company and Lundin, were clearly complicit in the gross human rights violations of the Khartoum government led by al-Bashir.

In the late 1990s, the Clinton Administration in the United States began to finally wake up to the fact that the NIF was not only pursuing genocide against its own people, but was also a haven for global terrorists and radical Islamic groups, including Bin Laden and Hizbollah. The dangers to the rest of the world of the Sudanese nurturing of global terrorists emerged with the simultaneous bombing of the American Embassies in Kenya and Tanzania on August 7, 1998. It was only when this realization included the possibility that the U.S. homeland itself was at risk of terrorist activity from Bin Laden and others that the Clinton Administration pressured the U.N. to impose multilateral sanctions against the NIF government and added to these its own sanctions. Faced with growing U.S. and international pressure, the Khartoum government finally forced Bin Laden to leave the country and find a more explosive exile, Afghanistan, after he was offered sanctuary by the brutal Taliban regime.

In the same time period, there was a growing rift between al-Bashir and the troublemaker Hassan al-Turabi, who was instrumental in making Sudan a terrorist haven. The American and international branding of the NIF government as a rogue administration and the faltering economy led to the final split between the two Khartoum leaders. In 1999, General al-Bashir declared a state of emergency and dissolved parliament which al-Turabi denounced as a coup. He was immediately removed from the NIF. Al-Turabi formed a new party, the Popular Patriotic Congress, and started agitating against al-Bashir and the NCP ruling party. He also moved to sign an alliance with the SPLM rebels in 2001 in opposition to the al-Bashir regime. For this and other acts of rebellion al-Turabi was jailed but later freed to make more trouble, first in the south and later in Darfur.

Faced with this internal dissent, at the end of 2002, al-Bashir signaled his desire to both consolidate his power and further marginalize al-Turabi by entering into a new round of peace talks with the SPLM, backed by the U.S. and a number of other foreign states. One thing that the international community pretended not to realize was that the Khartoum government had no intention of giving up its desire to control the oilfields and to have its radical form of Islam dominate the country. From the very beginning, many have doubted whether there was any long term interest in the al-Bashir regime giving up its desire to dominate all of Sudan. A further incentive for al-Bashir to agree to a peace agreement was the aftermath of the terrorist attacks in the U.S. orchestrated by a former honored guest of the Khartoum government led by al-Bashir, Salah Gosh and al-Turabi on September 11, 2001. After the Iraq invasion by the U.S., fear that Sudan could be the next 'regime change' target led the Khartoum government to scramble to be seen as a partner in the so-called 'War on Terror'. This new partnership assisted the ability of the U.S. and a host of other foreign mediators to enter the peace negotiations, despite the continuing outcry against the genocidal track record of the al-Bashir regime by Christian, human rights and humanitarian groups in the U.S. and elsewhere. These groups and others questioned whether, given the track record of the Khartoum government, they could be trusted to follow through on any final peace agreement. Some have argued that in the context of the so-called 'war on terror' and the need for an unholy alliance with the al-Bashir government, there was too much of an urgency to find a peace agreement. This resulted in the Comprehensive Peace Agreement (CPA) finalized between the Khartoum government and the SPLM in 2005. Some have suspected one of the other key motives of the al-Bashir government was to agree to the CPA in order to gain freedom to start another genocide in Darfur.[37]

The CPA, signed in January 2005 in Nairobi, Kenya, may only have created a hiatus in the war between Khartoum and the SPLM. The main terms of the agreement give the south the right to exercise regional autonomy and the right to self-determination and possible independence by referendum in 2011. The charismatic leader of the SPLM, John Garang, would become the first Vice-President of Sudan. After his untimely death in July of 2005, he was succeeded by the then Chair of the SPLM, Salva Kiir. Critical aspects of the deal would include the equal sharing of revenues of oil from the border region between northern areas governed by the Khartoum government and the southern part governed by the southern rebels in Juba. In addition, the northern forces would leave the southern region and some joint forces with the SPLM would be formed in the capital area around Khartoum. Finally, Islamic law or Sharia would not apply to the southern region.

There seemed a lack of memory that previous peace agreements in 1972 and 1979 had failed because of the determination of successive Khartoum governments that there would be a Muslim and an Arab dominated Sudan. Any agreement to the contrary would be a certain trigger for future conflicts and potentially lay the foundation for a future Khartoum government to walk away from the agreement. Yet the stated goal of the CPA was to lay the foundations of a democratic Sudanese state with a Muslim dominated north and a secular but Christian and animist dominated south. The CPA also guaranteed autonomy and possibly independence for the south, a proper and independent legal system and an equitable sharing of the burgeoning oil revenues.

Moreover, the CPA includes a further unworkable division of the region in the south into three levels of government. The North was also divided into two regions. One major potential future flashpoint is the region around Abeyei, an area the oilfields of which lie close to the border between the Khartoum controlled north and the SPLM controlled south. While the focus was on preserving the unity of the country, the actual constitutional framework seemed to invite disunity and potential further tribal and regional conflicts.

This contradictory result in part stemmed from the fact that the CPA was the product of agreement only between General al-Bashir's government, the NCP coalition ruling party, and the SPLM, the two major combatants at the time, ignoring the emerging conflicts in the Darfur region and the east of Sudan. Opposition to the CPA is growing, in part led by the now disgruntled al-Turabi and his Popular Congress party. There are reports that al-Turabi is involved with some of the Arab militias in Darfur, instigating rebellion against the al-Bashir government. Armed groups, aside from the SPLM, in other parts of the south have refused to follow an agreement in which they were not involved. The death of John Garang in a plane crash was a further blow to the survivability of the CPA, given his vision of a united Sudan that was democratic and able to reconcile long-standing ethnic and religious hatreds and rivalries. The deadly riots that followed his untimely death could be a harbinger of the future of the CPA. Finally, there are growing suspicions that the Khartoum government is fomenting discord among the southern tribes and the SPLM, hoping that such conflict could postpone the 2011 referendum on independence by the South. In conclusion, the CPA was a major step in putting a hiatus to one genocidal plan by the Khartoum government.[38] However, it may have given the Khartoum government the critical breathing room needed to start another genocide in Darfur. Given the miasma of hidden agendas, the lack of inclusiveness, the weak governance structures put in place and the failure to resolve the equitable division of resource revenues, it is questionable how stable the CPA will be in both the medium and long term.

Even before the Khartoum government was inching its way towards the peace agreement with the southern rebels, it was methodically putting in place the foundations of the second genocide in Darfur. The previous NIF government took over ownership of public property in Darfur and deliberately worsened the effects of the drought and the resulting famine in 1989–1990. It refused the offers of food aid from the international community. Darfur had seen inter-tribal conflicts for decades due to the increasing scarcity of land and water caused by the southward creep of the Sahara desert and poor farming methods. U.N. Secretary General Ban Ki Moon may have proclaimed the first major climate change war that threatens international peace and security in an opinion published in the *Washington Post*:[39]

Two decades ago, the rains in southern Sudan began to fail. According to U.N. statistics, average precipitation has declined some 40 percent since the early 1980s. Scientists at first considered this to be an unfortunate quirk of nature. But subsequent investigation found that it coincided with a rise in temperatures of the Indian Ocean disrupting seasonal monsoons. This suggests that the drying of sub-Saharan Africa derives, to some degree, from man-made global warming.

It is no accident that the violence in Darfur erupted during the drought. Until then, Arab nomadic herders had lived amicably with settled farmers. A recent Atlantic Monthly article by Stephan Faris[40] describes how black farmers would welcome herders as they crisscrossed the land, grazing their camels and sharing wells. But once the rains stopped, farmers fenced their land for fear it would be ruined by the passing herds. For the first time in memory, there was no longer enough food and water for all. Fighting broke out. By 2003, it evolved into the full-fledged tragedy we witness today.

Arab nomadic herders from the northern parts of Sudan had begun migrating southwards towards the areas cultivated by the African tribes in the south of Sudan. The clash over land and water between Arab nomads and African tribes was resolved before the climate changes and the emergence of the NIF regime through customary law and processes. Religion was not a complicating factor as both the African tribes and the Arab nomads were Sunni Muslim followers. The fact that the origins of the carnage in Darfur have been in part caused by the contributions of many nations to global climate change makes the inaction on Darfur another factor of culpability on the part of the planet's leading greenhouse gas emitters such as the U.S., Europe, China, India and Canada.

Even if the changes wrought by climate change could be peacefully dealt with between the African tribes and the Arab nomads, such a peace would not survive the NIF regime. Fearful that the non-Arab population of Darfur would link up with the southern SPLM rebels, the Khartoum government began the strategy of divide and conquer with the Darfur tribes. First the Khartoum government divided the territory of the African Fur tribe, the largest of the Darfurian peoples, into three subunit states. It made the Fur a minority in each state with the Arab elite dominating the administration. Second, it reinstated laws that voided the traditional hereditary rights of the Fur to their land. Likewise the traditional lands of the African Dar Masalit tribe were also divided into thirteen administrative 'emirates' with again Arab elites dominating the traditional lands and denying rights to unregistered hereditary lands.

With the traditional lands of the Fur and the Masalit carved up, the Khartoum government then commenced the familiar pattern of arming and coordinating with the Arab militia groups called the Janjaweed. These Arab militias are manned by individuals not only from Sudan, but also from Chad and Libya. These militias were organized and orchestrated by the NIF regime in the late 1980s to the mid 1990s when they began the genocide in Darfur against Masalit and Fur villages in earnest. The villages were attacked and burned, thousands of Masalit and Fur were killed and vast herds of cattle stolen. Over 100,000 African villagers fled across the border to Chad to seek refuge there.

In many examples, there was overwhelming evidence of Khartoum's involvement with Sudanese forces entering villages first to confiscate weapons, kill or arrest leaders and pressgang younger men for military service in the south against the SPLM. Then with seemingly routine occurrence, the Janjaweed followed on horseback or camels, shot the remaining villagers, raped the women and girl children and burned the houses and crops to prevent any return by the villagers. In southern Darfur, the genocidal pattern repeated itself where the main Arab militia was organized by the Khartoum government to start a similar offensive against the African Zaghawa tribe.

What added to the desperate plight of the Fur, the Masalit and the Zaghawa was the influence of a growing anti-African and racist ideology of Arab superiority emanating from the Arab Alliance in Sudan, Chad and Libya which lumped the African tribes of Sudan as '*zurqa*' (blacks) and '*abid*' (slaves). First among equals in the organizers of racist genocide is Musa Hilal, a leader from the Arab Rizayqat tribe, nurtured by the Khartoum government, which over several years was armed by allied anti-African elements in Libya. Hilal began a ruthless campaign of ethnic cleansing against the Zaghawa and extended his raids further north against the Masalit. This Janjaweed killer should also be regarded as an architect of crimes against humanity and genocide. His supporters in Libya and Chad should be regarded as equally culpable in the eyes of the international community, regardless of their attempts to deny involvement.

With the Fur, the Masalit and the Zaghawa targeted for massive ethnic cleansing and genocide by the Arab militias and the Khartoum government, it was only a question of time before there emerged several rebel groups from the Darfur African tribes; the Sudan Liberation Army (SLA) and the Justice and Equality Movement (JEM). When the SLA launched its first attack against the Khartoum government army outposts in Darfur in 2003, all out genocidal war against the civilians of Darfur began.

The killing machines of the Khartoum government started taking on the efficiency of those in the Third Reich. First, Antonov bombers bought from the Russians and old transport planes dropped bombs on villages filled with civilians. Then Chinese and Russian purchased helicopter gunships would arrive on the scene to destroy remaining buildings and spray anyone fleeing with gunfire. Finally, the Janjaweed would arrive on horses, camels or technical pick up trucks with militia or soldiers armed to the teeth to finish off the killing. First, women and girls would be raped and often branded to mark them for life as despoiled. Then any property or livestock would be carried off. Men and boys were lined up and executed or saved to become slaves. Anyone of no use to the marauders, including children and babies, was thrown into huts that were then set on fire to be burned alive. Finally the dead would be thrown into wells to pollute the water to prevent any returning survivors.

The purpose of this systemic killing was clear: to depopulate the region and prevent any survivors from returning. Many fleeing survivors were hunted down before they could reach the Chad border. By August 2004, the U.S. State Department had estimated that over 400 villages had been depopulated, over 200,000 had fled into Chad and over 1.2 million had been herded into internally displaced persons' camps where they would be subject to further grotesquely inhumane treatment by the pack of Janjaweed thugs who prowled on the outskirts of the camps near the town of El Geneina and other Darfur towns. These camps present scenes reminiscent of the concentration camps in World War II. The ever increasing numbers in the displaced persons' camps were being subjected to the cruelest of choices humans could possibly face. Families would either starve due to lack of firewood or the women and girls of the camp would resign themselves to go outside the camp to forage for firewood and face the most horrible of fates. The Janjaweed and some Sudanese forces would gang rape the women and girls as young as 10, brand them and shoot them in the legs, hurling racial insults as they dragged themselves back to the safety of the camp. If the men or boys ventured outside, they faced certain death.

While the numbers of those killed or forced by the Janjaweed and Sudanese forces to flee to the camps and Chad climbed, the Khartoum government engaged in what can only be described as surreal hypocrisy aimed at primarily preserving its image as genuinely interested in the peace process in the south of Sudan. The NCP government claimed that the accusations of mass killing and genocide in progress were false propaganda by the western media, NGOs, dissidents, neighboring hostile states and Zionists in the West and Israel. Instead, the Khartoum government asserted that any civilian casualties were the result of tribal conflicts which were out of control and should not overshadow the peace process in the south.

Not satisfied with the depths of human misery in the displaced persons' camps and those fleeing the bombers, gunships, technicals and Janjaweed, the Khartoum government initiated the final part of its genocide plan. It began to starve the remnants of the Darfur tribes in the camps by throwing up all sorts of barriers to humanitarian agencies, confiscating and stealing food destined for the starving in the camps. By the end of 2004, the U.N. estimated that 10,000 persons were dying in the camps due to the genocide by starvation. In the same year, the total death toll reached over 200,000 with approximately 2.5 million people displaced in the camps or refugees in Darfur and Chad. It was the world's worst international crime committed by people that the leading democratic nations like the United States were regarding as credible peace partners in the attempt to reach the comprehensive peace agreement in the south of the country. The mediating states, in particular the U.S. and Great Britain, chose to focus on achieving the Comprehensive Peace Agreement rather than turn the screws on al-Bashir. In particular, the keenness of the United States to get a peace agreement in the south seemed to encourage the rampage by the Khartoum government and its Janjaweed killers in Darfur to carry on the ethnic cleansing.

Civil society groups, international NGOs, the media and key legislators in North America and Europe were the critical opponents of the seeming willingness to ignore the tragedy of Darfur, while the U.S., Great Britain and other western mediators focused on concluding the peace agreement in the south with the killers in Khartoum. There seemed to be more interest on the part of the former Bush Administration in the U.S. in strengthening its partnership in the so-called war on terror with the genocidal killers in Khartoum than on helping to end the carnage in Darfur. Tragic ironies kept increasing when the U.S., in May of 2004, removed Sudan from the list of those who were 'against' the U.S. in the war on terror and had become partners, as witnessed by the visit of Salah Gosh to the CIA headquarters. Yet in 2004, U.S. Congressional members pressured the U.S. to do more in Darfur by sending to the Bush Administration lists of Janjaweed leaders and their Khartoum collaborators. Similarly, religious groups, university students, faculty and human rights organizations in the U.S. kept the pressure up, while the Bush Administration tried to use their focus on the peace process in the south to justify their inaction in the Darfur genocide.

5.   PEACE IN THE SOUTH BEGINS TO CRACK

The 2005 Comprehensive Peace Agreement (CPA) in the south of Sudan was supposed to end the genocide that caused the deaths of an estimated 2.5 million southerners and caused close to 5 million displaced persons and refugees. If the intentions of the Khartoum government were duplicitous in their concessions in the CPA and had intentions to either undermine it or treat it as a breathing room maneuver, the consequence could be an even worse carnage and bloodshed than Sudan has seen to date. The duplicitous intentions have begun surfacing and the consequences are predictable. It must be borne in mind that Darfur was downplayed and overlooked by the African and western mediators, particularly from the U.S. and Britain, in order to wrest the CPA from the world's most dubious peacemaker, the Sudanese government.

At first, the CPA seemed to be on the road to success. The supposedly autonomous government in the south had been established and had access to an estimated $3 billion in petroleum revenues transferred to the SPLM government in Juba. With refugees from the genocidal war in the south returning to their towns and villages, the economy was starting to grow. However, the Khartoum government soon started stalling on some of the most critical elements in the CPA regarding the south's interests. Beginning in March of 2007, the Sudanese government temporarily suspended the agreed upon oil revenues to the south, critically needed for the running of the government and army in the south. Two months later, in June of the same year, President al-Bashir canceled the withdrawal of elements of the northern army still based in the south as required by the CPA.[41] In addition, Khartoum was delaying on the establishment of an electoral law and the carrying out of a census, both of which were indispensable for the elections slated for 2009.

The first series of armed conflict did erupt around the town of Abyei, in the oil rich area of the south in latter months of 2007 and into May of 2008. Nicholas Kristof of the *New York Times* describes the reality of this town seemingly as that of Darfur, not of the so-called peaceful territory of south Sudan:[42]

> This dusty little town of rutted dirt streets is surrounded by Janjaweed, Arab militias armed by the Sudanese government and paid to do its dirty work.
>
> But this isn't Darfur, where the Janjaweed have played the central role in the genocide that has claimed hundreds of thousands of lives. Rather, Abyei is on the edge of southern Sudan, in a region that is supposed to be at peace.
>
> In the 1980s and 1990s, it was here that the government perfected the techniques that later became notorious in Darfur: mass rape and murder by armed militias, so as to terrorize civilians and drive them away. Now Sudan is coming full circle, apparently preparing to apply the same techniques again to Abyei and parts of the south. With international attention distracted by Darfur and the United States presidential race, the Sudanese government now is chipping away at the 2005 peace treaty that ended the north-south war in Sudan. If war erupts, as many expect, the flash point will probably be here in Abyei, where the northern government is pumping oil from wells it refuses to give up.
>
> 'War is going to take place,' Joseph Dut Paguot, the acting government administrator in the Abyei region, said bluntly.
>
> Chol Changath Chol, a representative of South Sudan in Abyei, agreed: 'If there are no changes, war will come. It will break out here and spread everywhere.'
>
> Since late November, there have been repeated clashes in the Abyei area between South Sudan's armed forces and a large tribe of Arab nomads, the Misseriya, which is armed and backed by the Sudanese government in Khartoum. Mr. Paguot said that several hundred people had been killed in these clashes, and that some of the gunmen were government soldiers who had taken off their uniforms to masquerade as tribal fighters.
>
> Mr. Al-Bashir's plan seems to be to encourage Arab nomads to drive out other ethnic groups from areas with oil. Then once fighting begins, he would have an excuse to cancel national elections next year – which he would almost surely lose – and he might be able to rally Sudanese Arabs behind him in a nationalist campaign to hold on to the oil fields.
>
> So remember this little town of Abyei. It's the tinderbox for Africa's next war, which will probably resemble Darfur but be carried out on a much wider scale.

'If there is just one bullet in Abyei,' said Col. Valentino Tocmac, the commander of the south's forces here, 'that will be the end of the peace.'

What the Khartoum government seems determined to undermine is the critical part of the 2005 CPA in which there was an agreement to end the dispute over the oil rich territory around Abyei. Both sides had agreed to abide by the decision of the Abyei Boundary Commission. Ultimately Khartoum rejected the finding of the Commission.

The duplicity of al-Bashir as regards his intentions on following through with his CPA promises had become clear. In the first week of October, 2007, the SPLM, led by Salva Kiir Mayardit, the President of the Government of South Sudan, withdrew its ministers from the Sudanese government of national unity which had been part of the CPA framework. One southern official asserted that the Sudanese President almost declared war and called on his dreaded proxy militias in the south 'to open training camps and gather the mujahideen not for the sake of war but to be ready for anything'.[43] There were reports that sizeable units of the armies of both north and south had begun stationing themselves in the disputed border areas. In May of 2008, Abyei itself was the site of heavy fighting with tens of thousands of residents fleeing.[44]

True to form, President al-Bashir, realizing that if war broke out his army might not win it, called for peace talks with President Kiir, and yet again on paper obtained what some would regard as an illusory agreement to deal by January 9, 2008, with the serious points of conflict. These included a cabinet reshuffle of a southerner who had become too close to Khartoum, the redeployment of northern troops from the south, some of the contentious issues dealing with oil revenues, marketing and management, the final demarcation of the border and proceeding with the census and its related process for the referendum on southern independence in 2011.[45] It comes as no surprise that many of these promises remain unfulfilled.

The oil rich territory around Abyei is potentially the spark that could reignite the war in the south. The international boundary commission had given the region to the south. The Khartoum government responded by sending hundreds of northern troops into the town. One report indicates that an estimated 50,000 civilians have fled from the town seeking refuge in the bush, leaving Abyei virtually deserted.

On August 9, 2008, the BBC reported that a deal had been reached on the region between the Khartoum government and the south. The agreement would establish an interim administration with a southerner being the chief administrator and a local Arab clan leader and a member of al-Bashir's NCP Party as his deputy.[46] In addition there was an agreement that the disputed territory around the oil rich territory would be submitted to arbitration at the Permanent Court of Arbitration in The Hague.

Despite this latest peace deal by the unreliable Khartoum government and the ruling of the Permanent Court of Arbitration on July 22, 2009, that gave much of the oil rich territory around Abyei to the North,[47] there is growing evidence that the Khartoum government may not be in full control of the northern forces in the area of Abyei, given the infiltration of local militias into its ranks. There may be a war ignited without the consent of Khartoum.

The SPLM has rejoined the national unity government, but the cracks in the CPA are only papered over. The U.N. Mission in the south, UNAMIS, seems helpless, even with its 7,000 soldiers and police to deal with flare ups of violence, as occurred with the Abyei dispute. As in Darfur, the Sudanese government hampers its ability to stop such conflicts from becoming even wider.[48]

It is becoming clear what the real intentions of the Khartoum government are in the south. It is desperately trying to surreptitiously undermine the census and election process leading to the nationwide elections in 2010 and the ultimate referendum in 2011. There is little doubt that the government of President al-Bashir will try to manipulate the elections as it has done with the census. Therefore the outcome will be contested by the southerners. Likewise, there is a virtual certainty that the south will opt for independence in the 2011 referendum. The Khartoum government seems determined not to lose any of the remaining oil production areas that are within the territory of the South after the ruling of the Permanent Court of Arbitration on July 22, 2009.

These probable electoral and referendum losses were known to the Sudanese government in 2005 when it signed the CPA. It is a logical conclusion to make that the CPA may well have been a stalling tactic by the Sudanese government. In the meantime, the Khartoum government and their proxies along with the African and western mediators were willing to sacrifice the people of Darfur for an illusory peace in the south. This is tragedy on a gigantic scale.

There are few certainties in Sudan, but two of them are the probability of rigged national elections, first scheduled for 2009 and then delayed until 2010, and a vote for independence by the south in the 2011 referendum. Both of these certainties occurring could plunge Sudan into a humanitarian catastrophe that would be much larger than any of the previous conflicts in Rwanda, Bosnia or anywhere else in recent decades. These are consequences that the Khartoum government may well have envisaged from the very beginning of its duplicitous engagement with the CPA process.

The possibility of the conflict spilling over into neighboring countries is high. These countries include Chad, Libya, Egypt, Uganda, Ethiopia and the Central African Republic. One could envisage millions of refugees streaming across borders or seeking refuge in countries which were the mediators in the north–south conflict such as the U.S., Britain and Canada. The dead, the wounded and the internally displaced would also be in the millions. A disintegrating Sudan would also be a magnet for the extremists bent on the slaughter of innocents who delight in their title as terrorists. The global supply of oil would also be affected, with attacks on the oil fields.

The bad faith of the al-Bashir government in keeping its commitments under the CPA which is so highly treasured by the fragile peace deal's western backers became apparent in the spring of 2009. There is growing evidence that the Khartoum government is nurturing violent inter-tribal clashes in the south in the hope that the SPLM government will fall before the scheduled elections and the referendum in 2011. The SPLM government is starting to be overwhelmed by severe cash shortages caused in part by low oil prices and the failure of Khartoum to give the south its fair share. In addition, large scale cattle raids involving thousands of livestock perpetrated by militias, some heavily armed by elements from the Khartoum government, are left unhindered by the southern military forces. The *Washington Post* reported in April of 2009 that militias from the Lou Nuer tribe captured an entire town, displacing 5,000 inhabitants while soldiers stood by and watched, with more than 700 people killed. The finger of blame is increasingly being targeted at al-Bashir's senior officials who are arming these militias as they did during the earlier civil war and undermining the southern government with the hope of destabilizing the region ahead of the 2011 referendum on secession by the south.[49]

6. LIMITING THE DAMAGE AND BRINGING THE PRESIDENT TO ACCOUNT FOR HIS CRIMES

Given the potential disasters that al-Bashir is flirting with both in the south and in Darfur, it is one of the most urgent tasks of the international community to ensure that a fully-resourced UNAMID force of the promised 26,000 soldiers and police is immediately deployed in Darfur and a much strengthened U.N. force in the south of Sudan to deter attempts by al-Bashir to undermine the fragile peace there. These forces should be backed by all the logistical and military equipment that is needed. European nations, Canada, the U.S. and other countries that so vigorously condemned the atrocities in Darfur must produce the very limited number of helicopters and military equipment needed by the UNAMID force.

What if none of these things stop these plans of the Khartoum government? Military intervention by NATO battalions or by some other coalition of the willing into Sudan to exert regime change is not a realistic option. The massive territory of Sudan would make the quagmires of Iraq and Afghanistan seem inconsequential. Both countries have shown the insurgencies that would arise would be impossible to subdue within any reasonable amount of time. Perhaps the best military solution would be to bolster the forces of the SPLM in the south. That army is now very formidable as it has been battle hardened by decades of guerrilla warfare in the south. It had shown the ability to beat back the larger Sudanese army forces during the late 1980s and the 1990s. In part this unexpected ability of the SPLM forces was a factor in al-Bashir and his government deciding to start negotiations on the CPA. The conflict was a major burden on the finances of the Khartoum government, and towards the end of the conflict the SPLM was close to threatening the oil fields the revenues from which the north depended on. The CPA may have just been a lifeline for al-Bashir and his government rather than a real intention to forge a lasting peace with the SPLM.[50] If true, perhaps peace in the south of Sudan is also dependent on al-Bashir being sent to the ICC to face trial in the hope that a more genuine peacemaker appears as the leader of the Khartoum government to cement peace under the terms of the CPA.

The indicted Sudanese President may well be attempting the same approach he took with the SPLM to an illusory and unsustainable peace process in Darfur. The evidence of this agenda by al-Bashir is mounting. While he professes to seek peace, his military and Janjaweed proxy militias are daily increasing the death toll over the 300,000 estimation, more women and girls are savagely raped, and the displaced in the world's most wretched camps climb daily over the 2 million figure in Darfur. His forces are increasingly not hesitant to kill U.N. soldiers and aid workers. He continues to place obstacles to a fully operational and manned UNAMID force and has become an expert in stalling and manipulating attempts to broker a peace agreement. Few of those involved in the negotiations can trust in his promises or his agreements. Finally, given the fact his actions and those of his Janjaweed proxies have led to the splintering of the rebel groups and infighting between themselves, there is little hope that a comprehensive peace agreement is likely anytime soon.

In this tragic environment, there is not really a realistic choice between peace and justice. There is only the hope that the moral and legal denunciation of the world that has fallen upon al-Bashir through the indictment as a ruthless international criminal will lead to his own people and elites rising up against him and eventually handing him over to face justice in The Hague. The prospect of al-Bashir before the ICC may also give small comfort to those who are the victims of this architect of mass slaughter of his own peoples that the rest of the world cares about their plight and is seeking justice on their behalf. Finally, it may also send a warning to other architects of grave international crimes that the time for them to be held accountable before the world will only be a matter of time and that they will be haunted by this prospect until their last breaths.

Yet, the most powerful and influential players at the U.N. Security Council and in the international community are attempting 'to make justice negotiable', in the words of Louise Arbour, the former U.N. Human Rights Commissioner and Chief Prosecutor of the International Criminal Tribunal for the Former Yugoslavia. The Arab League together with the African Union petitioned the Security Council to defer the charges against al-Bashir for twelve months (renewable), as permitted under Article 16 of the ICC Statute. There is evidence that four of the five permanent members of the Council, namely the United Kingdom, France, China and Russia, had given support to the suspension. Not unexpectedly, human rights groups have warned that such a deferral could spell the grave undermining of the ICC. Human Rights Watch has asserted that '[a]n Article 16 deferral will send a message to human rights abusers around the world that justice can be bargained away'.[51] Given that al-Bashir is already defying the Security Council by not handing over Humanitarian Minister Ahmad Harun and the Janjaweed leader Ali Kushayb who are also subject to ICC arrest warrants, the allegation that the U.N. would be tolerating impunity for gross human rights abuses if it agreed to the deferral would not be unfounded. A dangerous precedent for other indicted leaders such as LRA leader Joseph Kony and other present and future instigators of crimes against humanity and war crimes in Africa and around the world would also be set. There is hope on the part of human rights groups that the newly elected U.S. President Barack Obama will resist the attempt to give al-Bashir a get out of the ICC jail card.

On March 4, 2009, the Pre-Trial Chamber of the ICC issued the warrant for the arrest of al-Bashir on charges of war crimes and crimes against humanity in Darfur. However, with one judge dissenting, the Court did not find that the Chief Prosecutor had provided sufficient evidence to prove the specific intent needed to ground a charge of genocide against the President of Sudan. The Court held that al-Bashir 'is suspected of being criminally responsible, as an indirect (co-)perpetrator, for intentionally directing attacks against an important part of the civilian population of Darfur, Sudan, murdering, exterminating, raping, torturing and forcibly transferring large numbers of civilians, and pillaging their property'.[52]

The arrest warrants issued by the Court stated that the international crimes were allegedly committed during a five year counter-insurgency campaign starting soon after April 2003 by the Government of Sudan against the SLMA and the JEM and other armed rebel groups opposing al-Bashir's government. These crimes, according to the Court, were the result of a common plan agreed upon at the highest level of the al-Bashir government and other high-ranking Sudanese political and military leaders.[53]

The Court held that this campaign included unlawful attacks by both the Sudanese military and their allied Janjaweed militias on the civilian populations of Darfur belonging to the African Fur, Masalit and Zaghawa groups that were perceived to be close to the rebel groups. There was the added involvement in these civilian attacks by the Sudanese Police Force, the National Intelligence and Security Service and, most ironically, the Humanitarian Aid Commission according to the Court. The Court found that al-Bashir as the *de jure* and *de facto* President and Commander-in-Chief of the Sudanese military was suspected of having coordinated the design and implementation of the counter-insurgency campaign or was in control of the apparatus of the state that led to the international crimes being committed.[54]

The following are the counts in the warrant of arrest listing infractions by al-Bashir of the Rome Statute establishing the Court and as listed by the Court:

> On the basis of his individual criminal responsibility (article 25(3)(a)):
> five counts of crimes against humanity: murder – article 7(1)(a); extermination – article 7(1)(b); forcible transfer – article 7(1)(d);
> torture – article 7(1)(f); and rape – article 7(1)(g);
> two counts of war crimes: intentionally directing attacks against a civilian population as such or against individual civilians not taking direct part in hostilities – article 8(2)(e)(i); and pillaging – article 8(2)(e)(v).

As regards the findings on the count of genocide, the majority of the Pre-Trial Chamber, Judge Anita Ušacka dissenting, found that there was not sufficient evidence presented by the Prosecution to show reasonable grounds that al-Bashir had acted with specific intent to destroy in whole, or in part, the Fur, Masalit and Zaghawa groups. This ruling seems to follow the 2005 conclusion of the International Commission of Inquiry led by Professor Antonio Cassese that genocide was not being committed by the Khartoum government in Darfur, but finding instead acts constituting crimes against humanity and war crimes. The Court added that if additional evidence was to be gathered by the Prosecution, there would be no impediment to a request for an amendment to the warrant of arrest to include the crime of genocide. There was a strong dissenting opinion which was prepared to infer from the evidence provided a specific intent on the part of al-Bashir to indirectly perpetrate through others a genocide in Darfur. The majority and minority opinions will be more fully discussed in the context of comparing the criticism of the prosecutorial strategy of the Chief Prosecutor of the ICC with the actual judgments of the Pre-Trial Chamber. The Prosecutor has successfully appealed the decision of the majority on the genocide charge. On February 3, 2010 the Appeal Chamber of the ICC reversed the decision of the Pre-Trial Chamber of March 4, 2009, not to issue a warrant of arrest in respect of the charge of genocide. The Appeals Chamber directed the Pre-Trial Chamber to decide anew whether or not the arrest warrant should be extended to cover the charge of genocide. The Appeals Chamber overruled the Pre-Trial Chamber's conclusion that demanding that the existence of genocidal intent must be the only reasonable conclusion amounts to requiring the Prosecutor to disprove any other reasonable conclusions and to eliminate any reasonable doubt. While this burden of proof may be required at the trial stage, the Appeals Chamber found this standard of proof to be too demanding at the arrest warrant stage, which is governed by Article 58 of the Rome Statute. The Appeals Chamber ruled that the burden of proof imposed by the Pre-Trial Chamber on the Prosecutor on the charge of genocide at the arrest warrant stage amounted to an error of law.

Anticipating that al-Bashir would repudiate the arrest warrant, as he did claiming that it was not worth the ink it was written in, the Court has sought the cooperation of all States Parties to the Rome Statute and the U.N. Security Council members which are not parties to the Rome Statute in the arrest and surrender of al-Bashir. Finally the Court also noted that Sudan had still failed to arrest and surrender the previously indicted individuals Ahmad Harun and Janjaweed leader Ali Kushayb. The Court noted its ability under the Rome Statute, article 87(7), to refer this previous failure by the al-Bashir government to the U.N. Security Council. In addition the Court also noted that under U.N. Security Council Resolution 1593, all states, whether party to the Rome Statute or not, as well as international and regional organizations, had a duty to fully cooperate with the Court as regards the arrest warrants.[55]

President al-Bashir seemed eager to confirm the grounds of criminality listed by the ICC Chief Prosecutor the day after the Pre-Trial Chamber handed down the arrest warrants by expelling key aid groups from Darfur. These groups included Oxfam, Save the Children, the International Rescue Committee and Doctors without Borders as a form of grotesque retaliation against the ICC.[56] These expulsions threaten the lives and health of hundreds of thousands of those seeking a semblance of safety in the refugee camps and who rely on the most basic food, water and health necessities from these aid groups. These expulsions could well provide evidence not only of ongoing crimes against humanity by the al-Bashir regime, but also possible additional evidence of specific intent to commit genocide which the Pre-Trial Chamber was not able to find and therefore excluded from the arrest warrant. The expulsions were also an attempt to force the U.N. Security Council to postpone the proceedings against al-Bashir in the vain hope of getting the Khartoum regime to be genuine about a peaceful settlement in Darfur.

There is a growing opposition both within Sudan and in the international community to resist any deal with al-Bashir and support the ICC's attempt to stem the tide of impunity and ruthless calculations by despots that use such criminal tactics to avoid facing the justice that their victims demand. Nicholas Kristof of the *New York Times* reports that there are rumours that some leaders just below al-Bashir were contemplating overthrowing the President to save themselves.[57]

Officials from the Office of the U.N. Human Rights Commissioner are also warning that there may well be additional criminal charges against al-Bashir stemming from the expulsions. Officials at the Office are examining whether the expulsions could constitute breaches of the Geneva Conventions prohibiting the deliberate blocking of humanitarian aid in a conflict zone. The *Times* of London reported that a U.N. Security Council effort to call upon al-Bashir to reverse his decision was blocked by China.[58]

In his continuing show of defiance against the ICC arrest warrant, al-Bashir promised that no Sudanese would ever be prosecuted in The Hague. As if to prove him wrong, a Darfur rebel commander of a splinter group of the JEM, Bahr, Idriss Abu Garda, voluntarily agreed to appear before the ICC on May 18, 2009, in response to a summons to answer charges of war crimes in connection with the attack and killing of twelve African Union peacekeepers and the looting of the A.U. base in the Darfur town of Haskanita in September of 2007. It was the first time that one of the Darfur rebels had been charged with any of the serious crimes under the ICC Statute since the ICC had begun investigating the Darfur situation under the referral by the Security Council in 2005. Up to this point, the ICC prosecutions had focused on President al-Bashir, his top official, Harun, and the Janjaweed militia leader, Kushayb.

The voluntary appearance by the rebel commander under a summons meant that he is able to return to Darfur while the facts in his case are being examined and has the option to either appear in person on October 12, 2009 to hear and contest the confirmation of the charges or allow the confirmation to go ahead without his presence. At his appearance on May 18, 2009, Abu Garda was informed of the crimes he is alleged to have committed and his rights.

There was a calculated risk that Abu Garda's commitment to the ICC process is firm and that he will not repudiate it by not returning to face trial and possible conviction and sentencing. The rebel commander was confident that he would not be convicted. He is quoted as saying 'I will go, no problem, I know I was not involved'. Due to this willingness to stand trial, no arrest warrant was issued against Abu Garda. It is reported that it was his former group, the JEM, that has helped collect evidence against him.[59]

Prior to the dramatic appearance of the first Sudanese suspect before the Court, the Prosecutor had announced in June 2007 that it was monitoring attacks on peacekeepers and aid workers in the Darfur region. While there had been other attacks by Sudanese government and militia forces against U.N. peacekeepers, the Haskanita attacks were the most deadly of them all, resulting in the ICC Prosecutor opening up an investigation in December of 2007 regarding these attacks. In June of 2008, the Prosecutor confirmed to the U.N. Security Council that the investigation would be completed before the end of the year, noting that such attacks on peacekeepers have a direct impact on the delivery of vital services and thereby exacerbate the suffering of vulnerable groups and impact on the lives of thousands.[60]

On November 20, 2008, the ICC Prosecutor had submitted a sealed case against three rebel commanders believed to be behind the raid that killed and wounded the peacekeepers. Apart from Abu Garda, the names of the other two rebel commanders charged with similar war crimes against the peacekeepers have remained sealed.

Announcing the first voluntary appearance by a Sudanese alleged war criminal, the Prosecutor, Luis Moreno-Ocampo, paid tribute to the fallen peacekeepers in the following words:[61]

> By killing peacekeepers, the perpetrators attacked the millions of civilians who those soldiers came to protect. They came from Senegal, from Mali, from Nigeria, from Botswana, to serve and protect. They were murdered. Attacking peacekeepers is a serious crime under the Statute and shall be prosecuted.

The Prosecutor also stressed that the voluntary appearance of Abu Garda would not have been possible without the assistance of a number of African and European states which worked with the Prosecutor over eight months. These countries included Chad, Senegal, Nigeria, Mali and Gambia.[62] This cooperation is a growing indication of the fact that several

African states are beginning to break away from the criticism of the ICC by the African Union and the Arab League. Supporters of the ICC are also hoping that this cooperative action by the African states along with the appearance of the rebel commander will counter the assertions by the Court's critics that the ICC is biased against the Sudanese government and is unfairly targeting African perpetrators of war crimes.[63] To the surprise of the Prosecutor, on February 8, 2010, the Pre-Trial Chamber of the ICC declined to confirm the charges against Abu Garda. The Chamber was not satisfied that there was sufficient evidence to establish substantial grounds to believe that the accused could be held criminally responsible for the crime of which he was charged. The positive side of this ruling is that it should be evidence to other Sudanese individuals who have been indicted that the ICC can conduct fair and impartial prosecutions based on the presumption of innocence of those charged with the most serious of international crimes.

7. THE CRITICS OF THE ICC PROSECUTION STRATEGY ON PEACE AND JUSTICE IN THE SITUATION IN SUDAN AND IN PARTICULAR THE INDICTMENT OF PRESIDENT AL-BASHIR

Before the decision of the Trial Chamber handing down the arrest warrant for President al-Bashir, perhaps the fiercest critic of the prosecution strategy of Chief Proscutor Luis Moreno-Ocampo was the Sudan expert Alex de Waal. In a paper published on the U.S. Social Science Research Council website, de Waal makes the following critiques which could be grouped into four main categories.

First, the Prosecutor alleged not only genocidal intent on the part of the President, but also a central genocidal plan, which de Waal asserts would be a difficult basis on which to convict the President. In addition the charges are broad-ranging in that they covered the entire period of the conflict from early 2003 and the whole of Darfur though specifically referring to the Fur, Masalit and Zaghawa tribes. De Waal uses his expertise to claim that there were rudimentary ethnographic errors in the prosecution, such as the reality that the Dar Fur is not an ethnically defined domain, but contains multi-ethnic groups from other 'Dars'. His critique also asserts that racial categorization is at best problematic between victims and perpetrators as he claims the Prosecution strategy focused on. He uses the example of the two indicted perpetrators, Harun and Kushayb, being of either African origin or lineage despite being held out as the Arab persecutors of the Darfur African tribes. According to this critic, these points, although seemingly minor, could impact on proving the specific intent to commit genocide by al-Bashir. The use of specialized ethnographic knowledge to undermine the legal strategies of the Prosecutor is a well tried strategy of de Waal.

Focusing on the specific intent required for a genocide conviction, de Waal almost predicts the majority decision of the Pre-Trial Chamber in the al-Bashir case when he argues that the prosecution is required to show that genocidal intent is the *only* reasonable inference that can be made from the evidentiary basis of the prosecution. This is imposing a 'beyond a reasonable doubt' proof at the arrest warrant stage which is only required at the full trial stage. The Prosecutor has appealed the ruling of the majority in the al-Bashir case to the Appeals Chamber of the ICC. In a confusing ruling allowing the appeal, the Pre-Trial Chamber asserted that it did not really rule that the prosecution was required to show at the arrest stage that genocidal intent is the only reasonable inference that can be deduced from the evidence.[64] By such a ruling, the Chamber undermines the critique of de Waal.

If there are other reasonable inferences the case for genocide cannot be proven. De Waal then goes through the factors presented by the Prosecutor to prove genocidal intent and attempts to refute that they can be the basis of the reasonable inference. However, such an inference can only be made by situating the individual intent of al-Bashir within a broader organization or collective intent which requires the application of an implied socio-political theory of genocide. The mode of liability termed joint criminal enterprise is based on such a theory of genocide and was the basis for the prosecution of the Nazi leaders at Nuremberg. However, de Waal strongly critiques the Prosecutor for not testing his genocide on this basis, but rather deciding to prosecute on the basis of indirect perpetration. He then implies that the Prosecutor did not adopt the socio-political theory of genocide because it would have led to the same conclusion of the International Commission of Inquiry into Darfur headed by Antonio Cassese, which concluded that there was no evidence for a genocidal plan, implying that there was no collective intent but that individual acts of genocide may have been committed. This approach would have exonerated al-Bashir from the charge of genocide in the view of this critic. Instead he argues that the evidence presented by the Prosecutor gives no indication of any genocidal plan or policy. Rather the evidence demonstrates 'the kind of clumsy and violent counterinsurgency, targeted at civilian communities, that is how wars are conducted in Sudan and neighbouring countries'. One can put aside the fact that as a non-lawyer, de Waal was probably not aware that the prior decisions[65] of the Pre-Trial Chamber had effectively sidelined any possibility of charging al-Bashir under the joint criminal enterprise mode of liability. The fact that this critic could assert that the deaths of over 300,000 people and 2.7 million people being imprisoned in the most squalid conditions on earth amounts to just the results of a clumsy and violent counterinsurgency speaks for itself in terms of lack of perspective as regards the human dignity of the peoples of Darfur.

De Waal also argues that the Sudan military commanders armed all the militias in Darfur, including those belonging to the African tribes, but then turned against them when they deserted to the SLA. De Waal also questions the Prosecutor's two-stage theory of the genocide in Darfur as regards the huge numbers of internally displaced persons in the squalid and 'slow death' camps that are preyed upon by Janjaweed militias who practice the most horrific gender crimes against women and the girl child. Astonishingly this critic claims that because al-Bashir allowed substantial amounts of humanitarian aid, including Sudanese aid, to operate in the camps, it negates any aspect of genocidal intent or policy! The absurdity of this position also speaks for itself, but genocidal intent can be masked by permitting limited access to humanitarian aid that does not stop the overall death toll and displacement of entire groups from their homes from rising.

Second, de Waal concludes that the charges of crimes against humanity and war crimes are a reiteration of the charges laid against Harun and Kushayb, with additional recent incidents and the addition of al-Bashir as another perpetrator through the mode of 'perpetration by means'. De Wall argues that rather than opting for less complex modes of liability such as superior responsibility, the Prosecutor chose to pursue the ambitious and innovative mode of liability of indirect perpetration, which depends on the control of the state. This critic argued that the evidence according to his expertise did not support the contention that Bashir had total control over every relevant institutions of the state. The majority in the Pre-Trial Chamber, while seeming to agree with de Waal on the genocide charge, allowed the charges on crimes against humanity and war crimes to be the foundation for the arrest warrant against al-Bashir. As discussed above, the Prosecutor has successfully appealed the decision of the majority on the genocide charge with the decision of the Appeals Chamber of the ICC directing the Pre-Trial Chamber to decide anew whether or not the arrest warrant should be extended to cover the charge of genocide.

Third, according to de Waal, the Prosecutor's strategy as regards al-Bashir was not in the interests of justice, peace or democracy for Sudan. He alleged that pursuing an arrest warrant against a Head of State is tantamount to demanding regime change, which was in contradiction to the intense efforts of the international community to negotiate a peaceful settlement with the Sudanese government in both the south of Sudan and

Darfur. The prosecutorial approach was both a gamble with unknowable consequences and involving very large risk areas. It has also already contributed to negative reactions to the ICC from African governments and civil society. As has already been discussed in Chapter 1, the provisions in the ICC Statute that relate to 'the interests of justice' exclude the examination of 'political consequences', given the fact that the Court is a legal institution and not a political body. This critic fails to understand this most fundamental aspect of the mandate and operations of the ICC, including the prosecutorial strategy of the Chief Prosecutor.

Fourth, the ICC is ill-suited as a political leverage mechanism. Therefore while deferral by the U.N. Security Council of the charges against al-Bashir under Article 16 of the ICC Statute may be inadequate for safeguarding the principle of justice and Sudan's needs, de Waal asserts that a deferral is in the interests of peace and security in Sudan and its neighbors. This critic claims that three of the members of the Security Council, the U.S., Britain and France, have already discreetly canvassed this option. This author would suggest that if the Security Council were to defer the charges against al-Bashir under Article 16, it would severely undermine the legitimacy and credibility of the Court for the very reasons that have been covered in Chapter 1. The interests of justice require that those charged with the gravest of international crimes do not get a 'get out of jail free' pass. To do so would undermine the foundations of the ICC that are stated in the preamble that, *inter alia*, the goal of the ICC is to put an end to impunity for the perpetrators of the most serious crimes known to humanity and contribute to the prevention of such crimes. There is no doubt that architects of the worst atrocities in other parts of the world from Burma (Myanmar) to Zimbabwe would be taking comfort from any deferral of the charges against al-Bashir by the Security Council.

Given these flaws, de Waal advocated for the Pre-Trial Chamber sending the case back to the Prosecutor for comprehensive reconsideration. This did not happen. Instead the Pre-Trial Chamber issued, on March 4, 2009, the arrest warrant for Omar Hassan Ahmad al-Bashir for war crimes and crimes against humanity.[66] The Chamber ruled that he is suspected of being criminally responsible, as an indirect co-perpetrator, for intentionally directing attacks against an important part of the civilian population of Darfur. These attacks included murdering, exterminating, raping, torturing and forcibly transferring large numbers of civilians and pillaging their property. The Chamber ruled that al-Bashir's official capacity as an incumbent Head of State did not exclude his criminal responsibility under Article 27 of the Rome Statute. Referring to the evidentiary foundation provided by the Prosecutor, the Chamber found that these serious international crimes were allegedly committed during a five year counter-insurgency campaign by the Government of Sudan against the Sudanese Liberation Movement/Army (SLM/A) and the Justice and Equality Movement (JEM) and other armed groups opposing the Khartoum government in Darfur. The alleged crimes against the civilian population were alleged to have started soon after the April 2003 attack by the Darfur rebels on the El Fasher airport following a common plan agreed upon at the highest level of the Government of Sudan by al-Bashir and other high ranking Sudanese political and military leaders. These attacks on civilians continued until July 14, 2008, the date of the filing of the Prosecutor's application for the warrant of arrest for the President.

The Chamber ruled that the central component of the common plan was the unlawful attack on the civilian population of Darfur, belonging largely to the Fur, Masalit and Zaghawa groups, which was perceived to be allied to the Darfur rebels opposing the Khartoum government. The attacks against these groups were planned and implemented unlawfully by the Sudanese military and their allied Janjaweed militias, the Sudanese Police Force, the National Intelligence and Security Service and the paradoxically named Humanitarian Aid Commission. The Chamber found al-Bashir as an allegedly principal indirect and co-perpetrator for the crimes, as there were reasonable grounds to believe that he was in control of all branches of the apparatus of the state of Sudan and used such control to secure the implementation of the attacks on the civilian population during the implementation of the counter-insurgency campaign.

Despite these findings by an impartial judicial tribunal, critics like de Waal and Julie Flint continue to argue that justice and accountability for the most serious of international crimes must be trumped by the search for a peaceful solution in Darfur, especially when the joint U.N. and A.U. peacekeeping mission was attempting to establish an effective presence in Darfur that would prevent the region from going over the brink. These critics would prefer to have no action taken against the Sudanese officials until they no longer hold positions of power which they could use to retaliate against the peacekeepers and humanitarian organizations.[67] Could it not be argued that such a critique is advocating total submission to political and threatened criminal blackmail by these same Sudanese officials?

The Chief Prosecutor of the ICC, Luis Moreno-Ocampo, does not have a simple choice of justice over peace. But many of his critics do not see it the same way. Along with Alex de Waal, the Chief Prosecutor's other most strident critic in the west is Andrew Natsios, a former high level USAID official and the former special envoy for Sudan appointed by President George W. Bush. His critiques have made their way into the widely read *Foreign Affairs* journal.[68] He is fearful that the ICC indictment will condemn Darfur to a prolonged hell without any prospect of a peace agreement and will also endanger the CPA between the North and South. Natsios seems to ignore that Sudan has been in a prolonged hell for decades in the South and in Darfur, in large part, due to the actions of al-Bashir.

Natsios claims that the ICC indictment would foreclose peaceful options out of the crisis facing Darfur and Sudan and move the country closer to the failed state of Somalia, pre-genocide Rwanda or the Democratic Republic of Congo triggering the potential for widespread atrocities as those in power seek to keep it at any cost. He claims that the al-Bashir regime will now avoid any compromise that would weaken their already weakened position. Likewise Natsios fears the indictment will threaten a scheduled national election, or at least make elections more likely to be rigged.

He points to the expulsion of the thirteen western aid groups after the indictment was handed down as proof of his argument. With logic that would strike at the core of the achievements of not only the Rome Statute, but also all the international criminal tribunals since Nuremberg, Natsios seems to be arguing that there should be total impunity for a sitting Head of State who controls an army, a ruthless internal security force and other means to ensure means of reprisals at his disposal. Seeming not to have learned his own lessons from his time as U.S. envoy to Sudan, he points out that the sanctions that he designed against Sudan were met with reprisals by al-Bashir that included punishing the South and undermining the CPA. What further proof did this critic need to learn that al-Bashir's instincts are not for genuine peacemaking but raising the stakes of even higher levels of impunity? Instead of learning from his own hard experience as envoy to Sudan, Natsios warns about the lack of incentive of the rebels to seek peace due to the ICC arrest warrant against al-Bashir. Given the level of atrocities against the civilians in Darfur, Natsios astonishingly seems to suggest that the rebels may have been satisfied with 'blood money' as a precursor to making peace with Khartoum. Now, he claims, they are demanding the 'Western-style justice' as a condition for any peace deal. It will be a tragic day when demands for real accountability for the most serious crimes known to humanity are regarded as only 'Western-style justice'. In a somewhat contradictory statement, Natsios acknowledges that in his six years in Sudan refugees in Darfur and their leaders insisted for justice to be served as regards the Sudanese leaders, but also wanted the tens of thousands of Arab militias to also be prosecuted. He asserts that would be impractical. The ICC Prosecutor would agree and has stated that the focus of the Court should be on those leaders most responsible for the gravest of international crimes with others being tried in national courts or traditional justice settings.

Where Natsios has sadly legitimate concerns, as does the ICC itself, is in the reaction of the Arab and African governments to the arrest warrants. While al-Bashir had become increasingly isolated before the arrest warrant handed down by the ICC, both the Arab League and the African Union have strongly criticized the arrest warrant and urged their members not to cooperate in the arrest and surrender of the Sudanese President. On July 3, 2009, the African Union (with some countries dissenting) announced it was ending its cooperation with the ICC relating to the immunities for the arrest and surrender of al-Bashir.[69] It will be up to the Court, the U.N. Security Council and the rest of the States Parties to the ICC to remind other States Parties who are members of the African Union that they cannot pick and choose what legally binding obligations they can ignore without serious consequences, including potential linkages to financial and development assistance.

Like others, Natsios can also legitimately contest the exact number of casualties that are still dying at present in Darfur, and especially in the massive refugee camps, but to downplay the significance of even a thousand deaths resulting from the actions of the al-Bashir regime is to devalue the human lives of already the most traumatized individuals on the planet. Finally, Natsios has legitimately warned that if al-Bashir is deposed due to the ICC indictments, a worse leader could emerge, such as the sinister Hassan al-Turabi who brought al-Bashir to power. While this is a very real concern, it cannot be the rationale for allowing the present leader to continue having an impunity shield for the most serious of international crimes. Foundationally, the concern of Natsios is that the indictment of al-Bashir threatens to unravel the CPA, which he and other western officials worked so hard to accomplish. This is understandable from his personal perspective. However, a larger perspective would indicate that the CPA is already unraveling. Moreover, to sacrifice the millions of civilians in Darfur and fail to secure justice for those who have suffered the most serious of crimes for a peace that al-Bashir may not want himself, as discussed above, is to perpetrate a much greater injustice.

Human Rights Watch has detailed how the urgency to maintain peace agreements or attempts to negotiate them may often seem to make justice and accountability like a luxury that societies in conflict can ill afford in the short run. However, in the longer run, persistent impunity and lack of accountability for past atrocities can sow the seeds of new conflicts and atrocities by ruthless leaders who manipulate past injustices to their own political ends. The example of the former Yugoslavia is used to demonstrate this reality. The serious human rights abuses committed during the Second World War by certain individuals and groups such as Croatian pro-Nazis were used by ruthless nationalist Serb politicians such as Slobodan Milošević to divide communities in Bosnia, Croatia and Serbia and lay the ground for the serious international crimes, including those that were committed there during the 1990s.[70] Likewise in Burundi, Rwanda and Kenya, persistent examples of impunity practiced over several decades are demonstrated to have led to periodic inter-tribal violence as tribal groups and communities harbor collective fear of and anger regarding past inflictions of violence and human rights abuses leading to the advocacy by ruthless political leaders for the imposition of collective responsibility on entire communities that paves the way for even greater violence or in the case of Rwanda, genocide.[71]

Sadly the fierce critics by de Waal and Natsios, along with the foreign government critics of the ICC and its Prosecutor regarding the indictments of the three Sudanese officials, do not seem to have learned these lessons from history, namely that condoning impunity in the cause of a peace that is unlikely to be sustainable results in neither peace nor justice. It is time that we prove the German philosopher Friedrich Hegel wrong when he opined that the only thing we learn from history is that we learn nothing from history.

NOTES

1. See the BBC report of the attack, *U.N. fury at Darfur militia ambush* (9 July 2008) available at the following url: http://news.bbc.co.uk/2/hi/africa/7498811.stm and the report by Associated Press reporters Mohamed Osman and Maggie Michael entitled 'Seven Darfur Peacekeepers slain, 22 wounded' in *The Globe and Mail* on 9 July 2008 located at the following url: http://www.theglobeandmail.com/servlet/story/RTGAM.20080709.wsudan0709/BNStory/International/home.
2. *Ibid.*
3. Steven Edwards, 'Al-Bashir "masterminded" genocide; Sudanese leader ordered atrocities, prosecutor says' *Ottawa Citizen* (15 July 2008) A6.
4. See, to this effect, the decision of the International Court of Justice in *Reservations to the Convention on Prevention and Punishment of the Crime of Genocide*, Advisory Opinion [1951] ICJ Rep. 15 at 23.
5. (1951) 78 UNTS 277. For a critical analysis of the reservations by the United States and others to the Genocide Convention, see W. Schabas, *Genocide in International Law* (Cambridge University Press, 2000) at 521–528.
6. *Ibid.* at 2.
7. Adam LeBor, *Complicity with Evil: The United Nations in the Age of Modern Genocide* (Yale University Press, 2007) at 155.
8. *Ibid.* at 185.
9. *Ibid.* at 193.
10. BBC Panorama program entitled 'China's Secret War', first aired 14 July 2008. Details on the program can be located at the following url: http://news.bbc.co.uk/2/hi/programmes/panorama/7493934.stm (accessed July 15, 2009).
11. LeBor, *supra* note 7 at 193.
12. *Ibid.* at 194.
13. *Ibid.* at 198.

14.	*Ibid.* at 222.
15.	*Ibid.* at 200–201.
16.	*Ibid.* at 222–223.
17.	*Ibid.* at 202.
18.	'Selling Justice Short: Why Accountability Matters for Peace' *Human Rights Watch* (7 July 2009) at 73 and 102–103.
19.	Caroline Flintoft, 'Our silence on Sudan shames us' *The Globe and Mail* (16 June 2007) located at the following url: http://www.theglobeandmail.com/servlet/story/RTGAM.20080616.wcosudan16/BNStory/specialComment/?page=rss&id=RTGAM.20080616.wcosudan16.
20.	Chris Cobb, 'Darfur peace depends on a single arrest' *The Ottawa Citizen* (15 October 2007).
21.	'Sudan "crimes charges" worry U.N.' *BBC Report* (11 July 2008) located at the following url: http://news.bbc.co.uk/2/hi/africa/7501066.stm.
22.	See the BBC report of the A.U. and Arab league statements on the potential indictment of President al-Bashir, 'AU Warning of Sudan "Charges"' *BBC Report* (12 July 2008) located at the following url: http://news.bbc.co.uk/2/hi/africa/7503803.stm.
23.	M.W. Daly, *Darfur's Sorrow, A History of Destruction and Genocide* (Cambridge University Press, 2007) at 315.
24.	Jeffrey Gettleman, 'Darfur withers as Sudan sells a food bonanza' *New York Times* (10 August 2008) at 1 and 10 located at the following url: http://www.nytimes.com/2008/08/10/world/africa/10sudan.html.
25.	Louis Charbonneau, 'Darfur is now a low intensity conflict: U.N.' *Reuters* (27 April 2009) located at the following url: http://www.reuters.com/article/worldNews/idUSTRE53Q4LR20090427.
26.	*Ibid.*
27.	See 'War in Sudan's Darfur is Over' *BBC Report* (27 August 2009) located at the following url: http://news.bbc.co.uk/2/hi/africa/8224424.stm.
28.	*Ibid.*
29.	*Supra* note 23 at 235–255.
30.	*Ibid.*
31.	*Ibid.*
32.	*Ibid.*
33.	The United States Committee for Refugees (USCR) report 'Quantifying Genocide in Southern Sudan and the Nuba Mountains: 1983–1998' was researched and written by USCR consultant Millard Burr, former director of logistics for the U.S. Agency for International Development in Sudan. The report was published in 1998.
34.	*Ibid.*
35.	Cited in the U.S. Department of State's Report to the 57th Session of the U.N. Human Rights Commission, 2001 on Special Groups and Slavery in Sudan, which can be located online at http://www.state.gov/g/drl/rls/rm/2001/2751.htm (accessed 1 June 2008).
36.	Stephen Lewis, 'I too accuse him of crimes against humanity, Twice I begged him to stop collaborating with the Lord's Resistance Army and to return the abused children' *The Globe and Mail* (28 July 2008) A13.
37.	*Supra* note 23 at 272.
38.	Dr. Adlan Harallo, 'Possible Challenges/Impediments to the Peace Process in Sudan' University of Khartoum (20 August 2005) presented at SRG Workshop, London, UK, located at the following url: http://sudanrg.org/resources/Possible+Challenges_Impediments+to+the+Peace+Process+in+Sudan.pdf (accessed 4 June 2008).
39.	Ban Ki Moon, 'A Climate Culprit In Darfur' *Washington Post* (16 June 2007) A15.
40.	Stephan Faris, 'The Real Roots of Darfur' *Atlantic Monthly* (April 2007) located at the following url: http://www.theatlantic.com/doc/200704/darfur-climate.
41.	Andrew S. Natsios, 'Beyond Darfur, Sudan's Slide Toward Civil War' *Foreign Affairs*

(May/June 2008) 77 at 80. The same author states that the northern forces were removed by January 2008.

42. Nicholas Kristof, 'Africa's Next Slaughter' *New York Times* (2 March 2008) located at the following url: http://www.nytimes.com/2008/03/02/opinion/02kristof.html?_r=1&p agewanted=print&oref=slogin.
43. 'Bashir "Preparing for Sudan War"' *BBC Report* (20 November 2007) located at the following url: http://news.bbc.co.uk/2/hi/africa/7101285.stm.
44. 'The south is on the brink too' *The Economist* (24 May 2008).
45. 'Sudan Rivals try to resolve split' *BBC Report* (18 October 2007) located at the following url: http://news.bbc.co.uk/2/hi/africa/7050351.stm.
46. 'Deal agreed on Sudan oil region' *BBC Report* (8 August 2008) located at the following url: http://news.bbc.co.uk/2/hi/africa/7550223.stm.
47. See the analysis of *The Economist*, 'Line Drawn' *The Economist* (23 July 2009) at the Economist.Com Global Agenda, located at the following url: http://www.economist. com/agenda/PrinterFriendly.cfm?story_id=14070450.
48. *Ibid.*
49. Stephanie McCrummen, 'Precarious South Essential to Sudan' *Washington Post* (25 April 2009).
50. Natsios, *supra* note 41 at 84.
51. 'ICC fending off Darfur Challenge' *BBC Report* (20 November 2008) located at the following url: http://news.bbc.co.uk/2/hi/africa/7739577.stm.
52. ICC Press Release, 'ICC issues a warrant of arrest for Omar Al Bashir, President of Sudan' (4 March 2009) located at the following url: http://www.icc-cpi.int/NR/ exeres/0EF62173-05ED-403A-80C8-F15EE1D25BB3.htm.
53. *Ibid.*
54. *Ibid.*
55. *Ibid.*
56. For support of this view, see N. Kristof, 'A President, a Boy and Genocide' *New York Times* (9 March 2009) located at the following url: http://www.nytimes.com/2009/03/05/ opinion/05kristof.html.
57. *Ibid.*
58. Catherine Philp, 'Omar al-Bashir may face new charges for ousting agencies from Sudan' *Times on Line* (7 March 2009) available at the following url: http://business. timesonline.co.uk/tol/business/law/article5860726.ece.
59. 'Darfur Rebel to appear before the ICC' *BBC News* (18 May 2009) available at the following url: http://news.bbc.co.uk/2/hi/africa/8054455.stm.
60. ICC Press Release, Office of the Prosecutor, 'Prosecutor: "The attack on African Union peacekeepers in Haskanita was an attack on millions of civilians they had come to protect; we will prosecute those allegedly responsible"' (17 May 2009) ICC-OTP-20090517-PR412-ENG.
61. *Ibid.*
62. *Ibid.*
63. Colum Lynch, 'Rebels Charged with War Crimes in Sudan' *Washington Post* (May 18, 2009).
64. See the full text of the decision to allow the appeal at the following url: http://www. icc-cpi.int/NR/exeres/D01E1FEC-1E4D-4CCB-8DEE-53F8535B1E35.htm (accessed 19 June 2009).
    Essentially the Pre-Trial Chamber asserted that its decision was misinterpreted in the following manner: '. . . the Majority only required the Prosecutor to demonstrate that the only reasonable conclusion from the facts proven by the Prosecutor is that there are "reasonable grounds to believe" in the existence of genocidal intent (article 58 of the Statute evidentiary standard)'.
65. *The Prosecutor v. Germain Katanga and Mathieu Ngudjolo Chui*, ICC-01/04-01/07-717, Situation in Democratic Republic of the Congo, Decision on the confirmation of charges (30 September 2008) (International Criminal Court, Pre-Trial Chamber). In

this decision the PTC observed that the blameworthiness attached to principal criminal liability based on the joint criminal enterprise mode of liability would be inconsistent with the placement of common purpose doctrine under Article 25(3)(d), which the Chamber asserted was an accessory mode of liability.

66.   The full text of the Pre-Trial Chamber decision is available from the site of the ICC at the following url: http://www.icc-cpi.int/Menus/ICC/Situations+and+Cases/Situations/ Situation+ICC+0205/Related+Cases/ICC02050109/Court+Records/Chambers/ PTCI/1.htm.

67.   Julie Flint and Alex de Waal, 'Justice Off Course in Darfur' *Washington Post* (28 June 2008) located at the following url: http://www.washingtonpost.com/wp-dyn/content/ article/2008/06/27/AR2008062702632.html.

68.   Andre Natsios, 'Waltz With Bashir, Why the Arrest Warrant Against Sudan's President Will Serve Neither Peace nor Justice' *Foreign Affairs* (23 March 2009) located at the following url: http://www.foreignaffairs.com/articles/64904/andrew-natsios/waltz-with-bashir.

69.   See the BBC report of the A.U. decision, 'African Union in rift with court' *BBC Report* (3 July 2009) available at the following url: http://news.bbc.co.uk/2/hi/africa/8133925. stm.

70.   Human Rights Watch, *supra* note 18 at 75–76.

71.   *Ibid.* at 77–92.

3   Is it peace, justice or a military solution in the tragedy of Northern Uganda?

1.   THE NIGHTMARE OF THE LORD'S RESISTANCE ARMY

The lives of tens of thousands of people in Northern Uganda have been a daily living nightmare for the past two decades. A ghoulish armed militia called the Lord's Resistance Army (LRA) has inflicted the most horrible of crimes on the Acholi and other tribes in this area of Uganda that borders on the other troubled territories of southern Sudan and the Democratic Republic of Congo (DRC). The macabre actions of the LRA have resulted in the deaths of tens of thousands of civilian men, women and children and the displacement of almost 90 per cent of the population in this region of Uganda, accounting for close to two million people. While the LRA has moved the centre of its actions to the DRC and now plagues the border areas of Uganda, the DRC, Sudan and the Central African Republic, the nightmare remains for the people of Northern Uganda.

Although the LRA is led by a messianic leader, Joseph Kony, and a rag tag of adult rebels, it is largely comprised of abducted children from all of the countries mentioned above. These child victims are aged between 11 and 15 and are forced into becoming the most ruthless of killers. Many are initiated into the LRA through the most brutal of initiations, which include being raped, drugged, beaten and then forced to kill or mutilate their own families to cut the familial or tribal loyalties. The children are forcibly inducted into the spiritual teachings of Kony who claims that he is instructed in spiritual and military matters by holy spirits and is tasked with fighting evil by promoting the Ten Commandments of the Old Testament. He obviously has not learned that those Commandments include children honoring their parents and not committing murder.[1] This mental incongruence must be kept in mind when one thinks about whether someone with the mental and psychological makeup of Kony can ever be a reliable peace partner to even begin to start a discussion on peace and justice.

There is a link between the crimes of al-Bashir, the indicted President of Sudan, and the rampage of Kony's LRA. Kony had formed his group as a rebel movement after Yoweri Museveni seized power in 1986. The potential for peace in Northern Uganda had been undermined even before Uganda gained its independence in October of 1962. The British had recruited its army from the Acholi tribe in the North while favoring the South economically. After independence, the successive regimes of Milton Obote, interspersed by the savage regime of Idi Amin, used the Acholi tribe's domination of the military to keep power and dominate the country until he too was ousted by a coup led by an Acholi, General Tito Ochello. When Museveni took power, the Acholi people's power base disappeared and this led to the creation of Acholi resistance movements due to the marginalization of the formerly dominant Acholi tribes. One of these was the Lord's Resistance Army led by Joseph Kony. The political goals of Kony's LRA are extremely vague beyond his stated messianic objective of overthrowing the Museveni government and establishing a regime in Uganda based on the Christian Ten Commandments.

Kony's military objective was to accomplish a revolt against the Museveni government by the Acholi people in Northern Uganda. When Kony failed to get the majority support of the Acholi and saw his resources and ranks depleted, he moved his base to Southern Sudan in search of arms and resources to continue the rampage. He found an ally in the Khartoum regime and was granted refuge from the Ugandan army. The al-Bashir government used the LRA in its own genocidal campaign against the southern Sudanese tribes and the rebel Sudanese People's Liberation Movement (SPLM).[2] The Khartoum government offered the refuge as retaliation for Museveni helping the SPLM. In this fashion, the terrorized people of Northern Uganda also became victims in one of the most vicious proxy wars in Africa. However, by 1999, Sudan and Uganda were beginning to end the proxy wars which allowed the Ugandan army to conduct operations against the LRA within Southern Sudan.

Angered by the failure of the Acholi to support him, Kony began his murderous campaign against his own people with a vengeance. The LRA started a prolonged campaign of mass murders, mutilation, torture, rape, looting, pillaging and abductions. The impact on the Acholi children and their parents was particularly devastating. To escape from the marauding LRA rebels, approximately 40,000 children had to walk many miles from their villages to the relative safety of the town of Gulu and other urban centres every evening, sleeping in the open or any available public building only to return the next day to their villages and schools. The nightmare landscape of Northern Uganda was filled with the terror of small children and mutilated adults, many with ears, lips and hands cut off. An estimated 20,000 children were abducted and account for the overwhelming majority of the LRA ranks. These children are given the crudest of military training, often under the influence of drugs, and are abused as sex slaves and human shields in hostilities against the government forces. The children are often forced to commit the worst atrocities against their own communities and even their own families in order to alienate them from their social supporting networks and bind them to the LRA.[3] While some would argue that Kony is not a deranged personality who cannot be held accountable, it is clear that his mix of biblical ideology and messianic form of terror verges on the psychotic, a fact which hardly makes him a suitable partner for a sustainable peace. He is quoted as justifying his penchant for mutilation as follows:

> If you pick up an arrow against us and we ended up cutting up the hand you used, who is to blame? You report us with your mouth, and we cut off your lips. Who is to blame? It is you! The Bible says that if your hand, eye or mouth is at fault, it should be cut off.[4]

It is estimated that approximately two million people, amounting to almost 90 percent of the population, were displaced from the three main Acholi provinces, moving to squalid camps that lack most of the basic necessities. These internally displaced persons were supposedly protected by the Ugandan army or local militias which are not averse to preying on the refugees themselves and also committing serious crimes. The LRA have also managed to penetrate these so-called 'protected villages' to inflict their horrible crimes on the inhabitants.[5]

The Ugandan army tried over two decades to wipe out the LRA with very limited success. President Museveni tried throughout the 1990s to offer various incentives to get the rebels to enter into peace negotiations and surrender their armed struggle with some limited success. This included an amnesty law in the 1999–2000 period which purported to grant immunity to the LRA leadership and offered assistance for the demobilization and reintegration of the LRA rebels into Ugandan society. The clear intention of the Amnesty Act of 2000 was to provide inducements for LRA rank and file to defect from Kony's grasp as they were offered an unconditional amnesty without any fear of criminal prosecutions. It is reported that the Ugandan government then used the possibility of defections to engineer a meeting with top LRA leaders in 2004. The amnesty approach was backed by key allies of Uganda, including the United States, Britain, Norway and the Netherlands.

By 2005, some 14,000 soldiers had been enticed into taking up these amnesty offers and left the LRA, but thereafter the numbers dropped off.[6]

However, the nightmare of the people of Northern Uganda did not end, as Joseph Kony and the majority of his LRA followers did not accept the amnesty offers and continued committing the crimes against humanity that terrorized the local populations.[7]

Frustrated with the slow pace of the negotiations and with the continued macabre killing spree of Joseph Kony and his followers, on December 16, 2003, President Museveni rescinded the amnesty offers and decided to refer the LRA atrocities to the ICC. The Prosecutor of the ICC, Luis Moreno-Ocampo, also seized upon the impasse at attempts to reconcile peace and justice with someone as unpredictable as Kony and invited the President of Uganda to make the first referral by a sitting Head of State of a situation in his own country to the ICC.[8] In January 2004, President Museveni and the ICC Prosecutor, Luis Moreno-Ocampo, made a joint public appearance at the announcement of the referral in London, England. Some have criticized this joint appearance as it was argued that it militated against the appearance of impartiality of the ICC Prosecutor in any situation in which the ICC is called upon to investigate. The Prosecutor to this day justifies it as a key mechanism to ensure that the self-referral would go ahead and provide the much needed cooperation between the Court and the Ugandan government as the investigation unfolded.

Uganda ratified the Statute of the ICC on June 14, 2002, giving the ICC jurisdiction over the crimes enumerated in the Statute committed by Ugandan nationals or crimes committed in the territory of Uganda after July 1, 2002. However, under the Ugandan Constitution, the ICC Statute had to be implemented into domestic law to affect the rights and obligations of individuals there. There is serious question as to whether crimes listed in the ICC Statute can be recognized as crimes under Ugandan law without implementing legislation, other than those crimes which are regarded as *ius cogens* or universally applicable in all jurisdictions such as genocide. This would affect the issue of whether Uganda was able to exercise complementary jurisdiction over the crimes committed by the LRA in its own national courts. The Ugandan Ministry of Justice had prepared in 2004 draft implementing legislation, the International Criminal Court Bill, that was a product of the technical assistance with the Commonwealth Secretariat. However, after the Bill was introduced in the Ugandan Parliament, it lapsed at the Committee stage. It was reintroduced in 2006, but again lapsed before it could be passed. There is, at the time of writing, a third attempt to pass the legislation.

In addition to the Ugandan failure to implement the ICC Statute into domestic law, there has also been a failure to prosecute any form of international crime in the country, despite the alleged criminal actions of successive governments, especially that of Idi Amin, that could have amounted to indictable crimes under the Rome Statute. Uganda had implemented the 1949 Geneva Conventions into its domestic law, but had not yet implemented the 1977 Additional Protocol that would have criminalized attacks on civilians in violation of Common Article 3.

The President of Uganda used its jurisdiction as a country that had ratified the ICC Statute to grant the Court jurisdiction under Articles 13(a) and 14 of the Rome Statute which established the ICC.[9] As discussed in Chapter 1, these provisions allow for a referral to the Court of a situation in the territory or a national of the referring state. Justifying the referral, the Ugandan government stated that while it was both willing and able to prosecute the alleged perpetrators of the atrocities by the LRA, the Ugandan judicial system had been unable to secure their arrest because the alleged perpetrators had withdrawn from Ugandan territory and were now operating from bases in Southern Sudan, beyond the reach of Ugandan law. It had become clear that any arrest of Kony would require the cooperation of neighboring countries.

Some have argued that the referral by President Museveni of the LRA to the ICC was more of a means to bring the LRA to the negotiating table rather than a concern of human rights, including the human rights violations allegedly committed by his own military forces. This assertion was reinforced by the fact that Museveni had refused to cooperate with the ICC over possible human rights violations by his own military.[10]

The Chief Prosecutor, in part to deflect criticism of the joint appearance with President Museveni when the referral was announced in London, then declared that he would, at a future time, investigate not only the crimes committed by the LRA, but also any possible crimes committed by the Ugandan forces in their military actions against the rebel group and against civilian targets, but focusing on the most serious and grave alleged crimes.

Following a lengthy investigation by the Prosecutor of approximately 2,200 killings and over 3,200 abductions between July 2002 and June 2004 during over 850 attacks by the LRA, the Prosecutor determined there was sufficient evidence for seeking arrest warrants against the LRA leadership. On May 6, 2005, the Prosecutor presented an application to the Pre-Trial Chamber of the ICC for warrants of arrest for crimes against humanity and war crimes against five senior commanders of the LRA including Kony.

In July of 2005, the ICC issued the warrants under seal (later unsealed on October 13, 2005) for the arrest of the messianic LRA leader Joseph Kony and his core leadership consisting of Vincent Otti (who was later killed on the orders of Kony himself), Raksa Lukwiya (later killed by the Ugandan Army), Okot Odhiambo and Dominic Ongwen.[11] In view of the fact that the Ugandan Government had sought the referral, in part, to get the cooperation from neighboring states in obtaining the arrest of Kony and the top LRA leadership, the Registrar of the ICC sent out requests for cooperation in the arrest and surrender of the five suspects, not only to the relevant Ugandan authorities, but also to the Congolese and Sudanese authorities. Given that the DRC is also a State Party to the ICC Statute, it was also under an obligation to arrest the five indicted LRA leaders and hand them over to the Court in The Hague. As Sudan is not a State Party, the Registrar invited the Sudanese authorities to do likewise.

The announcement of these arrest warrants was one of the earliest and most important achievements of the Prosecutor and the ICC Court and was crucial to the early establishment of credibility of the Court in the eyes of the international community. However, in Northern Uganda itself, these early achievements of the Court were met with strong disapproval by some of the leading Acholi and Catholic Church leaders. The Ugandan Minister, Betty Bigombe, tasked with negotiating a ceasefire with the LRA felt she had been undermined by the arrest warrants, and claimed that the ICC had rushed too soon to unseal the arrest warrants when her negotiations with the LRA were at a crucial stage. She felt that the warrants had undermined LRA trust in the utility of future negotiations. Likewise, Catholic Archbishop Odama, a leading figure in the region, declared that the arrest warrants were a blow to the peace process and that negotiators with the LRA would be regarded as agents of the ICC. The Chairman of the Ugandan Amnesty Commission, Peter Onega, feared that the arrest warrants would decrease defections from the LRA as the rank and file would be told that it would be them that the ICC would go after next.[12]

What these well meaning, but frustrated, peacemakers may not have fully taken into account was whether Kony was using these domestic peace processes to gain time for getting more resources and arms for a determined and interminable struggle against the government of Museveni, as he would do later with the much larger and multinational peace talks at Juba in southern Sudan.

A very significant impact of the referral was the reaction of the regime in Khartoum that had been offering refuge, arms and money to the LRA killers. The Sudanese leadership, fearful of its own prospects before the ICC, ended its complicity with the LRA. In March of 2004, Khartoum agreed to permit the Ugandan army to launch attacks against the LRA from locations in the south of Sudan during a period in which the LRA was launching its most ferocious attacks on the people in Northern Uganda. The international attention and pressure that the ICC referral put on Sudan to stop nurturing the LRA killers is a key lesson to be learned in the narrow parameters of the peace versus justice debate. The involvement of the ICC justice process may well have the effect of putting pressure on those from within or outside the area of conflict who nurture indicted persons to withdraw such support. Such withdrawal of support is often the first step towards the defeat of those individuals on the battlefield, their surrender leading to a sustainable peace or the instigation of a more genuine desire to seek peace.

2. THE CHARGES AGAINST THE LRA LEADERSHIP AND THE BACKLASH AGAINST THE ICC

Joseph Kony was charged as leader, chairman and commander of the LRA. The ICC arrest warrant alleged that in 2002 he ordered his LRA forces to start a campaign against civilians in Uganda. The arrest warrant also alleged in 2003 that Kony ordered his LRA forces to kill, rob and abduct civilians, including children living in the internally displaced persons' camps. The warrant listed thirty-three counts of crimes against humanity and war crimes, including murder, sexual enslavement, rape, inhumane acts of inflicting serious bodily harm and suffering and forced enlisting of children.[13]

Vincent Otti, the vice-chairman and second-in-command, was alleged to have been in command of LRA attacks in 2003–2004, which included attacks on local communities and camps for internally displaced villagers resulting in killings, abductions, enslavement, recruitment of children as child soldiers and other crimes against humanity and war crimes. Mr. Otti was killed on orders by Kony on October 2, 2007. There is some indication that Kony feared that the LRA ranks were becoming more loyal to his second-in-command and that Otti, fearful of the trip to The Hague, seemed more genuinely interested in the peace talks than Kony himself. The infighting between indicted criminals is another possible ancillary offshoot of an ICC justice process that ultimately could lead to the dissolution or surrender of those under the arrest warrants. This is something again a narrow peace versus justice focus tends to overlook.[14]

Okot Odhiambo, a deputy commander of the LRA, was alleged in 2004 to have commanded two attacks on camps for internally displaced persons resulting in mass murder, enslavement, and forced enlisting of children and other crimes amounting to ten counts of crimes against humanity and war crimes.[15]

Dominic Ongwen, a former Brigade Commander of the LRA, is alleged to have ordered an attack against another camp for internally displaced persons, resulting in murder, abductions, enslavement, other inhumane acts, destructions of houses and other crimes resulting in seven counts of crimes against humanity and war crimes. He was reported killed in combat with the Ugandan army on October 10, 2005, but subsequently this was contested with a sighting in southern Sudan and in the Ituri region of the Democratic Republic of Congo.[16]

No sooner than when the indictments were announced, representatives of the Acholi villagers targeted by the LRA and even parts of the Ugandan government expressed severe misgivings about the ICC indictments, claiming that they would undermine the further implementation of the amnesty laws and potentially undermine any prospect of further peace negotiations with Kony. The Acholi leadership feared that Kony and his followers would have little incentive to pursue further peace negotiations. These strongly held sentiments of the local populations should not be discounted in any debate on peace and justice. There should also be awareness that when such populations are threatened with imminent death or atrocities, hope attaches even to the slimmest of possibilities of peace being restored. In that sense, justice may well take second place to desperate hopes and desperate fears.

The Acholi leaders had proposed that their traditional forms of conflict adjudication and resolution would provide a greater chance of peaceful reconciliation and forgiveness between them and the LRA than any ICC proceedings. These alternative traditional methods included the *Mato Oput* process which would entail elders bringing the LRA and victims together to identify the causes of the conflict through questioning. The process emphasizes that it is the tribal community or clan and its unity that come first and are superior to any individual demand for retributive justice. According to some proponents of the *Mato Oput* process, criminal activity is a manifestation of angry or bad spirits that have taken over the individual perpetrator which must be got rid of by traditional rituals for the sake of the entire tribal or clan community according to Acholi culture. Where deaths have occurred in inter-clan disputes, there is a particular need for ritual sacrifices or reconciliation. It is this traditionally held belief about criminality that requires the communal responses. At the same time, the individual perpetrator must take responsibility for his actions by confessing to his crimes, accepting the accompanying shame and allowing the community to determine compensation which is often directed against the community or clan of the perpetrator.[17]

The proponents of the *Mato Oput* process would argue that this process would hopefully lead to the guilty party accepting responsibility and showing repentance for their crimes against their brothers and sisters. The elders of the tribe would then establish the parameters for compensation for the victims of the LRA. Such compensation could take the form of cattle or goats as a price for rejoining their communities without further victimization. The guilty party atones by crushing a raw egg over his head to show a desire to begin anew and then symbolically steps over '*opobo*' bamboo sticks to represent themselves as cleansed from the past and brought into the present. At the end of the process, the perpetrator drinks from the bitter extract of leaves from the Oput tree to show that that they have faced up to the bitterness of their past wrongdoing and are promising to never indulge in such bitterness again.[18] Therefore, to counter criticism of the process from outsiders who would belittle this tribal practice, supporters of the *Mato Oput* process argue it does not only involve drinking a bitter concoction, crushing raw eggs and navigating over a stick; it was designed to stop internecine strife between clans in the tribal community and is representative of a form of restorative justice for the entire community. This type of traditional restorative justice is a long drawn out process that could take years to bring to a successful end with all the necessary elder mediated agreements on what is the truth of the dispute and the compensation between warring clans.[19]

The appropriateness and the effectiveness of such traditional methods have been both supported but also strongly critiqued. The main critique of the *Mato Oput* is as follows.

This traditional method is highly controversial as to the modern relevance of the process given the modernization of Ugandan society, including the influence of decades of British colonial rule over the peoples of the country, the introduction of the British model of criminal justice and the rule of law that focuses on the individual rather than the community. The chief proponents of the *Mato Oput* traditional process of reconciliation were the cultural groups which evolved the process, namely the Acholi. While the Acholi tribe of Northern Uganda has had longstanding grievances against the Ugandan government based in the South which the LRA tried to exploit, it, and particularly its children, has suffered the worst at the hands of the LRA. There was a desperate desire for peace at any cost among the Acholi, especially if it resulted in the return of their abducted children.

Therefore there is a conflicted relationship of the Acholi towards both the LRA and the ICC, while also having a distrust of the government that referred the situation to the Court. A delegation of Acholi leaders even traveled to The Hague to try and persuade the Prosecutor to drop the indictment against Kony and what they considered the ICC's form of retributive justice in favor of the *Mato Oput* or some other form of traditional justice process that favors restorative justice and reconciliation.

However, there is a substantial number of grounds on which to critique the benefits of the *Mato Oput* process asserted by the Acholi and some of the western supporters of this traditional process. To begin with, other Northern Ugandan tribes who have also been the victims of the LRA do not share the view of the effectiveness of the Acholi traditional justice process. Indeed, not only are other northern tribes such as the Madi, Teso and the Langi skeptical about the *Mato Oput* process, but so are many Acholi.[20] The International Crisis Group has also pointed out that such traditional processes are not appropriate even with the Acholi given the scale and nature of the conflict.[21] Traditional processes dealing with inter-clan disputes that may involve a single killing are hardly in the same category as the most serious international crimes involving mass murder amounting to crimes against humanity, war crimes, systematic rape, sexual enslavement and abduction of thousands of innocent children to be child soldiers. One simple fact demonstrates this more than others. The traditional process depends on some sort of relationship between the perpetrator and the victim. Many, perhaps most, of the LRA victims are strangers to their barbaric attackers, especially those outside the Acholi tribe and outside the borders of Uganda.

There is doubt that the Acholi always avoid retributive justice, with some writers asserting that many victims from the Acholi do not want to reconcile with the offenders. Such imposed reconciliation would place heavy burdens on the victims who have seen the LRA butcher their families and mutilate them.[22] Some of the Acholi advocated that the LRA offenders face prosecution and even proposed that they be executed. These same Acholi would show no mercy even to those whom the IRA had forcibly abducted and forced to be rebel fighters.[23]

A critical issue that cannot be forgotten in the pursuit of traditional justice processes in Northern Uganda is that the category of LRA victims now stretches beyond Uganda to the Congo, the Central African Republic and Sudan. With the crimes of the LRA go beyond those that have victimized the Acholi in Northern Uganda.

3.   THE PEACE TALKS AT JUBA

In late June 2006, the LRA publicly announced a willingness to start a new round of peace negotiations with the Ugandan government in the Southern Sudanese capital of Juba, with one condition: that the withdrawal of the ICC indictments would be a prerequisite to any final solution to the conflict. While the arrest warrants may have driven Kony and the top leaders of the LRA to enter into negotiations, the same warrants were starting to be a pawn in the peace negotiations. The tactic of seeming to want peace would soon begin to take on the appearance of one that was using the peace process to enable the LRA to get more breathing room for its ability to continue its intensely violent campaign.

Those who supported the indictments would counter that even with substantial numbers of rebels leaving the killing fields, Kony and most of his men continued with their terror against the innocent civilians of Northern Uganda. By the time the peace talks had begun, the LRA had transformed Northern Uganda into the most wretched of internally displaced camps. In these camps hundreds of thousands of men, women and children had sought safety but were ravaged by malaria, an emerging HIV/AIDS epidemic, starvation and periodic raids by the LRA that took place even during the peace talks in order to carry off new recruits, including children, and murder many others.

The unreliability of Kony and his LRA leadership as a partner in peace negotiations continued into 2006. In July of 2006, a new peace negotiator entered the scene in the form of the Vice-President of Southern Sudan, Riek Machar. This potential peacemaker had witnessed the savagery of the LRA on his own people during his decade long combat with the genocidal regime in Khartoum that had used the LRA as a local militia. On the other hand there was also evidence that Machar had colluded with the Khartoum regime in the past, including helping establish the links with the LRA, and therefore was not the most appropriate negotiator for peace. Because the LRA was still using Southern Sudan as a base to launch attacks on Uganda, Machar had hoped to finally rid his fledging autonomous region of the LRA for good now that the Khartoum government of al-Bashir had ostensibly given up support of the militia.[24]

During the initial stages of the Juba talks, Museveni also seemed determined to undermine the ICC justice process by promising total amnesty for Kony and his core leadership if they surrendered and terminated their attacks on the people of Northern Uganda. In addition, the Ugandan government also began pressuring the ICC to withdraw the arrest warrants against the LRA leadership. This request was met with a barrage of criticism by human rights groups outside Uganda but was supported by the Acholi leadership within Uganda. In late August 2006, after several weeks of negotiations, the parties began discussions on a possible ceasefire agreement under which the LRA would marshal its forces at certain locations in Southern Sudan to begin the process of disarming and demobilization. After negotiations on whether and how the Ugandan government would reciprocate, the LRA and the Ugandan government signed a truce on August 26, 2006. The truce required the LRA to vacate its bases in Uganda and assemble in areas designated in Southern Sudan where the government would guarantee its safety. Not surprisingly, the LRA did not live up to its commitments under the ceasefire agreements and talks ground to a halt. However, a second round of peace talks commenced in April of 2007.

The negotiations between the Ugandan government and the LRA then focused on the terms of a ceasefire and the terms of a longer peace agreement. Machar and the Ugandan negotiators had every reason to be skeptical about the commitment of Kony to peace negotiations. Just before the talks had even begun, Kony had given a video statement that he denied involvement in the litany of atrocities the LRA were alleged to have committed, and instead alleged that it was Museveni that was oppressing the Acholi.[25]

Not unexpectedly, on September 23, 2006, Kony threatened to again back out of any final agreement if the ICC arrest warrants were not withdrawn. This was clearly beyond the power of any of the negotiating Ugandan teams and indeed even beyond the power of the ICC Chief Prosecutor. On October 20, 2006, President Museveni joined the Juba talks hoping to salvage the negotiations. He soon came to the conclusion that the LRA was not serious about the negotiations, but nevertheless his involvement ultimately led to a second truce agreement being signed on November 1, 2006.

An emerging tactic by the LRA in the negotiations was to allege that the Ugandan army was violating the truce by killing its fighters and threatening to withdraw from the talks, while not following its own commitment for its fighters to assemble at designated areas in Southern Sudan. When both the Khartoum government and the Southern Sudan government's patience was exhausted, they requested the talks move to Kenya. The growing uncertainty as to the possibility of real peace talks with the mercurial LRA leadership and the frustration of the Sudanese negotiators prompted the U.N., Kenya, South Africa and Mozambique to join the failing peace talks, a development also demanded by the LRA. The result of the new round of talks was to extend the ceasefire until June 30, 2007.

At this second stage of the Juba talks, Museveni again offered amnesty to the LRA if they agreed to a ceasefire and to enter into comprehensive peace negotiations. He also allegedly made a commitment that none of these mass murderers would be arrested and transferred to The Hague. This was a violation of Uganda's commitments under the Rome Statute and potentially undermined the future prospects and credibility of the ICC. Justice Richard Goldstone, a former chief prosecutor of the International Criminal Court for the former Yugoslavia, asserted that Museveni was acting in contravention of international law as his government had signed the 1998 Rome Statute and offers of amnesty violated the letter of that legal commitment. Justice Goldstone warned both Museveni and other national leaders that the ICC could not be used opportunistically 'like a hot water tap that can be turned on or off'.[26]

Despite such warnings from the leading jurists in the world, on June 29, 2007, the Ugandan government reached an agreement with the LRA on the principles for resolving the conflict, which included only amnesties and domestic proceedings with alternative sentences for LRA soldiers which included the possibility of using the traditional *Mato Oput* reconciliation process. Opponents of the ICC indictments pointed to the partial success of the previous amnesty law and the peace negotiations by referring to the approximately 14,000 soldiers who left the LRA and other rebel militias because of the promise of amnesty. In addition, these opponents also pointed out that in some opinion surveys the Acholi supported amnesty for the LRA and voiced opposition to the ICC arrest warrants.[27] As mentioned, this majority support of amnesty for the LRA may not be too much of a surprise, given that these victimized people were desperate for the nightmare atrocities visited upon them and especially on their children to stop.[28]

In a June 29, 2007 document entitled Agreement on Accountability and Reconciliation, both sides agreed on justice and reconciliation principles that would include both formal Ugandan justice procedures, including the use of the traditional *Mato Oput* process detailed above. The agreement also included a reference to a body to be set up to examine the need for accountability on both sides to the conflict. Any such investigations of accountability could result in penalties that could be mitigated on the basis of status, such as being a child or a female perpetrator, the gravity of the crime and the need for reparations, reconciliation and rehabilitation.[29] It was clear that the Ugandan government would have to implement this agreement by legislation and amend the previous legislation that had given amnesty to the top LRA leadership.

Kony and his second-in-command, Vincent Otti, participated in some of the negotiations guarded in part by what looked like teenaged LRA fighters, with Kony continuing to deny that he had enslaved and enlisted children. To the surprise of many and perhaps signing his own death warrant, Vincent Otti declared a unilateral ceasefire leading up to the June 29, 2007 agreement.

One writer has noted the uncertainty about the interpretation of the Agreement. On one level the Agreement required formal criminal and possibly civil justice proceedings against the top LRA leadership, yet the LRA negotiators had repeatedly rejected any possibility of criminal prosecutions for these leaders. They may have been reinforced in this position by the fact that the Ugandan government had indicated that the traditional justice ceremonies, like the *Mato Oput*, would be a sufficient replacement for the formal criminal justice processes.[30]

Adding to the confusion, rather impetuously, the Ugandan government promised that the use of Ugandan justice and traditional processes would convince the Court to allow Uganda to use its complementarity jurisdiction. It was hoped that this would suspend the ICC process including the withdrawal of the arrest warrants. However, even if this were possible, it was not certain the Ugandan government would take any such steps before the LRA had fully surrendered and demobilized.[31]

Around this time on October 8, 2007, Kony ordered the assassination of his second-in-command, Vincent Otti. There have been suspicions that Kony did not want Otti to get too serious about, and committed to, the unfolding peace negotiations.

Not aware of the intentions of Kony to ignore any peace agreement, the Ugandan and LRA negotiators had endorsed the idea of creating a Special Division of the High Court of Uganda to initiate prosecutions against the LRA leadership in the July 29, 2007 agreement and to enter into consultations with victims regarding the alternative to the ICC process.[32]

These consultations dragged on for months into the Fall of 2007. By that time it had become clear that the LRA had succeeded in getting the Ugandan government to promise to put the LRA leadership under the traditional justice processes rather than formal judicial proceedings in Uganda or to submit to the ICC process. Indeed, the LRA had apparently asked the Ugandan government to pass legislation implementing the traditional justice processes. Surprisingly both the LRA and the Ugandan government were convinced such traditional processes were capable of meeting the complementarity requirements of the ICC Statute and therefore led to the deferment of the arrest warrants.[33] Given the lack of substance of the *Mato Oput* process discussed above, in terms of a genuine process of accountability for the most serious crimes known to humanity, it is unlikely that such legislation would satisfy the thresholds required for it to be regarded as complementary to the ICC jurisdiction.

When the Ugandan government decided to establish a deadline for the peace talks to end, the ceasefire was extended to the end of February 2008. Given the urgency of the situation, the European Union and the United States became observers to the talks.

On February 19, 2008, after a further period of consultations with victims and negotiations with the LRA, the parties agreed on an 'Annexure' to the previous agreement at Juba, Sudan. However, this new additional agreement raised further confusing issues, especially as regards the nature of the alternative and traditional justice procedure. The Annexure proposed what looked like a truth and reconciliation commission but also provided for a new division of the Ugandan High Court to try those alleged to have committed the most serious crimes. The provisions of the Annexure dealing with the establishment of a truth and reconciliation commission to be legislated into existence by the Ugandan government would focus on accountability of both the Ugandan government forces and the LRA. Any penalties handed down by such a commission would be subject to mitigation on gender and age and focus on the goals of reconciliation and rehabilitation. The commission would have the ability to offer reparations that would include restitution, compensation, apologies, memorials and commemorations.[34] Later reports have suggested that the Ugandan government has changed its mind on such a commission and does not intend to establish such a truth telling body.[35]

Yet there were still major doubts as to whether the LRA leadership would face any criminal prosecutions as the proposed legislation for the new High Court division would include the possibility of providing 'recognition of traditional and community justice processes in proceedings'.[36] Other provisions of the Annexure added weight to the suspicion that Kony and the LRA leadership indicted by the ICC could escape any form of criminal prosecution, and instead face some traditional forms of justice such as the *Mato Oput* process, and could even escape any form of punishment while only paying some form of reparation instead.[37]

There was much to be skeptical about in the ability of the Ugandan government to pass the required implementing legislation that would satisfy both the LRA and the complementarity provisions of the ICC Statute. It must be kept in mind that Uganda has not yet implemented the ICC Statute into domestic law. There is also evidence that President Museveni had admitted the LRA leadership would only undergo a system of traditional justice such as the *Mato Oput*, as he claimed the victims had opted for that process which was compensatory rather than retributive. The President further defended his retreat from the ICC process by saying that he had referred the situation in Northern Uganda to the ICC when the LRA was outside Ugandan territory, and that if the rebels returned, he would prefer the 'traditional blood settlement mechanism' to the 'Western type of justice'.[38]

Yet, after his demands for avoiding the certainty of criminal prosecution had supposedly been met by the Annexure Agreement, Kony engaged in many forms of delaying tactics designed to forestall the signing of the final agreement. After asking for clarifications about the Annexure agreement regarding the resort to the Ugandan courts and the traditional justice processes, he then demanded more financial and security guarantees. These delaying tactics were designed to buy time to build up his military support, especially from Sudan.[39]

The alternative theory was that Kony was looking to re-establish a military and political power base in Uganda while finally thwarting the ICC process. The LRA had walked out of the talks temporarily after being denied senior army and government posts in Uganda. After President Museveni agreed to consider such appointments some time in the future, a permanent ceasefire was signed by the parties on February 28, 2008. However, on the same day, true to form, once again the LRA demanded the suspension of the ICC arrest warrants. The Ugandan government promised only to request the U.N. Security Council to seek such a suspension after the LRA had demobilized. After such a demobilization and reintegration agreement had been signed the next day, the final peace agreement was awaiting the signature of the LRA leader.[40]

International human rights groups, such as Amnesty International, and many international jurists condemned the Ugandan government for promising to establish a national court to try Kony and the LRA leaders. At the same time, the government seemed willing to allow these same perpetrators of the most serious crimes to face a traditional justice process that was such an ineffective method of accountability and inappropriate punishment for such crimes.

Amnesty International and other human rights advocates vigorously asserted that, as party to the Rome Statute of the ICC, Uganda had the legal duty to fully cooperate with the Court in its investigations and prosecutions. Part of that duty is to cooperate in the arrest and surrender of any person charged by the Court. It is only once the surrender has taken place, Amnesty International and other supporters of the ICC argued, that the Ugandan government has the right to apply to the Court to return the indicted back to any special Ugandan court. It would also be up to the Pre-Trial Chamber of the ICC to determine whether the Ugandan authorities and courts were able and willing to genuinely investigate and prosecute the LRA leadership named in the arrest warrants. Amnesty International and other authorities on Uganda were also very doubtful whether any special court in Uganda would be able and willing to determine the guilt or innocence of the LRA leaders in a fair proceeding that was not a sham.[41]

Despite the fact that ICC Chief Prosecutor, Luis Moreno-Ocampo, refused to meet the LRA to discuss the withdrawal of the arrest warrants, stating that they remained in effect, Kony had agreed to sign the peace agreement. He had been given assurances that he would not be apprehended and transferred to the ICC by the Ugandan government and the peace negotiators.

While talks on implementing the peace agreement continued in March of 2008, the ICC gave the first indication that it was examining the possibility of Uganda exercising its complementarity jurisdiction. The Chief Prosecutor started inquiries into the nature and powers of the proposed Uganda war crimes court to see if it could properly conduct war crimes trials for the remaining LRA leaders under the ICC arrest warrants.

However, Moreno-Ocampo was adamant not to give in to what he termed LRA blackmail and extortion, and that the arrest warrants had to be executed, while acknowledging that the other traditional justice mechanisms could be useful for the LRA combatants lower down the hierarchy.[42] Finally, the Chief Prosecutor, like many other observers, worried that the peace negotiations were being used as a diversion for Kony to continue his atrocities and abduct children.[43]

When the ceasefire period expired, both sides adhered to it but extended the deadline for the signing of the final peace agreement to April 10, 2008. The deadline passed again without Kony coming out of the bush to sign it. He then claimed he had been misled by his own negotiating team and subsequently dismissed them, putting in place a new chief LRA negotiator. Negotiations continued again and Kony once more agreed to sign the final peace agreement in November of 2008. Again he did not show up. His failure to show up to sign the peace agreement was just one more sign of many that indicated the peace talks may have been doomed from the start and were essentially a hoax perpetrated by Kony.[44]

Frustrated, the Ugandan government declared the Juba Peace Process dead and decided to start a new military offensive against the LRA. Predictably Kony began to rearm and restart the abductions of children and other recruits, adding over 1,000 new forcibly enlisted fighters to his existing approximately 600 fighters according to BBC reports.[45]

Demonstrating his complete unreliability as a possible peace partner, Kony started attacking the people and army of his Southern Sudanese peace negotiator, Riek Machar. Kony also accused Machar of bias, demanding a new mediator from Kenya or South Africa. The Southern Sudanese government even started paying Kony to stop killing innocent civilians and abducting their children in Southern Sudan.[46]

Even the foreign governments and the U.N. envoy for Northern Uganda, former Mozambiquan president Joachim Chissano, involved in the mediation began to realize that the possibility of a genuine peace process with the unstable leadership of the LRA was unlikely and that the peace process was coming to an unsuccessful end.[47]

History may well confirm that the urgency to get on paper peace agreements that proved fruitless may have proved the weakness of the Juba process. The process managed to produce five agreements or protocols in twenty-one months to resolve over two decades of some of the most brutal civil conflicts that the African Continent has seen. What was left out may have been more important than what was in the agreements. This included a failure to address the impunity of the Ugandan army in its own actions against the LRA and the civilian populations.[48]

The remaining options seemed to be either a military victory over the

LRA or the arrest and transfer of Kony and the LRA indicted leaders to The Hague to face justice before the ICC. The U.N. Security Council recommended that peace efforts continue, but also continued to support the implementation of the ICC arrest warrants. The Chamber made its requests on February 29, 2008, and June 18, 2008. Uganda responded on March 28, 2008 and July 10, 2008 respectively. The Ugandan Attorney General in the first response asserted that the proposed Special Division of the Ugandan High Court was not meant to supplant the work of the ICC and that the individuals under the arrest warrants of the ICC would have to be brought before the Special Division of the High Court when it was established. The Attorney General of Uganda in his second response also confirmed his view 'that there must not be impunity for the perpetrators of the crimes in Northern Uganda'. The Attorney General also promised that the provisions relating to the proposed Special Division were 'without prejudice to Uganda's communities' under the ICC Statute and the 'Cooperation Agreement between the Government of Uganda and the Office of the Prosecutor'.[49]

4.   THE ADMISSIBILITY HEARING ON THE LRA CHARGES

On October 21, 2008, the ICC Pre-Trial Chamber decided to initiate proceedings *proprio motu* under Article 19(1) of the Statute to determine the admissibility of the case against the LRA leaders in accordance with Article 17 of the ICC Statute. The reason for this unprecedented move by the Court was that it felt that there were a plethora of uncertainties over the complementarity jurisdiction of the ICC regarding the signing by the Ugandan Government and the LRA of the Agreement on Accountability and Reconciliation between the Ugandan Government and the LRA and the Annexure Agreement. The Chamber granted the Ugandan government, the ICC Prosecutor, the Defense and the victims standing to submit observations in the proceedings. With the exception of the Defense, all other parties granted standing to make observations submitted that the case was still admissible.

In its decision to initiate the Admissibility hearing, the ICC, through the statements of its Registrar, is on record stating it was concerned that the responses of the Ugandan government were very ambiguous as to where and by whom the individuals under the ICC arrest warrants were to be tried. The Court also indicated that there was a lack of clarity on the respective powers of the Special Division of the High Court and of the national judicial authorities as regards who had the final authority regarding admissibility of the case against the indicted LRA leaders, and as a consequence of the exercise of that authority which judicial venue would prosecute the cases. There were also concerns about the position of the Ugandan government regarding any firm commitments regarding prosecution of the LRA leaders in the absence of the final peace agreement coupled with the ongoing military hostilities.[50] Finally the Court also decided to initiate the admissibility hearing, given the uncertainty about the Ugandan government's position about the fact that the provisions of the Agreement and the Annexure relating to indicted LRA leaders might resurface if and when the military hostilities were to cease and a final peace agreement were signed.[51]

The Pre-Trial Chamber of the ICC was sufficiently concerned about the June 29, 2007 Agreement and its Annexure to make a number of requests for information to the Ugandan government seeking clarification as to the status of these proposed national proceedings.

After receiving the clarifications and submissions from the relevant parties, the Chamber gave its ruling on admissibility on March 10, 2009.[52] In its ruling the Court, in effect, gave a warning that justice at the ICC will not be fooled by empty promises by a government of a peaceful settlement coupled with the promise of appropriate court or traditional justice processes between those who have committed the worst crimes known to humanity. The Chamber stated that until the adoption of all relevant texts and the practical implementation of the Agreement on Accountability and Reconciliation together with the provisions of the Annexure, the admissibility of the case remained the same as at the time of the arrest warrants against Kony and the top leadership of the LRA. The Chamber emphasized that it is for the ICC, not any national judicial authorities, to interpret and apply the provisions governing the complementarity provisions in the Rome Statute in order to make a binding determination on the admissibility of a given case.

The Court, in very strong judicial language, emphasized that there was total inaction by the Ugandan authorities to implement the justice and accountability agreement, and therefore there was no reason to review the determination of admissibility at this stage. Noting that the agreement and the Annexure had not been either signed or submitted to the Ugandan Parliament, the Court held that until both documents were fully effective and binding upon the parties, a final determination could not be made regarding any asserted inadmissibility of the case by the Ugandan government.

Moreover, the Court also stated the obvious that the intention to prosecute the four LRA leaders in a special division of the High Court of Uganda had been made irrelevant in the absence of a final peace agreement and the ongoing military offensive against the rebels in the DRC. The Defense has appealed the Pre-Trial Chamber's decision and a final determination on admissibility will be made by the Appeals Chamber of the ICC.

The Registrar of the ICC has emphasized that the decision of the Pre-Trial Chamber did not call into question the complementarity regime of the ICC. She asserted that the arrangements set out in the Agreement and the Annexure were welcome developments to be encouraged regarding LRA combatants not subject to the ICC arrest warrants.[53] The Registrar also stressed that if the Agreement and the Annexure were implemented, national proceedings got under way and Uganda decided to extend these proceedings to the LRA leaders under the ICC arrest warrants, the Chamber would then be in a position to determine whether these proceedings would satisfy the complementarity provisions of the ICC Statute. Until such time, the case against Kony and the other LRA leaders remains admissible and the ICC awaits the cooperation of all relevant states in arresting and sur-rendering the LRA indicted suspects to the Court in The Hague.[54]

By July 2009, 119 victims of the LRA had applied to participate in the prosecution against Kony and the LRA. Twenty-one victims have been granted victim status regarding the situation and forty-one victims granted the status in the case against Kony and the LRA. There will be a very significant burden of disclosure on the part of the Prosecutor if the trial against the LRA gets under way. Almost 5,000 documents have been accumulated under Article 54(3)e, which mandates confidentiality unless the provider consents. It is also expected that between sixty and seventy witnesses will testify to cover all the incidents and criminal liability against Kony and the LRA leadership. At present, two potential witnesses are under witness protection arranged by the ICC, and the Prosecutor has stated that he would rely on the Ugandan government to provide the secu-rity and safety for the other witnesses.

As if to confirm the correctness of the Pre-Trial Chamber's admissibil-ity decision and to conclusively demonstrate that Kony had no intention of making peace with the government and people of Uganda or other adversaries, he had long decided to continue his war crimes and crimes against humanity in areas that ranged from the Central African Republic (CAR) to the Democratic Republic of Congo (DRC) to his former refuge in Southern Sudan. It soon became apparent that Kony used the lengthy process of the failed peace negotiations to rearm, enlist and enslave more fighters in all three neighboring countries. During his ostensible desire to negotiate peace, the negotiating Ugandan government and other parties had supplied large amounts of money and food to Kony as an incentive to continue the negotiations. It has become clear that he used the money and food, some naïvely provided by foreign aid agencies from countries such as Denmark, Austria, Sweden and Switzerland, to buy arms and recruit more fighters. While the intentions of these foreign donors were admirable, namely to prevent the LRA from looting nearby civilian populations and encourage the LRA to stay with the peace talks, these good intentions resulted in the food being stockpiled and, in the view of Human Rights Watch, being possibly used to finance the re-arming of the LRA while the peace talks were continuing.[55]

The many excuses made by Kony and his core leadership that the ICC arrests warrants were an obstacle to peace may well have been a delaying tactic to get more weapons and fighters to continue the fight after the inevitable failure of the Juba peace talks.[56]

5.   THE PEACE AND JUSTICE CHALLENGES IN NORTHERN UGANDA MUST BE EXAMINED IN THE CONTEXT OF THE NATURE AND STAGE OF THE CONFLICT

In 2005, the International Center for Transitional Justice (ICTJ) and the Human Rights Center at the University of California, Berkeley, in partnership with Makerere University Institute of Public Health, conducted an in-depth survey of 2,585 residents of districts from northern Uganda that included both Acholi and non-Acholi residents. The survey objectives were the following:[57]

1.   Measure the overall exposure to violence as a result of war and human rights abuses in Northern Uganda since 1987;

2.   Understand the immediate needs and concerns of residents of towns, villages, and internally displaced person (IDP) camps in Northern Uganda;

3.   Capture opinions and attitudes about specific transitional justice mechanisms, including trials, traditional justice, truth commissions, and reparations; and

4.   Elucidate views on the relationship between peace and justice in Northern Uganda.

The main findings of the research included the following. The exposure to LRA violence was extremely high. Forty percent of victims had been abducted by the LRA, 45 percent had witnessed the killing of a family member and 23 percent had been physically mutilated at some point during the conflict. The respondents named the availability of food and sustainable peace as their top priorities.

The most relevant finding of the survey was that the people of Northern Uganda who participated in the survey did not see peace and justice as mutually exclusive. Rather, they would like to have both. About 76 percent wanted the LRA to be held accountable for their actions. The majority of those surveyed (66 percent) favored some kind of punishment ranging from trials and imprisonment to death, while 22 percent favored forgiveness, reconciliation and reintegration, with the remaining participants favoring confronting or confessing and the granting of compensation. Paradoxically, the majority (65 percent) favored some kind of amnesty process for some of the LRA members, but only 4 percent agreed that it should be given unconditionally, the viewpoint of the LRA leadership.

The survey also found that the people of Northern Uganda had high expectations that the ICC would contribute to both peace (91 percent) and justice (89 percent) but knew very little about the Court, while 36 percent favored the national court system to deal with the LRA offenders. These survey findings, although conflicting in nature, demonstrate that there are no simple choices between peace and justice, even by those at the frontlines of the conflict and who are the most victimized.

The survey did find a disparity between the responses of the Acholi and other Northern Uganda tribes. The non-Acholi responses were the highest in terms of favoring accountability with prosecution and punishment, including executions being the favored accountability option. The survey also showed that 56 percent of the Acholi favored peace with amnesty compared to 39 percent for the non-Acholi, while 61 percent of the non-Acholi favored peace with trials and punishment compared with 44 percent of the Acholi. Despite the strong showing for some kind of judicial accountability, one writer still insists that the 2005 survey showed both an Acholi and non-Acholi preference for outcomes through traditional justice processes rather than through the ICC.[58]

The conclusion of the 2005 survey was that the peace versus justice debate had become unnecessarily polarized over the ICC and was often put into false alternatives between peace and justice. The conclusion from the survey is that a comprehensive strategy was needed to integrate the strengths of all the mechanisms, both formal and traditional, to bring peace and justice in the task of ending the nightmare of the LRA in Northern Uganda.

One writer interpreted the results of the 2005 survey as showing that while the Acholi have favored amnesty, perhaps as a 'natural, familial preference' especially for children abducted into the LRA, they would support prosecution for the leaders.[59]

When the survey was repeated in 2007,[60] there were very interesting similarities and differences in the opinions of the residents of Northern

Uganda. However, the violent conflict situation had dramatically changed during this later survey. In late 2005 the LRA had already moved its fighters to the Garamba National Park in the DRC. In June of 2007, the LRA and the Ugandan government had signed the peace agreement that attempted to provide for domestic judicial processes together with alternative penalties. As discussed, the agreement did not last long. However, the withdrawal of the LRA to the DRC had improved the security of residents in Northern Uganda at the time of the second survey in 2007. Some displaced residents had begun moving closer to their villages, but fear still pervaded the region and would not subside until the LRA fighters were demobilized and the final peace agreement was signed, which Kony would not agree to until the ICC arrest warrants were withdrawn.

As in the 2005 survey findings, 70 percent of the Northern Ugandan residents insisted that those responsible for the atrocities committed on the residents should be held accountable, with 50 percent adamant that this should include the LRA leaders like Kony. Seventy percent felt the Ugandan army had also committed war crimes and human rights abuses, and 59 percent felt the perpetrators should also be put on trial. There was a very substantial willingness on the part of the surveyed residents to engage in truth-seeking through a truth commission (90 percent) and compromises through amnesties or pardons to allow the peace process to succeed.

Interestingly, by 2007 the residents were equally divided between the ICC (29 percent) and the Ugandan national courts (28 percent) in prosecuting both the leadership in the LRA and the Ugandan army most responsible for the crimes visited upon the people of the region. However, there was substantial agreement of 59 percent of the residents that the LRA leaders, including Kony, should stand trial. While a very substantial majority would favor peace with amnesty over peace with trials, the researchers felt this contradictory conclusion was the result of residents fearing that trials could jeopardize the talks that were going on during the survey. Given that those talks failed in large part due to the instability and unreliability of Kony, a future survey may find the residents reverting back to a strong desire for accountability for the top leadership of the LRA through trials. As in the 2005 survey, there were differences in responses to peace and justice as between the Acholi and the non-Acholi tribes and even among the Acholi.

What the results of these surveys of those who have been victimized the most do not reveal is that in other comparable situations blanket amnesties can lead, not to peace, but to further carnage and serious crimes. Human Rights Watch has documented how in certain conflict situations such amnesties may be short lived and could incite further armed conflict in which serious international crimes are committed. For example in Sierra Leone, three wide ranging amnesty provisions failed to create a sustainable peace, while in Angola, six amnesty provisions did not lead to reconciliation. Instead, in both situations, serious international crimes resumed shortly after peace agreements had been reached. Human Rights Watch also claims that the *de facto* immunity of the Khartoum government and its leaders for their actions in South Sudan may well have set a precedent for the atrocities committed in Darfur. The CPA, discussed in Chapter 2, did not include accountability for President al-Bashir and his government because the negotiators were concerned about jeopardizing the peace talks.[61]

Human Rights Watch has also pointed to the deterioration in Afghanistan's human rights situation to demonstrate that offering impunity to perpetrators of serious international crimes, and worse still incorporating them into the military and government, is a recipe for disaster which includes further crimes and lawlessness to persist and return. As an example of this reality, the government of President Harmid Karzai incorporated many of the warlords who had committed war crimes and crimes against humanity into his government. This has undermined the legitimacy of his government and increased the level of violence both by the warlords, who now have governmental authority, and by the opponents of the government like the Taliban. Another example is the attempt by the government of the DRC to include many who were alleged to have committed serious crimes into the military and in local or national government posts during the transition from full blown civil war to peace. The result has been the creation and support of numerous rebel groups who see benefits from continuing the armed conflict.[62]

6.   THE ULTIMATE CHOICE MAY NOT BE BETWEEN PEACE AND JUSTICE AS REGARDS KONY AND THE LRA BUT BETWEEN JUSTICE AND A MILITARY SOLUTION

There is a valuable lesson to be learned from the academic debate that raged over the conflict between peace and justice as regards the arrest warrants for Joseph Kony and the core LRA leadership. Several very thoughtful academics had painstakingly discussed the options open to the ICC in the so-called peace versus justice issue concerning the LRA.

As one example of the academic debate, Linda Keller focused on the possibility that the ICC or the Prosecutor could interpret the Rome Statute to allow deferral to the Ugandan 'Alternative Justice Mechanism' (AJM).[63]

She argued that such an interpretation could allow for four possibilities for stopping the prosecution of the LRA and deferral to the potential Ugandan AJM, in particular the *Mato Oput* process described above or the establishment of a Ugandan Truth and Reconciliation Commission.

The four possibilities outlined were (1) a Security Council deferral under Article 16 of the ICC Statute requiring the suspension of the arrest warrants as they constituted a threat to international peace; (2) applying the concept of *ne bis in idem* under Article 20 of the Rome Statute, treating the Ugandan AJMs as prior prosecutions blocking subsequent ICC proceedings; (3) prosecutorial discretion under Article 53 of the Rome Statute allowing the Prosecutor to decline to prosecute in the interests of justice; and finally (4) inadmissibility under Article 17 of the Rome Statute interpreting the principle of complementarity such that the Ugandan AJM could render the prosecution inadmissible.

Keller's analysis finds, after citing a wealth of other academic analysis, that none of these possibilities dictates deferral to the Ugandan complementarity jurisdiction, but each might allow it. She then concludes with a framework which the Court and the Prosecutor could use to allow such deferrals only if the Ugandan AJM furthered international criminal justice principles, including the theories of retribution, deterrence, expressivism and restorative justice.

These principles will be further discussed in Chapter 4. However, given the discussion in Chapter 1 of the approach by the Prosecutor to the 'interests of justice' provision in Article 53 and the decision of the Pre-Trial Chamber on admissibility of the prosecution against the LRA, and finally the impracticality of the *Mato Oput* process taken together with the fact that the Ugandan government did not set up a truth commission, it is only the possibility of a U.N. Security Council deferral of the LRA warrants that still exists as a possible avenue for those who insist that the Kony and LRA warrants pit peace against justice.

For the U.N. Security Council to defer any prosecution under Article 16, the request for a renewable twelve month deferral must be made under the Chapter VII power of the U.N. Charter which empowers actions by the Council against threats to international peace and security.

The use of Article 16 to defer the charges against Kony and the LRA leadership would be a very dangerous precedent for individuals or groups alleged to have committed serious international crimes around the world. The demand for such a deferral could be used to refuse disarming or continuing to carry out atrocities. It would also potentially undermine attempts at negotiating peace agreements as such rebel groups would have an incentive to defer critical concessions using the demand for such a deferral as a form of negotiating blackmail. This is precisely the tactic that Kony was employing by using the ICC warrants as a stalling tactic to get more resources for the LRA. There is one report that before every meeting, Kony demanded shipments of food for his 5,000 fighters, although he was believed to have no more than 800 fighters at any time, using the provisions for future actions against government forces and innocent civilians.[64]

One learned jurist, John Dugard, has rightly concluded[65] that it is hard to imagine that the refusal by the ICC to accept alternatives to prosecution such as amnesties or truth commissions could be a threat to international peace, while others have supported possible U.N. Security Council action to uphold alternatives to ICC prosecution.[66]

The possibility of deferral by the U.N. Security Council under Article 16 of the Rome Statute may be strongest if there is a legal obligation to prosecute in national courts some or all of those accused of the most serious crimes. There is much debate about to what level of actors and crimes such national prosecutions must reach if a U.N. Security Council deferral is to be a real possibility.

Keller points out that because Uganda has ratified the Geneva Conventions, the Genocide Conventions and the Convention against Torture it would have a duty to prosecute some of the crimes charged by the ICC, but not all of them, adding that there could be an emerging rule of customary international law to prosecute all international crimes. However, as another respected jurist, Diane Orentlicher, has noted, the prosecution of only the most responsible actors would be sufficient in some circumstances.[67] Given the limited capacity of the ICC to try all of the thousands of LRA fighters who may have committed crimes against humanity and war crimes, Orentlicher's position is the most practical of those of the academic writers on this issue. Finally one jurist, Michael Scharf, also questions whether the ICC would have to honor a U.N. Security Council deferral where the alleged perpetrators have been given amnesty that covers genocide or grave breaches of the Geneva Conventions.[68] When all these eminent jurists' analyses of the proper role of the U.N. Security Council in granting a deferral are taken into account, one remaining academic conclusion stands out as a warning. The indiscriminate use of this power under Article 16 of the Rome Statute in order to advance peace over justice has the potential to 'emasculate the ICC'.[69]

It is at this point in the analysis that jurists such as Keller fail to see that in situations such as the prosecution of Kony and the core LRA leadership it was never a choice between peace and justice, but a choice between justice and the military defeat and capture of the LRA leadership. Keller argues that the U.N. Security Council could have determined that the ICC prosecution could have threatened international peace and also impacted on the still fragile peace in Sudan. The main threat to the fragile peace in Sudan was and is the actions of the al-Bashir government itself, not the LRA. The argument for an Article 16 deferral is also based on the assertion that Kony would never accept anything less than a total guarantee of non-prosecution and would not surrender or disarm prior to such a deferral.

However, it is unlikely that the Security Council would grant such a suspension until the peace agreement was implemented and LRA compliance guaranteed. There was and is almost no possibility of the U.N. Security Council allowing Kony to remain free and armed to continue the atrocities that he carried out even while he or his representative were negotiating peace at Juba in the south of Sudan.

It is precisely this catch-22 that had always made the situation not one of peace versus justice in the context of Northern Uganda, but finding a way of either getting Kony and his LRA leadership to The Hague to face justice or face military defeat or capture.

The continuous and inhumane killing machine that is Joseph Kony and his LRA rebels reinforces this conclusion. His chief base of operations at the time of writing seems to be in several heavily armed defensive sites in the DRC, in particular in the Garamba National Park. The LRA also continues to carry out raids into the CAR and Southern Sudan. In the CAR there are reports that in one month alone, August of 2008, over 300 were abducted by the LRA.

Given this nightmarish killing and abducting spree in three countries, the militaries of the DRC, Uganda and Southern Sudan decided to join up to defeat the LRA and hopefully eliminate them as a threat to the peoples of the region. There was also the desperate hope that a defeated or captured Kony together with other top LRA leaders would result in the rest of the rebels surrendering, disarming and taking part in a comprehensive peace settlement.

On December 14, 2008, these armies attacked the DRC bases of the LRA in the Garamba National Park, a joint operation to stop the LRA atrocities and execute, if possible, the arrest warrants against Kony and the top leadership. The joint military action was called 'Operation Lightning Thunder'. American military advisers had pinpointed with sophisticated maps the camps the Ugandan helicopter gunship should be looking for in the hunt for Kony and his men. There is mounting evidence that the U.S. had decided that the only option was the military solution for the LRA's continuing atrocities, perhaps even eclipsing the ICC justice option. The U.S. had decided even while the attempts at negotiating a peace agreement with the LRA were going on, that the military effort to wipe out the LRA rebels should get underway. The *New York Times* reported on February

7, 2009 that the American military helped plan and pay for the Operation Lightning Thunder attack.

When the gunships reached the LRA camps they prematurely unleashed the barrage of rockets and gunfire on those in the camp, including on the many child soldiers recruited by the LRA. Those who were not killed fled into the jungle. When the joint military commandos finally reached the LRA camp, two days after the gunships had done their lethal work, they found a bloodsoaked empty camp that looked more like a permanent settlement than a makeshift camp. There were even well equipped military offices with computers, satellite cell phones and cultivated fields to feed the rebels.

The joint forces captured the vast stores of food that had been left behind as the LRA rebels had abandoned the camps. Perhaps the main object of the operation, the capture or killing of Kony, was not achieved because he had left the camp before the assault had begun after either being tipped off or learning of the impending attacks from intercepting radio communications. American military personnel and senior Ugandan military officials have criticized the poor planning and execution of the joint operation, including the failure to take into account basic risks such as poor weather conditions.[70]

This author has learned from a high ranking Ugandan official that there is evidence that President al-Bashir of Sudan had tipped off Kony to the impending assault, having got leaked information from one of the joint forces or their political masters and spirited Kony out from the DRC with the help of Sudan. If this is verified, it demonstrates the criminal partnership between the two men, both sought on arrest warrants for allegedly committing the most serious of crimes known to humanity.

The joint action in Operation Lightning Thunder did not stop the rampage of the LRA.[71] On December 29, 2008 the LRA massacred nearly 200 people in the DRC after the LRA fighters were attacked by the three nation army. The LRA hacked to death dozens of DRC villagers in their path as they fled. According to U.N. and Ugandan military officials in December 2008, most of the approximately 200 victims were women and children who were deliberately cut to pieces by the LRA.[72] A more recent report has claimed that Kony and the LRA have retaliated for Operation Lightning Thunder by slaughtering more than 1,000 Congolese villagers, burning entire villages and enslaving more children. The report asserts that roughly a quarter of a million people have fled their homes in the DRC and South Sudan in the wake of the LRA atrocities. The LRA has become even more deadly by splitting up into smaller groups to make any attempt to capture Kony more difficult.[73] The brutality of the LRA fighters in hacking, burning and shooting any Congolese villagers they met indicates that their goal is far from seeking peace, but instead creating a safe haven for themselves through a reign of terror in an ungovernable part of the DRC. The LRA have gone beyond any known precedents of brutality and criminal behavior. There are reports that these fighters have tried to twist off babies' heads in efforts to terrorize local inhabitants. Other reports have asserted that Kony and his men have forced new male recruits, including child recruits, to rape their mothers and kill their parents.

Peace negotiations require some basic element of humanity, which seems to be absent from the LRA fighters. Indeed, there are growing concerns that the Ugandan and Congolese forces are doing too little to protect villagers in the path of fleeing LRA fighters despite the long and savage history of reprisals by these fighters against civilians.[74]

In March of 2009, internal political pressures seem to have forced DRC President Joseph Kabila to demand Uganda's military to withdraw from Congolese territory. In an attempt to save face from what was a botched attempt to capture or kill Kony, the Ugandan Army is claiming that the LRA has been severely weakened by Operation Lightning Thunder and also in part by the withdrawal of support from the Sudanese government in Khartoum.[75] However, an American think tank, after studying the impact of Operation Lightning Thunder, has concluded that the operation ended prematurely and left civilians in northeastern DRC open to LRA reprisal attacks.[76] Paradoxically, the beneficiaries, albeit perhaps only temporarily, are the people of Northern Uganda. With the LRA fleeing to the DRC, the rampage by the LRA against the Acholi and others in the region has ceased. Internally displaced villagers are returning to their former homes and students are returning to local schools which have opened. There is growing fear that the LRA may return to wreak vengeance on Uganda and the local inhabitants.

Even though large numbers of the internally displaced Northern Ugandan civilians have returned to their homes, many are staying in the squalid camps which still have some of the most basic education and health services that have been destroyed in their Northern Uganda homes that have not been rebuilt due to fear of the return of the LRA.

That fear is now spreading to much of the Great Lakes area. While the LRA has moved its main military actions out of Northern Uganda it has spread to the border regions between the DRC, Sudan and the Central African Republic. There is also evidence that the LRA has mutated into a majority Sudanese rebel force as Kony has taken advantage of both the Juba talks and its transfer to Sudan in 1994 to recruit or abduct Sudanese civilians.[77] The military option is becoming increasingly difficult as the border regions of the three countries provide ample ability for the LRA to stymie intelligence gathering.[78]

It has also begun to resource its brutal activities by engaging in the illegal production and trade of gold, ivory, and diamonds. There is also evidence of support from the Ugandan Diaspora in Europe and Kenya who are opposed to the Museveni government by providing resources and advice to Kony and the LRA. There is also growing evidence that the al-Bashir regime is providing support to the LRA as a potential proxy army against the Southern Sudan army, should it become necessary to stop the national elections next year or the 2011 referendum on independence from the North.[79]

7.   CONCLUSION: PEACE AND RECONCILIATION SHOULD BE PURSUED IN NORTHERN UGANDA EVEN WHILE A MILITARY SOLUTION OR CONTAINMENT IS ATTEMPTED

One of the world's best conflict resolution organizations, the International Crisis Group, still considers there is a possibility of negotiating a peace agreement with Kony and the LRA leadership, which if properly structured could also allow the U.N. Security Council to promulgate an Article 16 deferral of the charges against them.[80] From the above analysis and description of the recent savagery of Kony and his fighters, it is hard to accept that the possibility of peace with or without justice or any form of traditional reconciliation exists with them.

However, groups such as the International Crisis Group have offered other very important ways in which peace can be striven for without the hope for any reconciliation with Kony and the LRA.

First, the stakeholders' conference agreed upon at one of the many Juba peace protocols should still be organized with key objectives in mind. These include the consultation and planning for a strong Truth and Reconciliation Commission. The Commission should be empowered to investigate all crimes committed since 1986, including those of the Ugandan army, and decide on appropriate reparations for victims of both the LRA and the Ugandan army. Victim protection should also be part of the truth telling exercise. The stakeholders' conference should include a wide representation of communities from Northern Uganda and even from the diaspora in Europe and elsewhere.[81]

Second, there should be efforts to redress the legitimate grievances and feelings of marginalization of the peoples of Northern Uganda to remove the LRA as a possible vehicle for the expression of the frustrations of the people they claim to fight for. This could include a revitalized Equal Opportunities Commission provided for in the Ugandan Constitution.

The Commission would focus on claims of disempowerment and regional disparities in allocation of public offices and benefits from natural resources. This may be especially important, given the discovery of large reserves of oil and gas in Northern Uganda. In addition, the Ugandan government should take measures to ensure that any reconstruction funds for the ravaged North, provided either by foreign donors or the Ugandan government, should be transparently managed and not be misspent or subject to bureaucratic paralysis and corrupt practices. Land allocation, especially for women and children, the primary victims of the conflict, should be undertaken to ensure that peaceful resettlement of the internally displaced populations takes place and in priority to any commercial or industrial planning. [82]

Third, the Ugandan government should proceed with the establishment of a special division of the High Court and credible elements of traditional justice. The International Crisis Group has also offered the suggestion that the Special Division of the High Court could be established in Arusha, Tanzania, to give any LRA fighters a greater comfort as to whether they would have fair trials, and could include provisions respecting security detail. While the International Crisis Group hopes that these mechanisms could induce the U.N. Security Council to defer the charges against Kony and the LRA leaders, the promised national court could be the tribunal to prosecute lower level LRA fighters who desert from Kony and the LRA leadership. The traditional processes could be part of reconciliation efforts between the fighters and local communities.[83]

The ultimate peace efforts that could actually result in a sustainable peace in Northern Uganda may not be anything that comes from negotiations with Kony and his increasingly savage fighters, but from the Ugandan government making peace with the peoples of Northern Uganda and thereby marginalizing the LRA leaders and consigning them to a militarily contained isolation and desperate infamy that they so richly deserve.

NOTES

1. Payam Akhavan, 'Developments at the International Criminal Court: The Lord's Resistance Army Case: Uganda's Submission of the First State Referral to The International Criminal Court' (2005) 99 *Am.J. Int'l.L.* 403.
2. H. Abigail Moy, 'The International Criminal Court's Arrest Warrants and Uganda's Lord's Resistance Army: Renewing the Debate over Amnesty and Complementarity' (2006) 19 *Harv. Hum. Rts. J.* 267 also located at the following url: http://www.law. harvard.edu/students/orgs/hrj/iss19/moy.shtml.
3. Tim Allen, *Trial Justice: The International Criminal Court and the Lord's Resistance Army* (Zed Books, 2006).

4. *Ibid.* at 44, also quoted in Linda M. Keller, 'Achieving Peace with Justice: The International Criminal Court and Ugandan Alternative Justice Mechanisms' (2008) 23:2 *Conn. J. Int'l Law*. 209 at 214.
5. *Ibid.*
6. *Ibid.* at 75–76.
7. Professor Eric Blumenson, 'The Challenge of a Global Standard of Justice: Peace, Pluralism, and Punishment at the International Criminal Court' (2006) 44 *Colum. J. Transnat' L*. 801, also located at SSRN website at the following url: http://papers.ssrn.com/sol3/papers.cfm?abstract_id=834004.
8. Interview between the author and the Chief Prosecutor of the ICC, The Hague, 13 May 2009.
9. Ted Neilson, 'The International Criminal Court and the "Peace versus Justice" Dichotomy' (2008) 3 *Australian Journal of Peace Studies* 34.
10. See Matthew Happold, 'The International Criminal Court and the Lord's Resistance Army' (2007) 8:1 *Melbourne Journal of International Law* 159.
11. *Situation in Uganda*, ICC-002/04-01/05 Warrant for the Arrest for Joseph Kony Issued on 8 July 2005 as Amended on 27 September 2005 (27 September 2005) (International Criminal Court, Pre-Trial Chamber) at 12–19. See also Akhavan, *supra* note 1, and Annan Hails, 'International Criminal Court's Arrest Warrant for Five Ugandan Rebels' *U.N. News Service* (14 October 2005).
12. 'ICC Issues Arrest Warrants for LRA Leaders' *IRIN News* (7 October 2005) available at the following url: http://www.irinnews.org/report.asp?ReportID=49420&SelectRegion=East_Africa&SelectCountry=UGANDA; 'The ICC and the Northern Uganda Conflict' *IRIN News* (9 June 2005) available at the following url: http://www.irinnews.org/S_report.asp?ReportID=47573; 'ICC Indictments to Affect Northern Peace Efforts, Says Mediator' *IRIN News* (10 October 2005) available at the following url: http://www.irinnews.org/report.asp?ReportID=49453&SelectRegion=East_Africa&SelectCountry=UGANDA.
13. See Amnesty International's report for a speedy arrest of the five indicted LRA leaders in 'Arrest Now! Uganda: Joseph Kony, Vincent Otti, Okot Ohhiambo and Dominic Ongwen' (28 November 2007) AI Index:AFR 59/008/2007, also located at the following url: http://asiapacific.amnesty.org/library/Index/ENGAFR590082007.
14. *Ibid.*
15. *Ibid.*
16. *Ibid.*
17. See 'Roco Wat I, Acoli: Restoring Relationships in Acholi-land: Traditional Approaches to Justice and Reintegration' *Liu Institute for Global Issues* (15 September 2005).
18. See the Institute for War and Peace Reporting, description of the *Mato Oput* reconciliation procedure, Katy Glassborow, 'ICC-Africe Peace Versus Justice in Uganda' *Institute for War and Peace Reporting* (7 September 2006) AR No 77, located at the following url: http://www.iwpr.net/?p=acr&s=f&o=324160&apc_state=heniacr200609; see also the critique of this process for serious international crimes by Francis Onyago, 'Mato Oput Not a Viable Alternative to the ICC' *Global Policy Forum* (11 July 2007) located at the following url: http://www.globalpolicy.org/intljustice/icc/investigations/uganda/2007/0711matooputnotviable.htm.
19. Liu Institute for Global Issues, *supra* note 17 at 55.
20. See Allen, *supra* note 3 at 167.
21. See 'Peace in Northern Uganda?' *International Crisis Group* (13 September 2006) Africa Briefing No. 41, at 16.
22. Keller, *supra* note 4 at 225–226.
23. *Ibid.*
24. See Alexis Okeowo, 'ICC-Africa Update, Uganda: New LRA Truce Offers Hope' *Institute for War and Peace Reporting* (20 April 2007) AR No. 109, located at the following url: http://www.iwpr.net/?p=acr&s=f&o=335016&apc_state=henpacr.
25. Report by Stuart Price, 'Uganda: A huge dilemma' *New African* (1 July 2006).

26. Institute for War and Peace Reporting, *supra* note 18.
27. Blumenson, *supra* note 7 at 810–812.
28. *Ibid.*
29. Keller, *supra* note 4 at 218.
30. *Ibid.*, citing the International Crisis Group's document, 'Northern Uganda Peace Process: The Need to Maintain Momentum' *International Crisis Group* (14 September 2007) Africa Briefing No. 46.
31. *Ibid.*, citing Samuel O. Egadu, 'Museveni Wants LRA Warrants for Now' *Institute for War and Peace Reporting* (25 July 2007) Ann. Rep. No. 123.
32. *Ibid.*, citing Frank Nyakairu, 'LRA to Consult Victims on Accountability' *Daily Monitor*, Uganda (13 June 2007).
33. *Ibid.* at 219, citing Paul Harera and Greace Matkiko, 'LRA Asks Government to Legalize Traditional Justice' *Monitor Online*, Uganda (22 June 2007).
34. *Ibid.* at 218.
35. See the website of Conciliation Resources, 'Ugandans talking peace with Sierra Leoneans' located at the following url: http://www.c-r.org/our-work/uganda/peace-talk.php.
36. Annexure to the Agreement on Accountability and Reconciliation between the Government of the Republic of Uganda and the Lord's Resistance Army/Movement, 19 February 2008, at para. 9(e).
37. Keller, *supra* note 4 at 219.
38. *Ibid.*, citing Adrian Croft, 'Uganda offers "blood settlement" to LRA rebels' *Reuters* (12 March 2008).
39. *Ibid.*, citing Daniel Wallis, 'Uganda rebel Kony "worried about security finances"' *Reuters* (11 April 2008).
40. Blumenson, *supra* note 7 at 810–812.
41. See Amnesty International news release, 'Uganda strikes deal with LRA on trials' (20 February 2008) located at the following url: http://www.amnesty.org/en/news-and-updates/news/uganda-strikes-deal-lra-trials-20080220.
42. Luis Moreno-Ocampo Address at Nuremberg, 'Building a Future on Peace and Justice' (24–25 June 2007).
43. *Ibid.*
44. For a view that the peace talks were doomed from the start, see 'Juba Peace Talks a Hoax?' *Institute for Strategic Studies* (14 May 2008) located at the following url: http://www.iss.co.za/index.php?link_id=29&slink_id=5945&link_type=12&slink_type=12&tmpl_id=3.
45. See 'Ugandan Rebels Prepare for War' *BBC Report* (6 June 2008) located at the following url: http://news.bbc.co.uk/2/hi/africa/7440790.stm.
46. See the Report of Human Rights Watch, 'Sudan: Regional Government Pays Ugandan Rebels not to Attack' *Human Rights Watch* (2 June 2006) located at the following url: http://www.hrw.org/en/news/2006/06/01/sudan-regional-government-pays-ugandan-rebels-not-attack.
47. See the Institute for Strategic Studies' analysis on the daunting task of the remaining negotiators such as former Mozambique president Joaquim Chissano: Wafula Okumu, 'Uganda: Chissano Has a Daunting Task to Resuscitate the Juba Peace Talks' (19 January 2007) located at the following url: http://www.issafrica.org/index.php?link_id=29&slink_id=3999&link_type=12&slink_type=12&tmpl_id=3.
48. See 'Northern Uganda: The Road to Peace, with or without Kony' *International Crisis Group* (10 December 2008) Africa Report No. 146.
49. The above information is based on an address by the ICC Registrar Silvana Arbia, given at the Grotius Centre of Leiden University at The Hague on 13 May 2009.
50. *Ibid.*
51. *Ibid.*
52. *Situation in Uganda in the Case of the Prosecutor v. Joseph Kony, Vincent Otti, Okot Odhiambo and Dominic Ongwen*, ICC-02/04-01/05-377, Decision on the admissibility

of the case under Article 19(1) of the Statute (10 March 2009) (International Criminal Court) located at the following url: http://www2.icc-cpi.int/iccdocs/doc/doc641259.pdf.
53. Registrar Silvana Arbia, *supra* note 49.
54. *Ibid.*
55. 'The Christmas Massacres: Recent International Action on the LRA, A Failed Peace Process' *Human Rights Watch* (16 February 2009) located at the following url: http://www.hrw.org/en/node/80769/section/13.
56. See the report by Robert Crilly, 'How Monuc unmasked Kony's Plan B' *Daily Monitor* (18 December 2008) located at the following url: http://www.monitor.co.ug/artman/publish/news/How_Monuc_unmasked_Kony_s_Plan_B_77023.shtml.
57. Phuong Pham et al., 'Forgotten Voices: A Population-Based Survey of Attitudes About Peace and Justice in Northern Uganda' *International Center for Transitional Justice*, located at the following url: http://www.ictj.org/images/content/1/2/127.pdf.
58. Keller, *supra* note 4 at 227.
59. *Ibid.*
60. Phuong Pham et al., 'When the War Ends: A Population-Based Survey on Attitudes about Peace, Justice, and Social Reconstruction in Northern Uganda' *International Center for Transitional Justice* (December 2007) located at the following url: http://www.reliefweb.int/rw/rwb.nsf/db900SID/EMAE-79ZSZP?OpenDocument.
61. 'Selling Justice Short, Why Accountability Matters for Peace' *Human Rights Watch* (July 2009) at 57–73.
62. *Ibid.* at 35–54.
63. Keller, *supra* note 4 at 238–239.
64. Scott Johnson, 'Hard Target: The Manhunt for Africa's last warlord' *Newsweek* (16 May 2009).
65. See John Dugard, 'Possible Conflicts of Jurisdiction with Truth Commissions' in A. Cassese et al., eds, *The Rome Statute of the International Criminal Court: A Commentary* (Oxford University Press, 2002) 693 at 701–702.
66. See, for example, Darryl Robinson, 'Serving the Interests of Justice: Amnesties, Truth Commissions and the International Criminal Court' (2003) 14:3 *E.J.I.L.* 481 at 503.
67. D. F. Orentlicher, 'Settling Accounts: The Duty to Prosecute Human Rights Violations of a Prior Regime' (1991) 100:8 *Yale L.J.* at 2595–2598.
68. Michael P. Scharf, 'The Amnesty Exception to the Jurisdiction of the International Criminal Court' (1999) 32 *Cornell Int'l L.J.* 507 at 523–524.
69. Nick Grono, VP, International Crisis Group, Remarks at the International Conference on Building a Future on Peace and Justice, Negotiating Peace and Justice: Considering Accountability and Deterrence in Peace Processes' (26 June 2007) quoted in Keller, *supra* note 4 at 242.
70. Andrew M. Mwenda, 'Seven UPDR Generals criticise Kony Attack' *The Independent* (22 January 2009).
71. See Scott Baldauf, 'Africans join forces to fight the LRA' *The Christian Science Monitor* (17 December 2008) located at the following url: http://www.csmonitor.com/2008/1217/p06s01-woaf.html.
72. Jeffrey Gettleman, 'Rebels kill nearly 200 in Congo, U.N. says' *New York Times* (29 December 2008) located at the following url: http://www.nytimes.com/2008/12/30/world/africa/30uganda.html.
73. Johnson, *supra* note 64.
74. Jeffrey Gettleman and Eric Schmitt, 'U.S. Aided a Failed Plan to Rout Ugandan Rebels' *New York Times* (7 February 2009) located at the following url: http://www.nytimes.com/2009/02/07/world/africa/07congo.html?emc=rss&partner=rss.
75. 'Uganda army says LRA rebels weakened' *Agence France Presse* (12 May 2009) available at the following url: http://www.reliefweb.int/rw/rwb.nsf/db900sid/ASAZ-7RYGTN?OpenDocument.
76. *Ibid.*

77. International Crisis Group, *supra* note 48 at i.
78. *Ibid.* at 14.
79. *Ibid.* at i.
80. *Ibid.*
81. *Ibid.* at i–iii.
82. *Ibid.*
83. *Ibid.*

4 Reconciling peace with justice in the ICC through positive international complementarity

The legitimacy and the credibility of the ICC depend on the development of what can be termed 'positive international complementarity' (PIC) as the way to reconcile peace with justice, not only at the ICC, but also in the international community. What is meant by PIC is a framework that requires nations afflicted by actions constituting international crimes and all nations, and not only the ICC, to be the champions of the fight against impunity and to ensure that the most serious crimes do not go unpunished.

To have a reconciliation of peace and justice worldwide a PIC framework must have the following key features:

(1)   The ICC focuses on situations that give rise to the most serious of international crimes where investigations lead to the prosecution of those most responsible. The initial goal of such investigations and potential jurisprudence coming out of the trials of such crimes should be to maximize prevention of future crimes while also potentially acting as a catalyst for domestic investigations and proceedings. Such advances in domestic criminal law are critical to maintaining the ICC as a court of last resort.
(2)   Exceptional situations in which either leaders or others further down the hierarchy of groups that are alleged to have committed the most serious international crimes face either fair domestic prosecutions if available or alternative justice mechanisms (AJMs) that meet the moral and philosophical foundations of international criminal justice.
(3)   Where those who are alleged to have committed the most serious crimes are discovered or seek refuge in the territory of neighboring or other nations, there is a duty to either prosecute or extradite in cases where prosecution is not feasible. The duty to prosecute or extradite could be the most recent evolution of the concept of universal jurisdiction that has undergone both substantial successes and challenges.

1. THE POSITIVE INTERNATIONAL COMPLEMENTARITY AND DOMESTIC IMPACT OF ICC PROSECUTIONS

One of the untold achievements of the ICC and in particular the Office of the Prosecutor (OTP) is the impact of publicizing the preliminary examinations and monitoring activities of the ICC prior to launching an investigation. Under Article 15 of the Rome Statute, the Prosecutor can proactively monitor and analyze information on alleged crimes in order to determine whether it is appropriate to open an investigation according to the parameters set down in the Statute. At the time of writing the Prosecutor is engaged in preliminary examinations and monitoring in ten situations, six of which have been made public, namely Afghanistan, Colombia, Côte d'Ivoire, Kenya, Georgia, and Palestine.

The OTP has asserted that such preliminary examinations seem to be having an impact on the level of on-going violence. The reduction of violence should be regarded as a form of peace advancement. The OTP is asserting that with respect to the impact of public monitoring, in the case of Côte d'Ivoire, Georgia and Kenya, the level of violence has significantly decreased after the commencement of ICC public monitoring. There is an acknowledgement that this may partly be due to the fact that the public monitoring commenced towards the last phase of the conflict or crisis after violence had peaked.[1]

The OTP also asserted that another impact of its preliminary examinations and public monitoring is that it acts as a potential or actual catalyst for national judicial proceedings against impunity. The Office points to Kenya as an example. Under the recommendation of a Kenyan independent commission of inquiry, Kofi Annan, who mediated the post-election crisis, was mandated to hand over the names of ten major suspects to the ICC if Kenya did not set up a national tribunal to try those behind the post-election tribal conflicts that killed over 1,300 people in tribal violence and caused 300,000 internally displaced refugees. According to some reports, the list prepared by Mr. Annan contains the names of leading politicians and elites. In February 2008, the OTP announced that it had begun a preliminary examination of the situation in Kenya. The ICC was being used as a catalyst for the setting up of a complementary national judicial mechanism to combat impunity in this key African nation without the pressure from the Court itself.[2]

By July of 2009, both President Mwai Kibaki and Prime Minister Raila Odinga were trying to change Kenyan parliamentary opposition to establishing a national tribunal to prosecute those alleged to be behind the post-election violence. Kenyan officials had promised the Chief

Prosecutor of the ICC that they would have a clear plan for a national tribunal by September 2009 and, if that did not occur, the ICC would be able to take over the investigation and prosecution. The Prosecutor of the ICC has also revealed that Kenya had cooperated to such an extent with the preliminary investigation of the Kenyan situation that the ICC would itself be ready to start the justice process by 2010 if the Kenyan tribunal had not been established.[3] On July 9, 2009, Kofi Annan handed over the list of suspects to the Chief Prosecutor of the ICC in a sealed envelope. The list is believed to include the names of Kenyan ministers and prominent business people.

The Prosecutor is reported to have stated that justice delayed is justice denied in the context of the failure to promptly set up a national Kenyan tribunal to prosecute the suspects in the electoral violence. He claimed that the people of Kenya wanted to see progress on ending impunity, without which lack of reconciliation between ethnic groups threatened the stability of this critical African country.[4] Just before Mr. Annan handed over the list of suspects, a high level delegation from the Kenyan Government had met with the Prosecutor in The Hague and stressed the government's commitment to prosecute the perpetrators of the violence in order to prevent repeat of the crimes in the 2012 elections. The Kenyan government also promised to refer the situation to the Prosecutor in accordance with Article 14 of the Rome Statute, unless the Kenyan Parliament established a genuine national mechanism to prosecute those most responsible for the crimes.

On September 30, 2009, the Prosecutor of the ICC announced his decision to prosecute those most responsible for the post-election violence. This action would be part of a three-pronged approach by the ICC and Kenyan authorities. The first approach would focus on international accountability for those most responsible for the violence. The second approach would promote domestic accountability with the establishment by the Kenyan Parliament of a Special Tribunal for other perpetrators. The third approach would focus on other reconciliation efforts, reforms and mechanisms such as the Justice, Truth and Reconciliation Commission to be established that would shed light on the full history of past events and suggest ways and mechanisms to prevent such crimes in the future. The Prosecutor stressed that with this three pronged approach, Kenya could be an example to the world on managing violence.[5]

The Kenyan government has stated that it will cooperate with the ICC in its investigation and prosecution of those most responsible for the alleged crimes in the post-election violence. Indeed, the Kenyan Justice Minister, Mutula Kilonzo, suggested that the ICC could hold its trials in Kenya where the suspects would be arrested and detained pending the hearings.[6]

The OTP has also asserted that such domestic impacts of ICC preliminary examinations and monitoring could also be occurring in Colombia. This State Party ratified the Rome Statute in 2002 but with a declaration that it would not accept the ICC's jurisdiction over war crimes until 2009. The ICC Prosecutor has commenced preliminary examinations and public monitoring of the alleged massacres, torture and forced disappearances of thousands of civilians by the paramilitary groups linked to elites in the Colombian government. The paramilitary groups and their political accomplices have evaded investigation and prosecution. The situation of impunity, condoned even at the highest levels of the Colombian government, remains unresolved in the view of many observers.[7]

Faced with potential extradition to the U.S. for drug trafficking-related offences, the paramilitaries managed to secure the transitional justice Law 975 also known as the Justice and Peace Law. This law has been severely criticized by human rights groups within and outside the country for offering paramilitary commanders responsible for the worst crimes reduced sentences of five to eight years if the paramilitaries agree to demobilize. The groups had been promised that extradition to the U.S. on drug trafficking charges would be forestalled. After four years, the Justice and Peace Law has not fulfilled the promised accountability for the most serious crimes. Indeed there are disturbing reports of the victims of these crimes along with prosecutors and judges being threatened or killed for participating in the processes under the so called Peace and Justice Law. Only one paramilitary leader was convicted and subsequently had his conviction annulled by the Colombian Supreme Court.

As a result of meetings during the negotiations for the Justice and Peace Law with the Colombian Attorney General, other high level officials and human rights NGOs, the Prosecutor made public efforts to trigger national judicial and executive responses to some of his demands on the question of impunity for alleged breaches of international criminal law. These demands have included seeking assurances that those most responsible for alleged crimes, not only from the rebel FARC group, but also those political leaders and members of the Colombian Congress connected to the paramilitary groups, will be brought to justice. After Colombia brought in the Justice and Peace Law in an attempt to demonstrate its desire to ensure that the paramilitary leaders were not being granted impunity indirectly, the Prosecutor also went further and has publicly demanded to know the extent to which national investigations promised by the Attorney General of Colombia would be hampered by the extradition to the U.S. of eighteen of the key paramilitary leaders connected to the political and other elites.[8] In August of 2009, the Colombian Supreme Court suspended further extraditions. The Court acknowledged that not only would the failure by those extradited to testify under the Justice and Peace Law seriously hamper any attempt to impose accountability for the serious crimes, but also the drug trafficking charges paled in comparison to the resulting impunity for the killings and disappearances of thousands of civilians.[9]

The fact that the Prosecutor has continued a very high profile monitoring action and given warnings that he is focusing on those most responsible for the alleged crimes and their political accomplices in a country classified by many as a western liberal democracy should also assuage those critics who have claimed that the ICC is imposing a western form of international criminal justice on certain African countries.[10]

In a similar fashion, these preliminary examinations and public monitoring activities may also have led individuals and groups to gather the necessary evidentiary materials which could assist national or international authorities to start national investigations and ultimately prosecutions that could well have come within the jurisdiction of the ICC. The OTP asserts that this has occurred in the case of the Kenyan monitoring. It is also asserted that the same effects of public monitoring are occurring with the Eastern European situation in Georgia after a substantial number of communications on the situation dealing with the conflict in South Ossetia was transmitted to the ICC. Finally, the OTP asserts that the public announcement of a public preliminary analysis and monitoring provides third parties such as national authorities, international organizations and NGOs with increased leverage in fulfilling mandates to combat impunity or call for an end to violence. The situations in Kenya and Georgia are again asserted as examples where the Prosecutor's preliminary examination and public monitoring enabled several actors to call for an end to the violence, ensure accountability and ensure that evidence of violations of international criminal law was preserved.[11]

In the Central African Republic (CAR), at the time of the public announcement of the start of the ICC investigation of the situation in the country after the government's self-referral, there were consistent reports in 2006 and 2007 of village burnings and mass killings, some perpetrated by the Presidential Guard. The OTP has reported that the allegations of such atrocities significantly decreased after the start of the ICC investigation. In addition, the ICC and other international actors have claimed that their actions led to the curtailment of reprisal actions by government forces against rebel militias. These incidental impacts of the ICC investigation in the CAR occurred even though the focus of the OTP investigations was on alleged atrocities committed during the armed conflict of the earlier 2002–2003 period.[12]

Where the Prosecutor decides to focus charges against an alleged perpetrator in a particular evolving area of international criminal law, there is also the possibility of worldwide attention being drawn to that area of criminal actions. Such publicity could well have a preventative effect larger than in the country in which the charges arose. The focused charges against Thomas Lubanga Dyilo, in the context of the DRC, provide an example.

While the Prosecutor has faced criticism for only charging Thomas Lubanga Dyilo with recruitment of child soldiers and not the other serious crimes of rape, torture and killings constituting crimes against humanity and war crimes, the focused charges have triggered an international awareness of the social, psychological and legal nature of what constitutes the crime of conscripting or enlisting children into militias and using them to participate actively in hostilities under Article 8 of the Rome Statute. There is an urgent need to establish a worldwide consciousness on the part of actual and potential perpetrators that the conscripting and enlisting of children is a most serious international crime, even though it may have become common practice in some parts of the world. The brutalization of the most vulnerable of children and youth anywhere in the world is an abhorrent criminal stain on the entire human family.

This historic codification of an international crime directed against the most impressionable of the human family needed a major prosecution to flush out the inhumane nature of the crime. In the first major trial at the ICC, the Prosecution submitted distressing evidence of how Lubanga had systematically recruited children under the age of 15 into his political group called the Union des Patriotes Congolais (UPC) and its armed militia called the Forces Patriotiques pour la libération du Congo (FPLC). Thomas Lubanga Dyilo was charged with being criminally responsible as a co-perpetrator under Article 25(3)e of the Rome Statute. The Prosecution intends to demonstrate that a common plan existed between Thomas Lubanga Dyilo and other co-perpetrators to seize, and maintain control over the violence that plagued the Ituri region of the DRC. This plan included augmenting their adult militia fighters with the conscription and enlistment of children under 15 to actively participate in hostilities.[13]

The children were trained to be armed killers who would indulge in killings, rape and pillage even against their own family members. Child witnesses brought before the Court explained how they were abducted and underwent forced military training in camps where severe punishment was meted out and instructed that their guns would be their new 'father' and 'mother' and their arms would be the mechanisms by which they would be fed by killing and pillaging innocent civilians in the DRC. Evidence led by the Prosecution would show that there was no minimum age for such child soldiers as the only qualification was the ability to carry a gun.

When forced into actual combat, the children were instructed to kill everyone who was from a specific tribe, the Lendu, including other children. The Prosecution, following earlier decisions of the Pre-Trial Chamber, has argued in the Thomas Lubanga Dyilo trial that the crime of conscripting or enlisting children will include not only forced conscripting or abduction, but also the crime of enlisting children. The latter crime will even include, according to both the Prosecution and the earlier Pre-Trial Chamber decision, children who would volunteer themselves out of fear or the urge to seek revenge or are volunteered by their families.

Such an interpretation of the crime involving children could have catalytic impacts on how children are regarded as potential combatants in many parts of the world, not only on the African continent. As the Prosecution has pointed out in the Thomas Lubanga Dyilo trial, there is no free will on the part of these children or their parents in the context of a violent struggle such as that in the Ituri Province of the DRC. The consent was brought about by the power of the gun rather than through free will or the law. The Thomas Lubanga Dyilo trial has revealed that there would be repercussions including death threats if a child refused to be a soldier, and in some cases family members would be killed and their property pillaged.

Moreover, the Pre-Trial Chamber, in confirming charges against Thomas Lubanga Dyilo, had determined that consent would not be a defense under Article 8 of the Rome Statute. The prohibition against the forced or voluntary conscription and enlisting of children under the age of 15 would be absolute under the Rome Statute with no exception, as was the intention of the drafters of the statute of the Court.

The OTP has reported that the pre-trial phase and the trial of Thomas Lubanga Dyilo have significantly raised awareness of the issue of child soldiers and the legal nature of the crime of conscription and enlisting in the DRC, while also assisting in the demobilization of child soldiers in the same country. While it is acknowledged by the ICC that recruitment of child soldiers has continued in the DRC, the awareness that such action, even where alleged perpetrators may assert the voluntary nature of any enlisting of such children, constitutes a serious international crime has reached the militia leaders who are major perpetrators of this crime. The same report claims that some former leaders are keen to let international observers know that they did not engage in such criminal activity involving children.[14]

There is a similar desire to focus on another rampant and terrifying international crime in the prosecution of Jean-Pierre Bemba. As discussed in Chapter 1, the arrest warrants were issued by the Pre-Trial Chamber on May 23, 2008, based on eight counts of crimes against humanity and war crimes involving rape, torture, outrages on personal dignity and pillaging.

On the following day, Bemba was arrested in Belgium and brought to The Hague. The charges based on the alternative modes of liability of co-perpetration under Article 25 of the Rome Statute (which was subsequently denied by the Pre-Trial Chamber[15]) and as a superior officer under Article 28 emphasized the scale and gravity of the sexual violence and rapes allegedly perpetrated against civilians by forces under Bemba's command in the CAR. The purpose behind such crimes seems to be to terrorize certain civilian populations into not supporting the rebels against the former President of the CAR, Ange-Félix Patassé, who has also been implicated in the same criminal activity. In what can only reinforce the importance of having prosecutions that focus on the increasing use of such sexual violence, rape and torture, the potential instigator of the horrors in the CAR, Patassé, announced he had the intention of standing as a candidate in the presidential elections in 2010, even though he may well be the next candidate to face the same charges as Bemba.[16]

On June 15, the Pre-Trial Chamber confirmed the charges against Bemba. It found that there were sufficient grounds to believe that he was potentially criminally responsible for five charges out of eight under Article 28 of the Rome Statute.[17]

The increasing use of systemic sexual violence, rape and sexual torture is one of the most horrifying aspects of mankind's inhumanity. The increasing mountain of evidence of sexual violence, rape and torture coming out of the trial of Bemba was some of the most distressing that this author had to witness while at the ICC. The nature of such evidence, too horrible to even describe in a text such as this, should be a call to action by the international community to marshal every effort and resource to prevent this most inhuman of criminal activity from becoming a widespread aspect of civil wars and conflicts around the world.

In these early years of the Court, it is evident that the Prosecutor is focusing the prosecutorial strategy on crimes committed against children and crimes involving sexual and gender violence. Given this focus, equal attention must be paid to how to protect the safety, both physical and psychological, of victims and witnesses in the investigation and prosecution of these crimes. Successful efforts in this regard may well also have a positive complementarity impact regarding how national authorities deal with such victims and witnesses in domestic trials.

An under-appreciated aspect of the positive complementarity of the work of the ICC is the outreach activities of the OTP and the Registry. The OTP has also asserted that its outreach operations have resulted in reconciliation between affected victim groups in the Ituri region of the DRC. Such visits by the Prosecutor and other ICC officials are conducive to helping consolidate peaceful cohabitation and reconciliation between

communities affected by the armed conflicts and violence in the Ituri province between 2002 and 2003.[18]

There is also growing evidence in the DRC that public investigations by
the ICC have acted as a catalyst for domestic courts to start prosecutions
and apply directly the Rome Statute in prosecutions for war crimes and
crimes against humanity, some under the provisions of Congolese law.
Field and interview research by William W. Burke-White concluded in 2005
that with the 'Prosecutor's September 2003 announcement that he would
closely follow the situation in the Congo, elements within the Congolese
government have responded by launching reforms of the national judiciary and establishing a Truth and Reconciliation Commission'.[19]

The same research has found that while at least one senior DRC official would prefer the primacy of national courts, in particular the DRC
Supreme Court, over the ICC, there is recognition that the underpaid and
politically weak top court would not be able to prosecute a major political leader. Despite this acknowledgement of the weakness of the DRC
courts, the effect of the ICC investigation has been to stoke a strong desire
by DRC officials to improve domestic judicial capacity even in the face of
serious resource constraints.[20] Some of this desire was motivated by some
of the senior DRC officials to avoid the ICC because they too might end
up in the cells of the Court in The Hague. Ironically, one of them, Jean
Pierre Bemba, was brought to The Hague, although his alleged criminal
liability stems from actions in the CAR.[21]

It is precisely because of the acknowledgement of self-referring countries, such as the DRC, that it may be unable to prosecute the top leaders
that the ICC has rightly focused on only those most responsible for the
most serious international crimes. It is also the reason why it is grossly
unfair to critique the Court for having a smaller number of trials in a
longer period of time than other criminal tribunals such as the ICTY and
the ICTR. Tribunals like the ICTY were not established as a court of last
resort and had primacy over national prosecutions. Therefore the ICTY
could establish a higher number of trials within a short time by focusing
on relatively low level perpetrators such as Dusko Tadič.[22] The mandate of
the Rome Statute requires the Prosecutor of the ICC to be guided by the
gravity of the alleged crimes. This resulted in the OTP adopting a policy
of focusing its efforts on the most serious crimes and on those who bear
the greatest responsibility for such crimes. As regards those deemed most
responsible, the policy of the OTP is to focus its prosecutorial strategy on
those at the highest levels of responsibility for the serious crimes, including
those who ordered, financed or organized the alleged crimes.

The determination of both gravity and those most responsible would
only be the result of a laborious and detailed evidentiary foundation

following an investigation into a situation. This does not mean impunity is granted to the other perpetrators. As the DRC and Kenya examples demonstrate, the onus is on the positive complementary jurisdiction of the countries involved to begin national prosecutions before competent and effective national tribunals.

Yet some of the OTP's critics, surprisingly William Burke-White himself, have claimed that the Prosecutor has moved away from a policy of what he terms 'proactive complementarity', instead focusing on direct prosecution of international crimes.[23] This author argues that instead of the OTP following a strategy of what he calls 'passive complementarity' the Prosecutor 'can and should encourage, and perhaps even assist national governments to prosecute crimes'.[24] This critic justifies his somewhat contradictory position by reference to his earlier research in the DRC by claiming that though the ICC had not intentionally sought to activate the Congolese domestic courts to try those lower down the hierarchy who had committed international crimes, the investigation had catalytic effects that could be expected to flow from an express policy of proactive complementarity. These effects included notable judicial reforms and actual prosecutions. Burke-White gives the example of military courts convicting one officer of war crimes and another of recruiting child soldiers. In another situation, forty-eight soldiers were convicted in the Equateur Province for rape and murder as crimes against humanity, while other verdicts and trials occurred in other DRC provinces.[25]

There is no evidence provided by Burke-White that the OTP and the Chief Prosecutor did not intend as a policy and strategy to have these catalytic impacts follow from the public investigations of the Court. The OTP claims that there was such a specific strategy that flowed from focusing primarily on those most responsible for the crimes. Perhaps the only difference is that the OTP had termed this approach to its mandate as 'positive complementarity' as opposed to 'proactive complementarity'.[26]

As regards the condition of gravity of the crimes, the OTP views factors such as the scale of the crimes, the nature and manner of commission of the crimes and the impact of these crimes. Such factors lead to viewing the first self-referrals by the DRC and Uganda to the ICC as the gravest admissible situations, even though to ill-informed critics of the Court it may have appeared that the Prosecutor was focusing only on Africa to begin the Court's first investigations. Some critics have pointed out that the Prosecutor could have used his *proprio motu* powers to start the DRC and Uganda investigations along with other non-African situations. What is ignored in such a criticism is that, given the relatively new status of the Court and its limited resources, the Prosecutor's strategy of welcoming self-referrals has greatly increased the likelihood of critical cooperation and on the ground support needed to carry out detailed investigations and prepare the necessary evidentiary basis for trial in the Pre-Trial Chambers.

The cooperation of the two countries' self-referrals was considered essential to have expeditious and focused cases that zeroed in on specific incidents that could satisfy the gravity requirement of the Rome Statute. For example, in Northern Uganda, the cooperation with the government led to the OTP selecting six incidents out of hundreds that were alleged to have occurred leading to the charging of Joseph Kony and the top LRA leaders with the most serious of international crimes based on incidents involving direct attacks on the civilian population, enlisting children as child soldiers and systemic rape and pillaging.

The OTP has admitted that there are situations where, given the complexity of local conflicts and politics, conflicting realities force the Prosecutor to concentrate on only one part of the alleged gravest crimes and the individuals most responsible. In the DRC, the Prosecutor had initially investigated many incidents giving rise to the range of the most serious international crimes. However, the OTP decided to focus its first case on one top leader who was alleged, among other crimes, to have enlisted and conscripted children aged under 15 and used them to actively participate in hostilities. That leader was Thomas Lubanga Dyilo who was under arrest for approximately a year in the DRC, but was close to being released. The Prosecutor felt compelled to charge him with the crime that had the most compelling evidentiary basis, namely the charges dealing with the conscription and enlisting of children as child soldiers.[27]

As discussed above, given the widespread use of child soldiers in this part of the DRC, the OTP also hoped that the decisions coming out of the pre-trial phase and the trial would act as a warning to other potential perpetrators about the absolute prohibition of such recruitment of children as child soldiers with no possibility of a defense of voluntary consent.[28]

2.   ALTERNATIVE JUSTICE MECHANISMS THAT MEET THE STANDARDS OF INTERNATIONAL CRIMINAL JUSTICE

There is a growing academic literature on the moral and philosophical foundations of international criminal justice which casts doubts on whether international criminal tribunals are the only mechanisms to serve the objectives of retribution, deterrence, expressivism/denunciation and restorative justice. Jurists such as Linda Keller[29] and Eric Blumenson[30] have produced detailed research into whether there are forms of alternative justice mechanisms (AJMs) that would permit the ICC to be open to and allow deferral of prosecutions on the basis that such mechanisms meet the objectives of international criminal justice. Keller in particular has compared the philosophical objectives of the international criminal justice to those proposed as alternatives to the ICC in the context of the Ugandan referral to the Court. In particular the possible future establishment of the Ugandan Truth Commission and the *Mato Oput* process were examined by Keller to determine whether they even came close to being regarded as sufficient alternative justice mechanisms to trigger the international positive complementary framework discussed above.

While agreeing with the need to examine the feasibility of such AJMs, the discussion and analysis in Chapter 3 and in this Chapter has concluded that there is little viability in the Ugandan AJMs being complementary to the jurisdiction of the ICC.

3. RETRIBUTION AND DETERRENCE AS OBJECTIVES OF THE ICC PROSECUTIONS AND ALTERNATIVE JUSTICE MECHANISMS

The Preamble to the Rome Statute refers to the moral and philosophical foundations of the Court when it states in the Preamble that 'the most serious crimes of concern to the international community as a whole must not go unpunished'. What is unique in the concept of retributive justice as applied to the ICC is that it requires a global form of retributive justice as the crimes that are within the jurisdiction of the Court are crimes against all humankind.

The Preamble also asserts that one of the aims of the Court is to put an end to impunity for the perpetrators of the most serious international crimes in order to contribute to the prevention of such crimes. This provision has been interpreted as meaning that deterrence as a fundamental principle of international criminal justice is a goal of the ICC. Deterrence as a principle of international criminal justice can refer either to specific deterrence relating to deterring future criminal actions of the accused or general deterrence that prevents others from committing similar crimes as the accused. For reasons discussed in Chapter 3, it is unlikely that there can be any potential specific deterrence of either ICC prosecution or AJM processes for messianic and grotesquely violent individuals like Joseph Kony. As will be discussed below, general deterrence of international crimes from ICC prosecutions or AJM processes is also highly debatable, at least along traditional deterrence theories. Deterrence theory also connotes the presence or threat of punishment. In addition, this theory of international criminal justice would require public knowledge of such actual or potential punishments.

In the context of the LRA atrocities in Northern Uganda, Keller offers a somewhat weak analysis of how the putative Ugandan truth commission and the *Mato Oput* process could offer some kind of deterrence value. Given the weakness of the latter process and the non-existence of the truth commission as described in Chapter 3, it is not surprising that Keller also concludes that the value of both ICC prosecutions and both types of Ugandan AJMs would fall short of providing real deterrence. As described in Chapter 3, the actions of Kony and the LRA have absolutely confirmed this conclusion. Their actions may also have confirmed the view of the former Chief Prosecutor for the ICTY, Justice Richard Goldstone, that deterrence should not be a goal of the ICC as international criminal tribunals could not in themselves accomplish the goals of deterrence.[31]

Many observers like Justice Goldstone question whether the consequentialist or utilitarian basis of deterrence should even be an appropriate practical or moral basis for determining the complementarity strategy of the ICC. Some jurists like Payam Akhavan[32] have argued that ICC prosecutions can have a deterrent effect, if not for leaders who are most responsible, then more likely some deterrent effect for subordinates. Others like Blumenson argue that the consequences of ICC prosecutions can be wide-ranging and unpredictable,[33] as illustrated in the case of Northern Uganda and Sudan. Such prosecutions have the potential to either aid reconciliation or increase the cycle of violence and vengeance. Much is dependent on the specifics of each ICC prosecution to make any predetermined outcome of the potential of deterrence value of such prosecutions. Blumenson also points out the epistemological conundrum whereby any cost-benefit analysis of the deterrence of ICC prosecutions is as elusive as they are crucial and contestable.[34] Even in domestic criminal jurisdictions, research has demonstrated that there is no certainty that past punishments and even the most severe potential punishments, including the death penalty, have produced any certainty of a deterrent effect. Therefore, there is much uncertainty that ICC prosecutions, at least in the short run, will have the type of deterrent effect that many supporters of the Court have hoped for.

Human Rights Watch has also asserted that, given the relatively recent development of international criminal justice, evidence of prosecutions acting as a deterrent should not be expected. However there is some indication that ICC prosecutions are having some lower level deterrent impacts in conflict zones such as Afghanistan, the DRC, Côte D'Ivoire and the Central African Republic. Examples include a rebel commander demobilizing child soldiers under his command after being made aware of the prosecution of Thomas Lubanga at the ICC, claiming he was not aware to conscript child soldiers was a crime.[35]

However, there is one variation of deterrence or, more appropriately, prevention as a principle of international criminal justice that the ICC can realistically assert and defend. This variation was the foundation of the analysis in Chapter 1 that linked the prevention of impunity with the emergence not only of the ICC, but also the previous international criminal tribunals and the lessons of history in the prevention of impunity.

This variation of deterrence or prevention can assert that ICC prosecutions can impact on the moral standing of those heads of state and leaders accused of the most universally reprehensible crimes against humanity: war crimes and genocide. The taint of such global pariah status could well act as a deterrent to other heads of state and leaders who wish to maintain their credibility and standing among their global peers. While such a pariah status is not the traditional form of actual or potential punishment underlying the deterrence principle, it does operate as a real world form of prevention.

One can reasonably speculate that the indictment of President Omar al-Bashir for the most serious of international crimes has had some deterrent impact on other African leaders, even while he demonstrates defiance against the Court and has rallied the African Union and the Arab League to his support. This writer has learned from confidential high level government sources that the deterrent impact of the prosecution of Charles Taylor in the Special Court for Sierra Leone and the indictment of al-Bashir by the ICC was partly the cause of the warring leaders in the post-election violence both in Kenya and more controversially in Zimbabwe forming coalition governments in an effort to avoid facing international criminal justice processes.

Other jurists have given another and perhaps a more realistic version of the deterrent impact of the ICC by asserting that the operations of the Court could lead to a new international moral culture whereby respect for the rule of law is heightened and a new global dynamic of accountability is established.[36]

Turning to the deontological basis of international criminal justice being rooted in the moral and philosophical principles of retributive justice, what must be emphasized is that ICC prosecutions must not be regarded as a form of global vengeance. The concept of retributive justice is a deontological principle that focuses not on the consequences of prosecuting or not prosecuting, but on the principle of 'just deserts'. This principle, as elaborated in its classical form by Immanuel Kant and modernized by leading present day academic jurists and moral philosophers, asserts that actions in themselves are right or wrong and do not depend on any outcomes of the actions.[37] The focus of this foundation of criminal justice is that perpetrators deserve to suffer prosecution and punishment in proportion to the crimes visited upon their victims who also deserve rectification of the crime.

Blumenson makes a distinction between what he calls 'strict retributivism' and 'victim-conscious retributivism' in order to promote the possibility of a deontological alternative to ICC prosecution in certain cases. The former would require ICC prosecution and punishment regardless of the consequences in terms of peaceful settlement of violent conflicts such as the atrocities of the LRA in Northern Uganda which have now spread to the DRC, Sudan and the CAR. Blumenson, among others, considers that this strict retributive principle may not be defensible regardless of the effects on third parties such as the Acholi people of Northern Uganda. Such an absolutist retributivist approach to ICC prosecutions, Blumenson argues, would ignore that justice is due both to the victim and the accused. This jurist advocates the alternative conception of retributive justice that treats the victim as an independent subject of justice. This approach of victim-conscious retributivism would argue that both society and the ICC would be treating victims unjustly in the aftermath of a crime by leaving them as outcasts and unrecognized as part of the social compact. Blumenson argues that not only Kant, but also other leading moral philosophers such as George Fletcher,[38] implicitly recognize this when they condemn society's failure to sanction crime as a form of complicity which includes the victims' blood on society's hands. This victim-focused form of retributive justice would then lead to other forms of punishment beyond the formal ICC prosecution process.[39]

The victim-focused form of retributive justice's paradigm is the South Africa Truth and Reconciliation Commission (SATRC), established in 1994 by the government of President Nelson Mandela. It is the exemplar of when there should be ICC deferral of prosecutions, if such a truth and reconciliation mechanism can avoid further massive bloodshed or tyranny that causes greater injustice to actual and potential victims. The SATRC is showcased as the pluralism paradigm that 'respects the diversity among states and conceptions of justice that a global institution such as the ICC would be wise to respect these differences to the fullest extent compatible with its mission'.[40]

Blumenson gives a detailed examination of how the SATRC, as a form of conditional amnesty, would both satisfy the pluralist imperative of a global institution like the ICC and respect the fundamental principles of a victim-focused retributive justice. This jurist gives a compelling and rich analysis of the moral and philosophical underpinnings of international criminal justice.

The SATRC was a compromise between the demands of blanket

amnesties from the former apartheid regime as a condition for giving up power and the demands of the African National Congress (ANC) for prosecution of the perpetrators of the most serious crimes. The crucial element of a peaceful transition to a multiracial democracy was the establishment of the SATRC which was empowered to grant amnesties only to those who agreed to give a full accounting and disclosure of their crimes during the apartheid regime. The amnesties would only be granted for those acts that were associated with political objectives and committed in the course of conflicts of the past. The eligibility for such amnesties was limited to those crimes with political objectives, and most amnesty requests were denied. Those who gave a full accounting of their crimes to the Commission would be relieved of personal criminal and civil liability for their crimes. Those who refused to give such full disclosure would still be at risk of criminal prosecution. The legislation that established the Commission also provided for the prospect of reparation for victims. The hearings of the SATRC were open to the pubic and were widely publicized by the electronic and print media.[41]

Blumenson differentiates this almost unique truth telling Commission that allowed for a peaceful transition in South Africa from the much criticized similar commissions in Chile, Haiti, Guatemala and other countries 'that had granted blanket amnesties to outgoing regimes in exchange for nothing'. He then argues that regardless of the consequentialist results of the SATRC, it fulfilled his victim-focused variation of retributive justice for the extreme crimes within its mandate. The arguments in this regard are as follows: first, the vast majority of black South Africans who were the victims of the apartheid regime supported the SATRC's policy of amnesty in exchange for truth. It allowed the revelation of many more disclosures amounting to admission of criminal guilt than would be possible under criminal prosecution. This resulted in widespread recognition among all South Africans of the scope of the criminal atrocities and finally permitted the condemnation of these crimes and the censure of institutional actors who were instigators or were complicit in these crimes. On these factors, the argument is that the SATRC was more capable and ultimately was more successful than any international criminal prosecution. The totality of amnesty applications, the great number of horror filled confessions and the 22,000 submissions from victims, families, subpoenaed witnesses and Commission hearings of institutional complicity led to the societal impact of the final report of the SATRC. The greatest impact was the report's ability to offer a comprehensive picture of individual and institutional instigation of and complicity in the crime against humanity called apartheid. There is acknowledgement that the detailed research of other experts has pointed out the several flaws in the SATRC process and its omissions.

However, the counter-argument is the countervailing uncertainty whether actual criminal prosecutions would have rectified these flaws and omissions. The aspect of the SATRC that overcomes the counterweight of the flaws and omissions is the focus on the public condemnations of the crimes and the reaffirmation of the rights of the victims. Of particular importance is the right of victims to confront their criminal oppressors, even if the process did not impose criminal penalties on the perpetrators.[42]

Ultimately supporters of the SATRC process like Blumenson would advise that global institutions such as the ICC should consider such truth and reconciliation bodies with similar victim-focused retributive justice features as legitimate complementary processes. At minimum it could be argued that ICC deferral of prosecutions should be considered, if not for those most responsible for serious international crimes, at least for those lower down the hierarchy of criminality. Such an approach presents a far more acceptable alternative to ICC prosecution for such subordinates in rebel militias or national armies who have committed serious crimes than the totally unrealistic *Mato Oput* process or truth and reconciliation commissions that offer blanket amnesties with little impact on victim affirmation or public condemnation of such crimes.

Human Rights Watch is decidedly less enthusiastic about the SATRC. It claims that the Commission hails from a different era and that it would be regarded as a step backwards by victims whose expectations have changed due to the greater demands for accountability today, in part due to the evolution of international criminal law. In addition, this analysis claims that once the fear of prosecution died after high-ranking officials were acquitted, the number of amnesty seekers diminished along with the effectiveness of the Commission. Likewise according to Human Rights Watch, there was not a coherent program of prosecution for those denied amnesty or who had failed to apply for it. These failings continue to cause opposition by victims who, as recently as March, 2009, have sought to prevent formal pardons for politically motivated crimes without hearing from the victims and other relevant persons.[43]

This analysis of the SATRC as an appropriate alternative to ICC prosecution, while convincing from a moral and philosophical perspective, misses one reason why the Commission was a success in the peaceful transition to a multiracial democracy and a viable alternative to criminal prosecutions. The leaders of the last apartheid regime led by Prime Minister de Klerk and his former adversary Nelson Mandela first made the fundamental and critical decision to establish a sustainable new social contract between former bitter adversaries to avoid what was becoming over almost three decades an ungovernable society and end the pariah status of this major African nation.

Without such a genuine desire for a peaceful and sustainable social contract, realistically there can be little prospect of a successful alternative justice mechanism that respects the victim-focused retributive justice principles described by Blumenson. This notion of a social contract between two adversary groups usually engaged in violent armed conflict can be regarded as an adaptation of the concept first proposed by French philosopher Jean Jacques Rousseau.[44] The classical theory is focused on individuals joining together into civil society through the social contract and relinquishing whatever rights they had in the state of nature. As a consequence, they can preserve social order and remain free. Rousseau argued that the submission by individuals to the general will of the people is the best guarantee against subjugation to the will of others and to ensure that the rule of law is the ultimate sovereign. The adaptation of Rousseau's social contract theory proposed here acknowledges and avoids the pitfalls of this political philosophy identified by other major thinkers relating to the potential support to authoritarian regimes and intolerance of diversity stemming from the idea of the general will.

In the context of violent armed struggle between governments and rebel militias or other groups, a South African-type social contract requires the genuine consent by leaders of such warring entities to end the actions that have resulted in potential serious international crimes and submit themselves and their followers to the rule of law. Any social contract that would follow must include accounting for such crimes, reconciliation and the reparations for victims. Only then would a South African-type alternative justice mechanism represent the general will of all the people in the society torn apart by violence and conflict. The general will would be focused on the fight against impunity under the rule of law.

Nothing exemplifies the desire for such a sustainable peaceful social contract more than the words that Nelson Mandela uttered at his inauguration:[45]

The time for the healing of the wounds has come. The moment to bridge the chasms that divide us has come. The time to build is upon us.

We have, at last, achieved our political emancipation. We pledge ourselves to liberate all our people from the continuing bondage of poverty, deprivation, suffering, gender and other discrimination. We succeeded to take our last steps to freedom in conditions of relative peace. We commit ourselves to the construction of a complete, just and lasting peace.

We have triumphed in the effort to implant hope in the breasts of the millions of our people. We enter into a covenant that we shall build the society in which all South Africans, both black and white, will be able to walk tall, without any fear in their hearts, assured of their inalienable right to human dignity – a rainbow nation at peace with itself and the world.

We must therefore act together as a united people, for national reconciliation, for nation building, for the birth of a new world. . . Never, never and never again shall it be that this beautiful land will again experience the oppression of one by another and suffer the indignity of being the skunk of the world.

These sentiments were not as strongly replicated by the head of the apartheid regime, President de Klerk. He was motivated more by recognition that minority rule would make the country ungovernable and that there would not be any possible consent to white rule by the ANC leadership. Given these circumstances de Klerk realized that there was an urgent need for a new covenant, to use the words of Nelson Mandela.[46]

The desire for such a social contract underlies the relative success of the SATRC in comparison with other less effective AJMs around the world in the aftermath of conflict. There is certainly no equivalent possible social contract between the government and the LRA underlying any possible truth and reconciliation commission or the *Mato Oput* process in Uganda.

Sadly, for all the reasons discussed in Chapter 2, there is very little prospect of a similar genuine social contract between the Sudanese government, led by an indicted President, and the fractured rebel groups in Darfur that would allow alternative justice mechanisms to trump ICC prosecutions.

Those who advocate such AJMs as an alternative to ICC prosecution must look at the broader socio-political framework to fully understand their feasibility and potential for eventual successful outcomes. If a South African social contract framework exists, then there are compelling moral, philosophical and complementarity imperatives that could allow the ICC to defer to AJMs such as the South African Commission as least for subordinates in the hierarchy of criminal liability.

Human Rights Watch has also pointed out that the negative consequences, such as renewed instability, arising out of pressing for accountability often do not come to pass. For example, the peace agreements and ceasefires in the DRC did not include amnesty provisions for the most serious of international crimes, despite the fear of many that this would result in the collapse of the negotiations. Between 2002 and 2008 the DRC rebels had proposed broad amnesties without success, and did not imperil the peace talks.[47]

4. EXPRESSIVISM/DENUNCIATION AND RESTORATIVE JUSTICE AS OBJECTIVES OF THE ICC PROSECUTIONS AND ALTERNATIVE JUSTICE MECHANISMS

A lesser known basis for ICC prosecutions and AJM processes is what is known as expressivism or denunciation. The focus of this moral and philosophical principle of criminal justice is the message of affirmation of society's values that criminal prosecution sends from an authoritative societal or governmental institution. This principle is not, strictly speaking, an aspect of retributive justice which requires no societal messaging. Expressivism or denunciation focuses on the message of moral condemnation that results from prosecution and punishment. While ICC prosecutions and punishments can result in global moral condemnation messaging, Keller worries that the expressive value of such prosecutions would decrease in value if impunity continued in a specific situation.[48]

A counter-argument would take the form that even in a situation where an ICC prosecution is obstructed due to the failure of authorities to fulfill legal obligations to execute arrest warrants, as in the case of the Sudanese officials discussed in Chapter 2, there is still the possibility of a global message of moral condemnation for the failure to face justice, at least among the States Parties to the ICC.

Keller asserts that the *Mato Oput* process and the Ugandan truth commission that failed to materialize could possibly fulfill the expressivism or denunciatory basis of international criminal justice and so permit deferral of any ICC prosecution.[49] As discussed throughout this work, given the character and track record of Kony and the LRA, this conclusion was too unrealistic.

Finally as regards the restorative justice principle as the basis for international criminal justice, the Rome Statute and the policies of the ICC fully incorporate this principle in many provisions, policies and practices on victim participation and reparations. The present case law has seen a very substantial number of victims seeking to be actively involved both as witnesses and as active participants from the investigation stage through to Pre-Trial Chamber hearing and even on appeal.

While all aspects of ICC proceedings can be infused with the restorative justice principle, it is certainly possible that AJMs can also satisfy the imperatives of this principle of international criminal justice. Restorative justice is also fulfilled by truth telling and reporting on the individual and institutional causes of the conflict and the international crimes while giving victims the full rights of participation and to reparations. Such AJMs can accomplish the restoration of society from the harms arising out of the atrocities of international crimes while giving rise to the necessary reforms. Here again Keller offers the *Mato Oput* process and the potential Ugandan truth commission as possible AJM alternatives to ICC prosecutions.[50]

Since these conclusions were reached, events have demonstrated that the *Mato Oput* process was never a realistic option for a peaceful reconciliation with Kony and the LRA. They were waging war even as they talked peace at Juba, while the fact that the Ugandan truth commission never materialized, demonstrated that there was never the slightest trace of a potential social contract between the Ugandan government and its rebel opponents.

5. THE INTERNATIONAL CRIMINAL JUSTICE DUTY TO PROSECUTE OR EXTRADITE AND THE EVOLUTION OF THE PRINCIPLE OF UNIVERSAL JURISDICTION

On February 19, 2009, an international court case of historical significance in the global fight against impunity commenced before the International Court of Justice at the Peace Palace in The Hague. In the case, Belgium, the Applicant State, had instituted proceedings against the Respondent State of Senegal under the compulsory jurisdiction of the Court which both states had accepted. The case was also commenced under the dispute settlement provisions of the U.N. Convention against Torture. The case was brought on the grounds that the government of the latter state had failed to comply with what Belgium asserted was its international legal obligation to prosecute the former President of Chad, Hissène Habré, or, in the case of failure to prosecute, to extradite him to Belgium for the purposes of criminal proceedings there. The fundamental issue to be determined by the ICJ is whether, under multilateral conventions and customary international law, there is a duty to either prosecute the most serious international crimes or extradite to a jurisdiction that will seek accountability for such crimes. The sources of this duty have been detailed elsewhere in the most important conventions of the past century, including the Genocide Convention, the Convention against Torture, the Geneva Convention (IV) and the decisions of domestic, regional and international courts and commissions.[51]

In addition, Belgium had also asked for provisional measures in order to protect its rights pending the Court's Judgment on the merits regarding safeguarding the presence of Habré in the territory of Senegal where he had been living in exile since 1990. Given the possibility of Senegal lifting the house arrest imposed on Habré, Belgium asked for provisional measures requiring the Respondent to take 'all the steps within its power to keep Mr. H. Habré under the control and surveillance of the judicial authorities of Senegal so that the rules of international law with which Belgium requests compliance may be correctly applied'. Subsequently, on May 28, 2009, the ICJ denied the request for provisional measures, ruling that Belgium had not proved that irreparable prejudice would accrue to its rights under international law before the Court rendered its final decision.

Acting under the principle of universal jurisdiction, in 2001, a Belgian national of Chadian origin and Chadian nationals, under a Belgian statute that gave its courts universal jurisdiction over human rights offenses such as genocide, crimes against humanity, and war crimes, filed similar complaints in the Belgian courts against Habré alleging torture and crimes against humanity. Belgian authorities had issued numerous writs for judicial investigations to Senegal and had issued an arrest warrant for Habré in 2005 which was ignored by the Senegalese courts or dismissed for lack of jurisdiction ruling that they had no jurisdiction regarding an extradition request against a former Head of State. This ruling was not unexpected as a previous Senegalese court had ruled in 2000 that it had no competence to pursue charges over extraterritorial crimes committed by foreigners. In March of 2006, the U.N. Committee Against Torture concluded that Senegal had violated the Convention that the Treaty Body oversees by failing to prosecute or extradite Habré. In 2006, the African Union itself had urged Senegal to prosecute Habré on behalf of Africa.

While Senegal had amended its penal code in 2007 to include the universal jurisdiction offence of genocide, war crimes and crimes against humanity, its authorities claimed it did not have the financial and other resources to bring Habré to trial. Belgium contends in the ICJ that Senegal violated its obligations under the U.N. Convention against Torture for its failure to prosecute or extradite. In addition it argued that under customary international law 'Senegal's failure to prosecute Mr. H. Habré, or to extradite him to Belgium to answer for the crimes against humanity which are alleged against him, violates the general obligation to punish crimes against international humanitarian law which is to be found in numerous texts of derived law (institutional acts of international organizations) and treaty law'.[52]

The details of the allegations against Habré are reminiscent of the alleged crimes committed by al-Bashir in Sudan. Reed Brody describes how Habré was brought to power in a coup against the then government of Goukouni Wedeye in 1982 with the help of France and the United States. Habré's regime started a violent campaign against certain ethnic groups in both the north and the south of the country. These included the

Sara, the Hadjerai and the Zaghawa, the last group being also the target of the al-Bashir regime in Darfur. Habré is accused of ordering the arrest, torture and killing of members of these groups when he perceived they were a threat to his government. Before being disbanded by the present incumbent, Idriss Deby, Habré's Presidential Guard is alleged to have killed more than 300 political detainees at a secret prison in the President's headquarters in the capital, N'Djamena. While the number of victims is not known, a Truth Commission established by the new government of Idriss Deby has claimed the victims of Habré's regime could go into the tens of thousands who were killed during large scale massacres, political murders and systemic torture.[53]

The basis of the attempts to prosecute Habré both in Senegal and Belgium was the international criminal law principle of universal jurisdiction. Simply defined, universal jurisdiction permits any national court to prosecute alleged offenders for serious international crimes in circumstances where the prosecuting court lacks the traditional jurisdictional nexus with either the crimes, the offenders or the victims.[54]

The overall positive and negative aspects of this emerging norm of customary international law have been examined in detail elsewhere in the literature.[55] The focus of the analysis here in the context of the ICC and the peace and justice challenges will examine the practical opportunities and obstacles for universal jurisdiction to act as a final aspect of positive international complementarity for the Court.

There is a compelling argument to be made that universal jurisdiction can become a critical mechanism to assist the ICC in the global fight against impunity. When states prosecute under the principle of universal jurisdiction they are acting as partners with the Court and agents of the international community to ensure that the most serious of international crimes do not go unpunished. The evolution of international criminal law and the work of international criminal tribunals can have a major impact on domestic jurisprudence and law dealing with those most responsible for crimes anywhere in the world. The prosecution in Britain of General Pinochet and the rulings of the House of Lords, which have been discussed extensively elsewhere,[56] although ultimately unsuccessful, triggered other nations like Belgium, Spain and Switzerland to exercise universal jurisdiction against individuals involved in the Rwanda genocide and against the military leaders during Argentina's dirty war. Ultimately these examples of universal jurisdiction prosecutions in Europe led to the Chilean courts overcoming domestic constitutional barriers and immunities to start prosecutions against the former leader of the country and to Argentina successfully prosecuting the former military and police officials. While Pinochet may have died without being convicted for serious international crimes, his infamous legacy demonstrates the catalytic impact of combating impunity with the weapon of universal jurisdiction.

However, the most effective prosecutions under the principle of universal jurisdiction will only occur where states have effectively implemented the principle in domestic legislation as part of their obligation to implement the Rome Statute as States Parties. In the case of non-member states, the best scenario for universal jurisdiction is for the incorporation in domestic legislation of the provisions and procedures similar to those in the Rome Statute relating to the most serious international crimes.

In addition, there should also be judicial and prosecutorial mutual legal cooperation model agreements developed by the international community for investigation and prosecution of serious international crimes. There are precedents for such cooperation in other areas of law regarding the combating of international criminal activity by member states of the U.N. and other international and regional organizations such as the European Union and Interpol. There is growing evidence that even with states predisposed to exercise universal jurisdiction, there is a lack of political and prosecutorial will to start investigations. In addition, the obstacles in terms of investigative procedures relating to evidence gathering and challenges to effect extradition are serious impediments to the exercise of universal jurisdiction becoming complementary to the ICC prosecutions.

Amnesty International has documented the failings of the international community in this regard. While the Amnesty research has found that almost two-thirds of all states have some forms of legislative frameworks to exercise universal jurisdiction, many of these frameworks are seriously flawed relating to the crimes included and their definitions and the inclusion of defenses which undermine the application of universal jurisdiction.[57] Amnesty has correctly pointed out that the best way to remedy these defects is for states to amend their criminal laws and procedures to effectively implement the Rome Statute of the ICC. This would include incorporating the provisions relating to the definition, defenses and procedures contained in the Rome Statute as the basis for the exercise of universal jurisdiction leading to a global uniformity of prosecutorial practices and hopefully jurisprudence in the fight against impunity.[58]

The literature has also documented the growing challenges to universal jurisdiction being a complementary mechanism to the ICC, not only in the area of deficient legislative frameworks and prosecutorial obstacles, but also due to the growing backlash, much of it instigated by the U.S. under the former administration of President George W. Bush.

As a result of very high profile but strategically disastrous cases launched in Belgium, Germany and Spain, among other jurisdictions, against incumbent and former heads of state and other high level officials such as defense and foreign ministers, national courts have narrowed the exercise of universal jurisdiction, in some cases improperly using legal concepts such as sovereign immunity and other defenses. Proceedings initiated in Belgium, Germany and Spain have included the attempt to exercise universal jurisdiction against figures such as George W. Bush, Donald Rumsfeld and Israeli Prime Minister Ariel Sharon.

The political and legal backlash that followed resulted in states such as Belgium and Spain being pressured into weakening their legislation authorizing the exercise of universal jurisdiction. This was strategically disastrous for universal jurisdiction, given that such high profile actions had very little chance of success and never even led to formal investigations. The deleterious impact resulted in less political and prosecutorial will to start even compelling cases, while the U.S. Congress, American and other global media outlets and even respected academics joined the backlash and began to argue for limiting the scope of the principle against incumbent heads of state and high officials of foreign states in national courts.[59]

This academic backlash was supported by the decision of the ICJ in the *Congo v. Belgium* ruling that limited Belgium's ability to exercise universal jurisdiction in national courts against an incumbent foreign minister under international law.[60] Adding to the backlash has been one of the most influential jurists in international criminal law, Antonio Cassese, who first argued as an academic that universal jurisdiction should be limited to situations where the accused is present in the territory of the prosecuting state.[61] Subsequently, as head of the U.N. Commission of Inquiry on Darfur, Professor Cassese proclaimed that not only should the accused be present in the prosecuting state, but there must first be an inquiry as to whether the state where the crimes were committed and the state of the accused's nationality were willing to institute proceedings and request extradition.[62]

In Spain, the backlash has been against the crusading Judge, Baltasar Garzon, who had triggered the Pinochet rulings in the U.K. House of Lords[63] by seeking a warrant for the arrest of the former Chilean dictator. As a judge of the Audiencia National Court of Spain which had been given extensive leeway to exercise jurisdiction by the Spanish Constitutional Court, Justice Garzon along with his National Court fellow justices have attempted high profile universal jurisdiction investigations. These investigations have targeted six advisors of George W. Bush for establishing the legal basis for torture, along with former Vice President Dick Cheney and former Secretary of State Condoleezza Rice. Judge Garzon's colleagues have focused on investigating high profile Chinese officials for systematic attacks on the people of Tibet and Israeli politicians and military officials for actions in the military incursion in Gaza. Political pressure from the U.S. and other states against these high profile, but strategically unwise, exercises of universal jurisdiction has led the Spanish government of President Zapatero and the Spanish Parliament to initiate legislation to severely limit the exercise of universal jurisdiction. The legislation would limit such jurisdiction to situations where the victims were Spanish or there was some connection to Spain before any exercise of jurisdiction could proceed and that no national court had taken up the case.

Given the mounting backlash, even in countries committed to the global fight against impunity which are also strong supporters of the ICC, there is a need for a more strategically wise approach to universal jurisdiction. One approach that would assist the positive international complementarity approach of the ICC is for the exercise of jurisdiction by national prosecutors to not focus on accused who, while not the top leaders, have controlled the apparatus of the state or militia groups. Instead the focus should be on lower level subordinates who have been instrumental in the criminal strategy being carried out.[64]

Such a legal strategy for universal jurisdiction would counter arguments that the exercise of universal jurisdiction is a form of political justice carried out against foreign adversaries or western justice imposed on other cultures or is overburdening already overstretched courts. Such an approach would also avoid the claims to immunity, especially given the ruling by the ICJ in the *Congo v. Belgium* decision.[65]

Such a strategic approach to the exercise of universal jurisdiction would tie in with the present prosecutorial strategy of the Prosecutor of the ICC and cases before the Court. It is clear that the present prosecutorial strategy of the Prosecutor is to focus on the top leadership who controlled the apparatus of the state, as in the case of al-Bashir, or those who headed the key militia groups involved in the commission of serious crimes such as Thomas Lubanga Dyilo, Bemba and the leadership of the LRA.

The Canadian justice system has provided a solitary but finally good example of the strategic use of universal jurisdiction implemented under legislation that entrenched the country's obligations under the Rome Statute of the ICC. On May 22, 2009, Canada's first war crimes trial under the 2000 Crimes Against Humanity and War Crimes Act[66] that implemented the Rome Statute and permitted the prosecution of international crimes in Canada ended with a conviction in a Quebec court of Désiré Munyaneza, a Rwandan refugee claimant. He was accused of being one of the key co-ordinators and participants in the extermination of the Hutus through mass murder, sexual violence and psychological terror during the 1994 genocide in Rwanda. Munyaneza was charged with two counts of genocide, two counts of crimes against humanity and three counts of war crimes. In one of the most graphic of criminal judgments, Justice Denis described how Munyaneza intentionally killed hundreds of Tutsi, 400 of whom had sought refuge in a church, seriously wounded others, sexually assaulted many Tutsi women, beat to death children trapped in sacks and looted homes and businesses. In contrast to the prosecutions by the ICC Prosecutor against the militia leaders in the DRC, Uganda and the Central African Republic, Justice Denis pointed out that Munyaneza could have refused to participate or refrained from participating in the atrocities, but instead chose to be one of its driving forces.

The decision to convict Munyaneza by Superior Court Justice André Denis in a 350 page judgment is regarded as a historic event, not only for Canada but also for the global fight against impunity.[67] The Canadian justice system demonstrated how it was implementing the proactive international complementarity burden of the ICC by the two year long trial, one of the most complex war crimes trials in Canadian history. The hearing was conducted through five countries, heard sixty-six witnesses from both the prosecution and the defense and had a total cost of four million dollars. Rwanda has expressed its approval of the trial and conviction of Munyaneza but it has also asked Canada to extradite others involved in the genocide who have sought refugee status in Canada.[68]

The goal of prosecutions and convictions similar to the Munyaneza trial would be to present a warning to other actual and potential international criminals who are leading implementers of atrocities that they cannot ensure their impunity by seeking refuge in other countries once they are no longer safe in their own country. The worldwide publicity given to the trial and conviction of Munyaneza in Canada may well have assisted in promoting the global fight against impunity in this regard.

Some of the hundreds of such Rwandan refugee claimants and potential international criminals from other countries are being investigated by officials from the Canadian Department of Justice, the national police force, the RCMP and other agencies of the federal government, with the cooperation of the relevant Rwandan officials. Even from a relatively wealthy country like Canada, the emerging duty to prosecute or extradite has proved extremely burdensome in terms of financial and human resources. This situation has led to an emphasis on deportations back to the country of origin by revocation of unlawfully obtained citizenship, which amounts to extradition on the cheap without the attendant due process safeguards against the potential for torture or the death penalty.[69] Further prosecutions of alleged war criminals in Canada may depend on the outcome of any appeal in the Munyaneza conviction and could well set a precedent for other western jurisdictions that are genuine about implementing the positive international complementarity under the Rome Statute of the ICC.

On October 29, 2009, Munyaneza was sentenced to life in prison with no chance of parole for twenty-five years by Mr. Justice André Denis of the Quebec Superior Court. This is the most severe penalty under Canadian law that is usually handed down for those convicted of the most heinous murders in Canada.

The task facing even a relatively wealthy country like Canada is formidable and, despite the Munyaneza conviction, it could be argued that the country has not carried its weight in the positive international complementarity regime. The number of permanent resident visa cases being investigated for possible war crimes by the Canadian War Crimes Program in the fiscal year 2006–2007 was revealed to be 146. But during the same period, a total of 361 persons were prevented from coming to Canada due to possible involvement in war crimes or crimes against humanity. In addition the inventory of refugee cases still under investigation on March 31, 2007 doubled from 346, a year earlier, to 691 refugee claimant cases that could involve war crimes or crimes against humanity.[70] Given these increasing numbers, Canada, and perhaps other western nations, are being targeted as safe havens for those who have committed the most serious crimes. The single conviction of Munyaneza could be hiding the impunity iceberg under the immigration and refugees system of Canada and other western nations.

Other countries have successfully exercised universal jurisdiction, some without the implementing legislation based on the Rome Statute. Investigations and prosecutions have taken place in some thirteen European countries with a small, but significant number of convictions. In the U.S., the son of former President Charles Taylor was also convicted on charges of torture,[71] while progress is occurring in similar trials in Latin America, Asia, Eastern Europe and Africa, with some of the trials ending in convictions.[72] There is a growing consensus that there should be a coordinated legal strategy for the exercise of universal jurisdiction by national jurisdictions that wish to develop a globally coherent strategy on the fight against impunity.

Experts and leading human rights advocates such as Amnesty International suggest that one approach to such a coordinated strategy would be for legal counsel and NGOs representing and advocating on behalf of victims of serious international crimes to agree on a set of guidelines. These guidelines would include a risk assessment that would focus on whether filing a particular action on the basis of universal jurisdiction would set back the development of the law for other victims of international crimes and also not compensate for any benefits to the victim behind any particular planned action. There have also been attempts by NGOs and legal counsel to develop good practice manuals and checklists to assist in efforts to exercise universal jurisdiction more effectively. There have been parallel efforts at the inter-governmental level in the European Union and Interpol to get more coordination between police and prosecutors in this area that has led to a focus on lower level individuals suspected of serious international crimes. These include those who are no longer in any type of official function so that there is no immunity claim or that their former governments have been replaced.[73]

However, the difficulties in devising such a global legal strategy are not to be underestimated. There may be victims, legal counsel and even prosecutors who are determined to use the exercise of universal jurisdiction to shine the political spotlight on political and military leaders who are regarded as ultimately responsible for serious international crimes and therefore should be the subject of a 'shaming' process in the court of public opinion, even if the legal action stands little chance of success. This will no doubt continue and focus on present or former leaders of major world powers who have not become States Parties to the Rome Statute of the ICC, such as China, Russia and the United States.

The representation of these same world powers in the U.N. Security Council will also negate any possibility of referral of any allegations of serious international crimes to the ICC by the same body in which they have veto powers. These same world powers have been the source of pressure on countries such as Belgium and Spain to narrow their domestic legislation that permits the exercise of universal jurisdiction. There is little doubt that this trend will continue if other countries enact legislation that permits the exercise of universal jurisdiction without substantial connection of the accused or the crime to the prosecuting jurisdiction. Inevitably this potential or actual impunity of present and former leaders of major powers and even those of their closest client states will raise the allegation of hypocrisy and double standards in the global fight against impunity. There is no easy response to this legitimate critique.

There is only the hope that as the proactive international complementarity strategy of the ICC becomes successful in other states and the effective exercise of universal jurisdiction along with the emerging duty to extradite or prosecute engenders a global denunciatory impact in the international community, there will be a 'preventative effect' even on the leaders of the major world powers. We may be seeing the first signs of this 'preventative effect' in the decision by China, Russia and the United States not to veto the referral of the situation in Darfur to the ICC. Even though Sudan is a client state of China, which has invested heavily in the energy sector in that country and is a major arms supplier, as discussed in Chapter 2, Chinese leaders may have felt there were limits to condoning and supporting the worst humanitarian crisis in the world at the time of the passing of U.N.

Security Council Resolution 1593 and therefore quietly abstained. Within their own borders, the major world powers are attempting to hide their worst human rights abuses behind the fight against terrorism in the court of international public opinion.[74] The geopolitical impact of a substantial part of the international community not accepting this justification may well be the next very small step in the 'preventative effect' of the positive international complementarity of the ICC and its supporters in the international community.

In conclusion, the international community should not be looking at the ICC in isolation as regards the peace and justice challenge. The Court should be viewed as a catalyst in the global fight against impunity that promotes peace with justice throughout the world. The catalytic effect comes from its own positive complementary strategy outlined above, but reinforced by the international community acting as agents for global peace with justice by developing the prosecute or extradite international law norms and effectively implementing universal jurisdiction frameworks within national justice systems.

The development of this positive international complementarity has and will face considerable legal challenges, human and financial shortfalls and above all political backlash which could well threaten the whole enterprise. However, there is perpetual hope that the thirst for peace with justice in the human spirit will overcome any obstacles placed before it.

NOTES

1. The Office of the Prosecutor (OTP), 'Report on the activities performed during the second three years (June 2006–June 2009)' The International Criminal Court, The Hague (12 September 2006).
2. *Ibid.*
3. Andrew Cawthorne, 'Kenya seeks to present court plan by September – If Kenya fails to create tribunal, ICC will step in' *Reuters* (7 July 2009) located at the following url: http://www.alertnet.org/thenews/newsdesk/L7185415.htm.
4. See 'Annan acts on Poll Suspects' *BBC Report* (9 July 2009) available at the following url: http://news.bbc.co.uk/2/hi/africa/8142263.stm.
5. See the ICC announcement on the decision to investigate and prosecute those most responsible for the post-election violence, ICC Press Release, 'ICC Prosecutor Supports Three-Pronged Approach to Justice in Kenya' (30 September 2009) ICC-OTP-20090930-PR456 available at the following url: http://www.icc-cpi.int/NR/exeres/7766129C-79D4-447A-80AE-283E86DC58CD.htm.
6. See the BBC Report entitled 'Kenya backs poll violence trials' *BBC News* (2 October 2009) available at the following url: http://news.bbc.co.uk/2/hi/8286733.stm.
7. OTP Report, *supra* note 1.
8. See the letter of the Prosecutor to the Colombian Government at the site of the Colombia Support Network, 'The international criminal court has requested information from the Uribe Government' (18 August 2008) available at the following url:

http://www.colombiasupport.net/news/2008/08/international-criminal-court-has.html (accessed 15 June 2009).

9. See 'Militias march again' *The Economist* (29 October 2009) at 45–46, also located at the following url: http://www.economist.com/world/americas/displaystory.cfm?story_id=14744897.

10. For a documentary record of the *proprio motu* investigation by the Prosecutor and its impacts at the highest levels of the Colombian government see 'The Reckoning', a documentary film by Skylight Pictures available through the following website: http://skylightpictures.com/site/film_detail/the_reckoning/ (accessed 15 June 2009).

11. OTP Report, *supra* note 1.

12. *Ibid.*

13. *Ibid.*

14. *Ibid.*

15. See the decision of the Pre-Trial Chamber in *The Prosecutor v. Jean-Pierre Bemba Gombo,* ICC-01/05-01/08, Decision Adjourning the Hearing pursuant to Article 61(7)(c)(ii) of the Rome Statute (3 March 2009) (International Criminal Court, Pre-Trial Chamber) located at the following url: http://www2.icc-cpi.int/iccdocs/doc/doc638848.pdf.

16. Melanie Gouby, 'Central African Republic: Patassé Reveals Presidency Bid' *Institute for War and Peace Reporting* (15 June 2009) situated at allAfrica.com at the following url: http://allafrica.com/stories/200906150098.html.

17. See the full decision of the Pre-Trial Chamber in *The Prosecutor v. Jean-Pierre Bemba Gombo,* ICC-01/05-01/08, Decision Pursuant to Article 61(7)(a) and (b) of the Rome Statute on the Charges of the Prosecutor Against Jean-Pierre Bemba Gombo (15 June 2009) (International Criminal Court, Pre-Trial Chamber) located at the following url: http://www.icc-cpi.int/iccdocs/doc/doc699541.pdf.

18. OTP Report, *supra* note 1.

19. William W. Burke-White, 'Complementarity in Practice: The International Criminal Court as Part of a System of Multi-level Global Governance in the Democratic Republic of Congo' (2005) 18 *Leiden J. Int'l L.* 557 at 570.

20. *Ibid.* at 571.

21. *Ibid.* at 569.

22. For the details of the prosecution and the ultimate disposition of this early prosecution of the ICTY see Michael P. Scharf, *Balkan Justice: The Story Behind the First International War Crimes Trial since Nuremberg* (Carolina Academic Press, 1997). The final disposition of the case was handed down in *The Prosecutor v. Dusko Tadič,* IT-94-1-A, Judgment on Appeal (15 July 1999) (International Criminal Tribunal for the Former Yugoslavia, Appeals Chamber).

23. William W. Burke-White, 'Proactive Complementarity: The International Criminal Court and National Courts in the Rome System of International Justice' (2008) 49:1 *Harv. Int'l L. J.* 53 at 55.

24. *Ibid.* at 56.

25. *Ibid.* at 106.

26. OTP Report, *supra* note 1.

27. *Ibid.*

28. *Ibid.*

29. Linda M. Keller, 'Achieving Peace with Justice: The International Criminal Court and Ugandan Alternative Justice Mechanisms' (2008) 23: 2 *Conn. J. Int'l Law* 209.

30. Eric Blumenson, 'The Challenge of a Global Standard of Justice: Peace, Pluralism and Punishment at the International Criminal Court' (2006) 44 *Colum. J. Transnat'l L.* 801.

31. See Richard J. Goldstone & Nicole Fritz, '"In the Interests of Justice" and Independent Referral: The ICC Prosecutor's Unprecedented Powers' (2000) 13 *Leiden J. Int'l L.* 655 at 659.

32. Payam Akhavan, 'Beyond Impunity: Can International Criminal Justice Prevent Future Atrocities?' (2001) 95 *A.J.I.L.* 7 at 9–13.
33. Blumenson, *supra* note 30 at 825.
34. *Ibid.* at 827.
35. See 'Selling Justice Short, Why Accountability Matters for Peace' *Human Rights Watch* (July 2009) at 123–127.
36. Blumenson *supra* note 30 at 828. See also Neil J. Kritz, 'Coming to Terms with Atrocities: A Review of Accountability Mechanisms for Mass Violations of Human Rights' (1996) 59:4 *Law & Contemporary Problems* 127 at 128; Aryeh Neier, *War Crimes: Brutality, Genocide Terror and the Struggle for Justice* (Times Books, 1998) at 103–104.
37. See Immanuel Kant, *The Metaphysics of Morals* (Cambridge University Press, 1996) at 105. Modern retributive theorists include C.S. Lewis, 'The Humanitarian Theory of Punishment' in J.R. Burr & M. Goldinger (eds.) *Philosophy and Contemporary Issues* (McMillan, 1972) at 71; Herbert Morris, 'Persons and Punishment' (1968) 52 *Monist* 475.
38. See for example George Fletcher, *With Justice for Some: Protecting Victims' Rights in Criminal Trials* (Addison Wesley, 1995) at 203.
39. Blumenson, *supra* note 30, at 830–841.
40. *Ibid.* at 853–854.
41. *Ibid.* at 860.
42. *Ibid.* at 860–868.
43. See *Human Rights Watch, supra* note 35.
44. See Jean Jacques Rousseau, *The Social Contract or Principles of Political Rights* (Wordsworth Classics of World Literature, 1998) (trans. H. J. Tozer).
45. The full text of Nelson Mandela's Inaugural Address on 10 May 1994 can be found at the Washington State University website at the following url: http://www.wsu.edu:8080/~wldciv/world_civ_reader/world_civ_reader_2/mandela.html (accessed 15 June 2009).
46. See the presentation by de Klerk at Stanford University entitled 'The Miracle Revisited' on January 29, 2001 located at the de Klerk Foundation website at the following url: http://www.fwdklerk.org.za/speeches.php (accessed 15 June 2009).
47. *Human Rights Watch, supra* note 35 at 3.
48. Keller, *supra* note 29 at 273–274.
49. *Ibid.* at 274–275.
50. *Ibid.* at 276–277.
51. For an excellent overview of both the international law sources of the duty to prosecute or extradite and against blanket amnesties see *Human Rights Watch, supra* note 35.
52. See the ICJ Press Release on the Proceedings, 'Belgium institutes proceedings against Senegal and requests the Court to indicate provisional measures' (19 February 2009) No. 2009/13 located at the following url: http://www.icj-cij.org/docket/files/144/15052.pdf.
53. For details of these allegations and the proceedings against Habré in Senegal see Reed Brody, 'The Prosecution of Hissène Habré – An "African Pinochet"' (2001) 35:2 *New Eng. L. Rev.* 321 at 322.
54. For a good overview of the historical, contemporary practice and international law basis of universal jurisdiction, see Kenneth C. Randall, 'Universal Jurisdiction under International Law' (1988) 66 *Texas. Law Review*. 785; Cherif M. Bassiouni, 'Universal Jurisdiction for International Crimes: Historical and Contemporary Practice' (2001) 42:1 *Va. J. Int'l L.* 81.
55. See for example Kenneth Roth, 'The Case for Universal Jurisdiction' (Sept/Oct 2001) 80:5 *Foreign Affairs* 150 and Henry A. Kissinger, 'The Pitfalls of Universal Jurisdiction' (July/Aug 2001) 80:4 *Foreign Affairs* 86.
56. *R v. Bow Street Metropolitan Stipendiary Magistrate, ex parte Pinochet Ugarte* [1998] 3 W.L.R. 1456 (H.L. 1998) annulled by *R v. Bow Street Metropolitan Stipendiary Magistrate, ex parte Pinochet Ugarte (No.2)* [1999] 2 W.L.R. 272 (H.L. 1999); *R v. Bow*

Street Metropolitan Stipendiary Magistrate, ex parte Pinochet Ugarte [1999], 2 W.L.R. 827 (H.L. 1999). For a legal discussion of the Pinochet cases see also J. C. Barker, 'The Future of Former Head of State Immunity after ex parte Pinochet' (1999) 48 *Int'l & Comp. L. Q.* 937; Christine Chinkin, 'In Re Pinochet' (1999) 93 *Am. J. Int'l L* 703. For an excellent analysis of the transnational impact of the two Pinochet rulings by the House of Lords see N. Roht-Arriaza, *The Pinochet Effect: Transnational Justice in the Age of Human Rights* (University of Pennsylvania Press) 2006.

57.   See 'Universal Jurisdiction, Improving the effectiveness of state cooperation' *Amnesty International* (13 June 2007) AI Index: IOR 53/006/2007 also located at the following url: http://asiapacific.amnesty.org/library/Index/ENGIOR530062007?open&of=ENG-385.

58.   *Ibid.*

59.   See for example D. Akande, 'International Law Immunities and the International Criminal Court' (2004) 98 *Am. J. Int'l L.* 407 at 409–410.

60.   *Case Concerning the Arrest Warrant of 11 April 2000 (Democratic Republic of the Congo v. Belgium)* [2002] I.C.J. Rep. 3.

61.   A. Cassese, 'Is the Bell Tolling for Universality? A Plea for a Sensible Notion of Universal Jurisdiction' (2003) 1 *Journal of International Criminal Justice* 589 at 594.

62.   Report of the U.N. Commission on Inquiry on Darfur, 25 January 2005, available at www.un.org/news/dh/sudan/com_inq_darfur.pdf, at para 614.

63.   *Supra* note 56. For a discussion of the legacy of the Pinochet rulings see Francis Webber, 'The Pinochet Case: The Struggle for the Realization of Human Rights' (1999) 26 *Journal of Law and Society* 4, 523–537. Judge Garzon was recently suspended by Spain's General Council of the Judiciary for opening an inquiry into the human rights abuses of General Francisco Franco during Spain's civil war. This seemed to be the ultimate backlash against the foremost global champion of universal jurisdiction, see the BBC report at http://news.bbc.co.uk/2/hi/europe/8682948.stm.

64.   For a detailed advocacy of this strategy see Christopher Hall, 'Universal Jurisdiction: Developing and Implementing an Effective Global Strategy' in W. Kaleck, M.Ratner, T. Singelnstein, & P. Weiss (eds.) *International Prosecution of Human Rights Crimes* (Springer Berlin Heidelberg, 2007) at 85.

65.   *Ibid.* at 89–91.

66.   Crimes Against Humanity and War Crimes Act, S.C. 2000, c. 24. The full text can be located at the following url: http://www.canlii.org/en/ca/laws/stat/sc-2000-c-24/latest/sc-2000-c-24.html.

67.   *R. v. Munyaneza*, 2009 QCCS 2201, 22 May 2009. The full judgment is located at the following url: http://www.jugements.qc.ca/primeur/documents/r_c_munyaneza-22052009_an.doc.

68.   See the report by Michelle Collins, 'Rwanda welcomes war crimes conviction, wants extraditions' *Embassy Magazine* (3 June 2009) also located at the following url: http://www.embassymag.ca/page/view/rwanda-6-3-2009.

69.   The budgets of the Canadian federal departments involved in the investigation and prosecution of potential war criminals have been frozen at $15.6 million Canadian dollars for the past 10 years with the major part of that amount spent on deportations, with only approximately 7% being spent on investigations and prosecutions by the Department of Justice and the RCMP. The focus on deportations also arose out of the failure of the previous unsuccessful prosecution of another alleged war criminal, Imra Finta, which after a lengthy and expensive trial and acquittal resulted in the Supreme Court of Canada in *R. v. Finta* [1993] 1S.C.R. 1138 impeding any further such prosecutions by imposing an obligation on the prosecution to prove that the accused knew or ought to have known that a state of war existed and that his defense of following superior orders would prevail unless it would shock the conscience of the world.

      Following the Supreme Court of Canada ruling, Canadian government policy was to avoid further such unsuccessful trials by obtaining federal Cabinet approval through an Order in Council to seek the deportation of alleged war criminals who had obtained their citizenship unlawfully. However, more recently the Supreme Court of Canada in *Suresh v. Canada (Minister of Citizenship and Immigration)* [2002] 1 S.C.R. 3 has imposed a duty on Canada not to deport to countries where there is a substantial risk of torture except in exceptional circumstances. Given the curtailment of the defense of superior orders under Article 33 of the Rome Statute, under which orders to commit genocide and war crimes are manifestly unlawful, the obstacles imposed by the Imra Finta case to prosecutions of such war criminals in Canada have been substantially removed in Canada and in the jurisdictions of States Parties to the Rome Statute.

70. See the website of Canada's Program against Crimes Against Humanity and War Crimes, Tenth Annual Report, 2006–2007 available at the following url: http://www.cbsa-asfc.gc.ca/security-securite/wc-cg/wc-cg2007-eng.html#c5.

71. Taylor's conviction was the first conviction under the 1994 Extraterritorial Torture Statute, 18 U.S.C. 2340 and 2340A, which was enacted to implement U.S. obligations under the Convention Against Torture. See the report of the conviction by Human Rights Watch entitled 'US: First Verdict for Overseas Torture' (30 October 2008) at the following url: http://www.hrw.org/en/news/2008/10/30/us-first-verdict-overseas-torture.

72. For details of some of these convictions see Hall, *supra* note 64 at 92, footnote 16.

73. *Ibid.* at 89–92.

74. See the report of the Eminent Jurists' Panel on Terrorism, Counter-Terrorism and Human Rights of the International Commission of Jurists entitled 'Assessing Damage, Urging Action' (2009) located at the following url: http://icj.org/news.php3?id_article=4453%E3%80%88=en.

5 The future of the Court: reassuring Africa, investigating Gaza, integrating America and seeking help from global finance

1. IS THE ICC FOCUSING ON AFRICA UNFAIRLY FOR POLITICAL PURPOSES?

An opinion editorial by a leading Cameroon jurist, Roland Abeng, in the new high profile online journal, *The East African*, offered a unique perspective on the future of the International Criminal Court. Pointing out that the majority of cases before the Court were from Africa, he asked whether Africans and the African Union (A.U.) had an alternative to the Court. He further asked provocatively whether there were even five African countries with judicial systems that could try grievous international crimes fairly and equitably through effective national court structures. The way the question was posed removed the necessity for an answer. For those who advocate a continental judicial alternative to the ICC, the jurist seemed equally skeptical.[1]

The conclusion of this African jurist's perspective was that the ICC is a court of last resort because it is doing the job of failed judicial systems in many African countries. Contrary to the views of many authoritarian leaders in Africa, the A.U. and the Arab League, this provocative African perspective argued that the ICC had not replaced viable national judiciaries, but had helped attain justice where other options were not possible. The only other alternative to the ICC would have been the creation of numerous ad hoc international criminal tribunals to address serious international crimes in that continent. This African self-critique continued that many African governments are infamous for waiting until the situation deteriorates completely and then blaming the U.N., Europe or the U.S. for non-intervention. In concluding its analysis, the editorial writer reinforces the view of many supporters of the Court that there is a need for the Prosecutor to expand its cases beyond Africa and increase the number of States Parties to combat impunity wherever it occurs. In this regard, this

African perspective could be satisfied because the Prosecutor is expanding his *proprio motu* public preliminary examinations and monitoring outside the African continent to include countries such as Afghanistan, Colombia and Georgia.

It remains critical to the future of the Court that the opposition of the A.U., the Arab League and the Organization of Islamic Conference to the Court, following the arrest warrant for President al-Bashir, not undermine its global fight against impunity.

The opposition of the African Union is particularly worrisome. In February of 2009, at its meeting in Addis Ababa, Ethiopia, the A.U. expressed its deep concern at the indictment of President al-Bashir and requested a special meeting of African States Parties to the Rome Statute to exchange views on the work of the ICC in relation to Africa. In particular it called for the examination of processes initiated against African personalities, and the submission of recommendations on what actions to take. Underlying the concern was the unfounded accusation that the Prosecutor and the Court were concentrating on Africa for political reasons. As Chapter 1 has revealed, the situations before the Court dealing with serious crimes from Africa were either self-referrals or, in the case of Sudan, referred to it by the U.N. Security Council. If there were any political reasons for the focus on Africa, they were not coming from the Court but from Africa itself or from the U.N. Security Council.

There was much apprehension within the ICC and among its supporters around the world that the calling of the special meeting of African States Parties would focus on the withdrawal of the thirty African States Parties to the Rome Statute. If this were to occur, it would constitute a deadly blow to the legitimacy and credibility of the ICC. The meeting of the African States Parties had been orchestrated by Libyan leader Muammar Gaddafi, who held the current Chairmanship of the African Union. Gaddafi was clearly attempting to get African states to withdraw their support from the ICC. Already a few African countries, including Senegal, Djibouti and Comoros, had advocated the simultaneous withdrawal of all African states parties to protest the focus of the Court on Africa and in particular on the indictment of President al-Bashir.

On June 8 and 9, 2009, the African States Parties met in Addis Ababa, in what some regarded as a test of survival of the ICC. The meeting was attended by South Africa, Benin, Botswana, Burkina Faso, Burundi, Chad, Congo, Djibouti, Gabon, Gambia, Ghana, Kenya, Lesotho, Liberia, Malawi, Mali, Mauritius, Namibia, Niger, Nigeria, Uganda, Senegal, Sierra Leone, Tanzania and Zambia.

The supporters of the Court around the world breathed a sigh of relief when the meeting confirmed the African States Parties' continued support for the Court. The States Parties did consider proposals regarding possible withdrawal from the ICC or withholding cooperation. These proposals failed to win a consensus from the minsterial level meeting from which Libya, Sudan and other non-States Parties had been excluded. Instead the meeting reaffirmed the commitment of African member states to the ICC and the fight against global impunity.

However, the African States Parties did adopt key recommendations that included the following: first, that the A.U. Assembly should inquire into examining the feasibility of strengthening the African Court of Human and Peoples' Rights to take on the role of the ICC by dealing with serious international crimes in a complementary manner to national jurisdictions in Africa. This would require greatly strengthening the mandate and resources of the African regional human rights court. Second, the States Parties recommended monitoring the ICC cases dealing with African situations with regard to the question of legal immunities and appeals procedures. Third, States Parties recommended that national legal systems should be strengthened to allow prosecution of the most serious crimes. Fourth, States Parties agreed to prepare for the ICC Review Conference scheduled for 2010 in Kampala, and in particular focus on the issues relating to immunities of non-States Parties and the ability of the U.N. Security Council to refer and defer cases to the ICC. In regard to the latter issues, States Parties reaffirmed the importance of the ability of the U.N. Security Council to defer prosecution against President al-Bashir in the interest of a peaceful settlement of the situation in Darfur. The most potentially damaging agenda for the Court was the allegation that the ICC was unfairly focusing on Africa. This was the agenda that the A.U. leadership was keen to taint the Court with. Instead the member states largely accepted the recommendations of a restricted circulation working paper of an A.U. Commission, prepared in large part by a leading African jurist, Dapo Akande.[2] The conclusions of the Commission were as follows.

First, considering that African States constituted the largest regional grouping of States Parties, it was not surprising and more likely statistically that more prosecutions would arise from African States. Second, the paper confirmed the thesis in Chapter 1 that three of the four situations before the Court were referred by African states themselves and so could not be regarded as unilateral external intervention. The paper added that these referring countries had considered the ICC to be more appropriate to address the serious crimes as their own national courts were 'not properly positioned to undertake criminal proceedings against the suspects in question'. Particular reference was paid to the fact that the highest court in the Central African Republic had specifically ruled that it was unable to carry out the necessary criminal proceedings against Jean Pierre Bemba and other perpetrators. The Court had cited difficulty in the most basic areas of prosecutorial competence, such as the collection of evidence. Likewise, as regards the prosecution of Joseph Kony and the LRA leadership, the government of Uganda had specifically stated that the LRA leaders indicted by the ICC were 'triable' by that Court.[3]

The working paper nevertheless aimed a critical barb at the Prosecutor of the ICC regarding the fact that he had not used his *proprio motu* powers to a greater extent to instigate investigations or prosecutions outside the African continent. While accepting that state party referrals made the cooperation and the gathering of critical evidence more likely, the paper insisted that the Prosecutor cannot rely solely on self-referrals as that was not contemplated by the Rome Statute.[4] It should be noted that the Prosecutor has initiated the possible start of such *proprio motu* public preliminary examinations by commencing preliminary examinations and public monitoring of situations outside Africa, including in Colombia and Georgia. Therefore this critique may already be outdated.

As will be discussed later in this chapter, much of the perception of the unfair targeting of Africa seemed be coming from the view of many African and Arab leaders and opinion makers that the ICC should be accepting jurisdiction over Israeli military actions in Gaza, regardless of the difficulties of the Court exercising jurisdiction over such actions.

The working paper of the A.U. Commission also tackled the view that the ICC was imperiling peace efforts in civil conflicts in the continent by initiating prosecutions. The paper accepted that in relation to Northern Uganda it had to be borne in mind that it was the government of Uganda which considered the situation 'triable' while in Sudan it was the U.N. Security Council that had referred the situation to the Court. Regarding the core peace and justice challenge, the authors made a key conclusion that African states had not taken the view that one should necessarily prevail over the other or that the two could not be reconciled.[5]

In a statement that may not please some of the leaders of the A.U. or specific countries, such as Robert Mugabe or Libyan leader Muammar Gaddafi, the working paper noted that the Constitutive Act of the A.U. had mandated that impunity for international crimes would not be tolerated and that the widespread ratification of the Rome Statute by African states reaffirmed African leaders' belief that prosecutions ought to follow where serious crimes had been committed. Therefore while the authors refuted the fact that there was no African support for the Darfur referral to the ICC, it drew attention to the fact that opposition had arisen over whether the Prosecutor and the ICC had exceeded their powers in indicting and prosecuting a sitting Head of State in the person of al-Bashir. The paper also engaged in a lengthy discussion as to whether Sudan was bound by Article 27 of the Rome Statute which negated any immunities that al-Bashir could claim and seemed to agree with the views expressed below by this author on this issue. The authors of the A.U. Commission paper felt compelled to point out that there were some unnamed experts who disagreed on this crucial point.[6]

Overall, the States Parties focused on legal recommendations and refused to be embroiled in the political controversies surrounding the conduct of the Prosecutor, the proposal for a unified request to the U.N. Security Council to defer the proceedings against al-Bashir and in particular to withdraw *en masse* from the Rome Statute.

Analysis from the Institute of Security Studies, a leading African research institute, of what transpired at this crucial meeting of African member states has warned that while the threat of a mass withdrawal from the ICC was averted, there has to be a greater coordinated cooperative effort between the A.U. and the ICC. Both bodies have a duty to make greater efforts in this regard. The opening up of an ICC liaison office within the A.U. could facilitate this work, as would greater outreach efforts on the part of the ICC with the A.U. and the States Parties to ensure that the Court is operating in a non-partisan way in the continent.[7] Likewise the same research institute has rightly noted that the lesson learned from the African States Parties' meeting is the need for capacity building at the regional and national levels for those who have ratified the Rome Statute, but have not passed the appropriate implementing legislation. The record of States Parties passing the necessary implementing legislation is far from satisfactory. Only thirty-nine States Parties have passed implementing legislation as required by the Rome Statute.

The role of civil society expertise would also be critical to capacity building and pressing for the passing of legislation implementing the Rome Statute. Finally, the ICC should also organize pre-ratification activities for those African states that have not ratified the ICC Statute in order to promote greater knowledge and appreciation of the Statute.[8]

As discussed in Chapter 2, sadly three weeks later, the A.U. Assembly had decided on July 3, 2009 that its members should withhold any cooperation with the ICC in the arrest and surrender of President al-Bashir. Yet, the same body restated what it regarded as 'the consistent position of the A.U. of unflinching commitment of A.U. member states to combating impunity and promoting democracy, the rule of law and good governance on the continent as enunciated in the constitutive Act of the Union'.[9]

In urging non-cooperation with the ICC in relation to the immunities and arrest of al-Bashir, the A.U. had lashed out at what it called the 'publicity-seeking approach of the ICC Prosecutor'.[10] Also not spared condemnation was the refusal by the U.N. Security Council to accede to the request by the A.U. and its allies for deferment of the indictment against President al-Bashir of Sudan, under Article 16 of the Rome Statute of the ICC.

It has become clear that the African States Parties and the other members of the A.U. have reserved their greatest ire for the indictment of al-Bashir. There is a growing sentiment among the legal advisors to the African states parties and indeed to the entire A.U. that the ICC exceeded its authority in indicting a sitting Head of State. This opinion is based on a specific provision of the Rome Statute, Article 98(1), that has triggered legal and political confusion as to whether immunities still attach to heads of state and other senior state officials. Article 98(1) states the following:

Article 98(1) Cooperation with respect to waiver of immunity and consent to surrender

1. The Court may not proceed with a request for surrender or assistance which would require the requested State to act inconsistently with its obligations under international law with respect to the State or diplomatic immunity of a person or property of a third State, unless the Court can first obtain the cooperation of that third State for the waiver of the immunity.

This provision seems contradictory to an earlier provision of the Rome Statute, Article 27, which was excerpted in Chapter 1 and, repeated here, states the following:

Article 27: Irrelevance of official capacity

1. This Statute shall apply equally to all persons without any distinction based on official capacity. In particular, official capacity as a Head of State or Government, a member of a Government or parliament, an elected representative or a government official shall in no case exempt a person from criminal responsibility under this Statute, nor shall it, in and of itself, constitute a ground for reduction of sentence.

2. Immunities or special procedural rules which may attach to the official capacity of a person, whether under national or international law, shall not bar the Court from exercising its jurisdiction over such a person.

To determine why it was inevitable that the Prosecutor and the Court of the ICC had to eventually seek the indictment of President al-Bashir it is necessary to examine and get an inside look at the prosecutorial strategy that first led to the arrest warrants against al-Bashir's senior officials before the Prosecutor and the Court had to then turn to the possible indictment of the President himself.

The starting point for any attempted exercise of jurisdiction by the ICC must be based on the provisions of Articles 12 and 13 of the Statute which have been described in Chapter 1. These provisions limit such exercise of jurisdiction only where there is involvement of States Parties or their nationals. Non-States Parties can also declare their acceptance of jurisdiction under Article 12(3).

Finally there is the exercise of jurisdiction by the U.N. Security Council. The referral by this highest body of the international community is essentially what started the process that led to the arrest warrant for al-Bashir, which is often forgotten by adversaries of the Court in the A.U., the Arab League and others.

The Prosecutor is limited to investigate situations only where the most serious crimes listed in Article 5 (genocide, crimes against humanity or war crimes) have allegedly been committed. Article 53 then gives guidance to the Prosecutor to decide whether or not to initiate an investigation and also guidance on case selection within a situation that it has been decided is within the jurisdiction of the Court. Critical to the decision to initiate an investigation and select specific cases is the flow of information and evidence that comes to the Prosecutor.

In the case of Darfur, since the U.N. Security Council had made the reference to the Court, it had been predetermined by the international community that there was a reasonable basis to proceed with an investigation and that the Court would have complete jurisdiction over any crimes that would be uncovered by the investigation. Subject to Sudan being willing or genuinely able to carry out the investigation or prosecution, there was no complementarity obstacle to the exercise of jurisdiction over the Darfur situation.

As with any investigation by the Prosecutor, it will first focus on 'the situation' as a whole and, as the evidence gathering proceeds, the prosecutorial strategy will focus more and more on individuals who may be most responsible for the alleged serious crimes. There is as much a duty on the part of the Prosecutor to collect exculpatory evidence for the benefit of any alleged perpetrator as there is to collect evidence that will strengthen the prosecution's case. These preliminary prosecutorial stages in the case of Darfur were conducted by the Prosecutor following the referral by the U.N. Security Council under Resolution 1593.

There could be little doubt, as confirmed by the Pre-Trial Chamber, that the Security Council did not prohibit the ICC from investigating the possible criminality of President al-Bashir. Indeed, the Security Council could not make such a prohibition, as it had mandated the Prosecutor to investigate within the rules of the Rome Statute that included Article 27, which clearly stated the irrelevance of the official status, capacity and immunities of any high state official of Sudan.

After a lengthy investigation the Prosecutor determined that Sudan did not show any willingness and ability to carry out any investigations or prosecutions genuinely and that the interests of justice did not prohibit the prosecution. The fruits of the first investigations by the Prosecutor in Darfur led to the issuance of arrest warrants by the Pre-Trial Chamber of the ICC against two individuals lower down the hierarchy than President al-Bashir. As discussed in Chapters 1 and 2 these were the former Minister of State for the Interior, Ahmad Harun, and the Janjaweed militia leader, Ali Kushayb, who were charged with crimes against humanity and war crimes.

It became clear there were no complementarity obstacles to the prosecution of these two individuals when, as described in Chapter 2, the Sudanese authorities did the opposite of taking steps to investigate, arrest and prosecute them. The Minister was promoted and the Janjaweed leader was released after a brief detention, as discussed in Chapter 2.

It was at this stage that the Chief Prosecutor, Luis Moreno-Ocampo, informed the U.N. Security Council that further investigations had revealed evidence that the two individuals under arrest warrants were receiving protection from the entire state apparatus of Sudan which seemed to be involved in the commission of the serious crimes in Darfur.[11]

The fact that the person who was most in control of the entire state apparatus in Sudan was the President gave the Prosecutor little choice but to seek the indictment of al-Bashir himself for genocide, crimes against humanity and war crimes committed through those linked to the state apparatus which he controlled. As discussed in Chapters 1 and 2, on March 4, 2009, the Pre-Trial Chamber, after seeing the evidence collected since the start of the investigation into the Darfur situation, agreed that an arrest warrant and request for surrender be issued against al-Bashir for crimes against humanity and war crimes. As discussed in Chapter 1, the Chamber refused to issue the arrest warrant on the charge of genocide.[12] The arrest warrant and request for surrender were issued not only to all ICC States Parties and Sudan, but also to all Security Council members who had started the whole process in the first place.

The Pre-Trial Chamber ruled definitely that the position of al-Bashir as a sitting Head of State had no effect on the ability of the Court to exercise jurisdiction over him due to the wording of Article 27 of the Rome Statute detailed above. Indeed the Court argued that the very Preamble to the Statute required that impunity for the most serious crimes not go unpunished.[13] The implication was that to exclude sitting heads of state would blow a huge hole in this rationale for the existence of the Court. A legitimate criticism of the decision of the Chamber is that it failed to discuss the relevance, if any, of Article 98(1) of the Rome Statute and how it relates to Article 27 of the same Statute.

The Pre-Trial Chamber also implied that the U.N. Security Council must have realized that there was a possibility that any investigation and prosecution by the ICC could lead to the highest officials in Sudan and that these individuals could not be offered impunity due to their status and function.

It is these basic factual and legal considerations that should have placated the African member states and indeed the A.U. from any concern that the ICC was deliberately targeting a sitting African Head of State unfairly and for political considerations. However, there were other legal precedents and Article 98(1), which seems to have led even some of the most supportive of African member states to question whether the ICC overstepped its mandate and jurisdiction in order to seek the indictment of al-Bashir.

First, the customary international law principle enunciated in the Judgment of the International Court of Justice ('ICJ') in the *Yerodia* case (*Belgium v Congo*),[14] briefly discussed in Chapter 4, has been cited by A.U. opponents of the indictment of al-Bashir as a legal reason why the ICC overstepped its jurisdiction. In that decision, the ICJ ruled that in the domestic courts of foreign states, a sitting Head of State from another state, and indeed certain other high level officials such as the Minister of Foreign Affairs in the case itself, enjoyed inviolability and immunity even for war crimes and crimes against humanity.

What has been omitted by those who use this decision against the indictment of al-Bashir, is another part of the ruling of the ICJ in the same decision that an exception to this customary international law principle is where an international court exercises criminal jurisdiction over such high level officials including a sitting Head of State.[15] Despite the use of this decision by those who have opposed the indictment of al-Bashir, it is clear that under customary international law principles accepted by most international law experts, with regard to the criminal prosecution of al-Bashir before the ICC, any immunity *ratione personae* (personal immunity) and immunity *ratione materiae* (subject matter immunity) can be set aside.[16] It must be noted that this ruling only applies where the treaty establishing the international criminal tribunal expressly or impliedly removes the ability of perpetrators to claim immunities. This is precisely what Article 27 of the Rome Statute does. It must also be noted that such removal of claims to immunities does not extend to non-states parties.

As discussed in Chapter 1, the legacy of this exception can be found in the Charter of the Nuremberg Tribunal (and also in the Tokyo Tribunal) that mandated that any 'official position of defendants, whether Heads of State or responsible officials in Government Departments, shall not be considered as freeing them from responsibility or mitigating punishment'.[17]

The opponents of the indictment of the President of Sudan go on to argue that Article 27 does not apply to states which are not party to the Rome Statute. While this is absolutely true, it cannot be relevant to Sudan, because once the U.N. Security Council referred the situation to the ICC, the Rome Statute applied in its entirety to that country.

The U.N. Security Council was also aware of the possibility of grave crimes being committed by high level officials from the report to it by the International Commission of Inquiry as described in Chapter 2.Therefore it was also not unaware that this could lead to the prosecution of high level officials, including even the sitting Head of State. There is no doubt that the U.N. Security Council can exclude immunities of the most senior state officials as it did with the establishment of the Yugoslavia and Rwanda Tribunal Statutes which had provisions similar to Article 27 of the Rome Statute. It becomes a matter of indisputable logic that once the U.N. Security Council referred the situation in Darfur to the ICC without laying down any procedure, it could only have intended that Sudan would be bound by the provisions of the Rome Statute that includes Article 27.

Resolution 1593 (2005) of the Security Council that made the referral to the ICC was passed under the Chapter VII powers of the U.N. Charter under which members are obliged to accept and carry out the decisions of that body. Despite the views of some A.U. members, this means that all States Parties to the Rome Statute, the ICC itself and Sudan are legally obliged to accept the complete jurisdiction of the Court over prosecution of alleged serious crimes in Darfur. It is only non-states parties, excluding Sudan, by the very terms of Resolution 1593 that are not bound to accept the outcome of any investigations and prosecutions of such crimes.

However, the A.U. and some of the member states and their legal advisors are insistent that the provisions of Article 98(1) extracted above could override all other provisions of the Rome Statute, and indeed customary international law, to result in the ICC exceeding its jurisdiction in indicting al-Bashir. The claim by the A.U. and some of its member states is that this provision prohibits the ICC from requesting any form of surrender or assistance from the national judicial institutions of any state, including ICC States Parties, as it would amount to making them act inconsistently with their obligations under international law regarding the various forms of state or diplomatic immunity of a sitting Head of State like al-Bashir. The only exception would be where the ICC can first obtain a waiver of the requested state of the immunity attaching to al-Bashir.

What has been obscured in the reliance on Article 98(1) by the A.U. opponents of the indictment of al-Bashir is that its provisions relate *not* to whether the ICC has jurisdiction over a sitting Head of State, but about the duty of States Parties to cooperate with the Court in the *surrender* of a person normally subject to state immunity. This duty to cooperate is absolute with regard both to States Parties and to Sudan flowing from U.N. Security Council Resolution 1593.

The logical conclusion from this interpretation of Article 98(1) and Article 27 of the Rome Statute is that Sudan cannot claim any form of immunity with respect to al-Bashir, and therefore it cannot claim any form of immunity for him against any state party whether in Africa or elsewhere on a request by the ICC for the arrest and surrender of the President. Put in simpler terms, if neither al-Bashir nor Sudan can claim immunity before the Court, there is no immunity to be claimed in the jurisdiction of any State Party to the ICC as regards the surrender of the indicted President to the Court.[18] In effect there is also an implied waiver of any immunity for al-Bashir or indeed any indicted high official by States Parties because of the operation of Article 27. The same applies to non-states Parties, like Sudan, which have become the subject matter of a referral to the ICC by the U.N. Security Council.[19]

A final and extremely weak argument that could be made by States Parties is that Article 27 of the Rome Statute is not applicable as regards the exclusion of liability for high state officials, as any surrender request for such officials under Article 98(1) has to be received and decided upon by the domestic judicial or administrative authorities of the state in which the indicted official is situated. Therefore it is purely a domestic legal affair and not connected to any external legal obligation of the States Parties' own national governments. The only reasonable response to this assertion is that such domestic authorities of member states are carrying out their duties as agents of the ICC under the international legal obligation of the relevant State Party under the Rome Statute. Any other interpretation could potentially render meaningless the provisions of Article 27, the decision of the Pre-Trial Chamber that issued the arrest warrant against al-Bashir and potentially undermine the effectiveness of the Court and indeed the entire Rome Statute.[20]

The clear conclusion from the above analysis is that, much as the A.U. may wish to have Article 98(1) stand in the way of African States Parties or any other State Party to the Rome Statute cooperating in the arrest and surrender of al-Bashir, there is no sound legal basis for this advocacy as was promoted by the A.U. resolution on July 3, 2009.

The remaining legal option that was proposed by the restricted circulation A.U. Commission working paper that was largely accepted by the African states parties indicated a less adversarial approach, but one that could still undermine the independence of the Prosecutor and the ICC. In addition to quite appropriately suggesting that Sudan, African member states or even the A.U. participate in any appeals regarding the indictment of al-Bashir and focus on the fact that the Pre-Trial Chamber that issued the arrest warrant did not even mention the relevance of Article 98(1), there was one more contentious recommendation that was suggested.

African States Parties and the A.U. were encouraged to consider steps to influence prosecutorial discretion where there is a view that such investigations or prosecutions could impact negatively on peace processes in Africa. The suggested way to do this would be to broaden out the view of the Prosecutor of when such prosecutorial strategies would not 'serve the interests of justice' under Article 53(2)(c), as discussed in Chapter 1. The working paper suggests that the existing policy of the Prosecutor, namely that the curtailment of any investigation or prosecution in the interests of justice should be exceptional, is too narrow and, as such, African states should call for a revision of the policy. The way in which the policy could be changed could be by a revision of the Rome Statute or by the Assembly of States Parties developing guidelines to broaden out the scope of what constitutes the interests of justice. The Prosecutor would then be obliged to take these wider considerations into account in making prosecutorial decisions. The least intrusion into the independence of the Prosecutor would also be the African states advocating that the Prosecutor revise his own policy concerning the interests of justice.

Paradoxically, while the A.U. Commission working paper was critical of the record of the present Prosecutor on several grounds, including the timing and nature of the indictment of al-Bashir and the early challenges regarding non-disclosure of confidential evidence in the Thomas Lubanga Dyilo trial, it recognized the dangers of seeking the dismissal of such an important player in the ICC. Most importantly, the paper recognized that such a move would permanently damage the independence of the Office and potentially that of the entire Court.

Yet, the move to prescribe the prosecutorial strategy of the Prosecutor in terms of setting parameters on when investigations and prosecutions must be stopped in the interests of justice could result in the very same undermining of the Office of the Prosecutor and indeed the Court itself. If the focus of any expanded definition of 'interests of justice' is to desist from prosecuting heads of state or high officials or make political attempts at peace settlements trump ICC investigations and prosecutions, the future of the Court could be imperilled. These are profoundly political considerations that could undermine the independence of the Prosecutor of the ICC and ultimately the Court itself.

The hard fought struggle to establish the ICC had as its core the objective to stop political considerations trumping the global fight against impunity. The Rome Statute was designed to prevent the ICC from making political considerations become the main motivating factor in the decision to prosecute or not prosecute the most serious crimes known to humanity. Indeed the Rome Statute itself makes it clear that if political decisions have to be made it is the role of other organs of the international community.

In particular, the Rome Statute in Articles 12 and 13 makes it clear that it is only states that can determine whether to become States Parties and accept the jurisdiction of the ICC. Likewise, it is only the U.N. Security Council that can make referrals to the ICC that target non-States Parties. In addition it is also the U.N. Security Council that can decide to defer prosecutions for a renewable period of one year under Article 16.

For these fundamental reasons that were the rationale for the establishment and structure of the Court, the Prosecutor or any organ of the Court must not be coerced into taking political considerations. Perhaps the most compelling counterintuitive reason for resisting the politicization of prosecutorial discretion is that it would give greater incentives to those responsible for the most serious crimes to increase the political consequences of any potential attempt to prosecute them. The catastrophic result would most likely be an increase in the number of innocent victims. President al-Bashir has confirmed this outcome by first attacking and killing U.N. peacekeepers and subsequently expelling the international aid groups in retaliation to the arrest warrants against him, as described in Chapter 2.

2. THE ARAB WORLD DEMANDS ACTION AGAINST ISRAELI ACTIONS IN GAZA TO DISPEL THE UNFAIR FOCUS ON AFRICA

Behind much of the animosity of some of the leaders of the African Union and the Arab League towards the ICC is the view that, while the Court has focused extensively on Africa, it seemed to be ignoring the possibility of investigating and prosecuting Israeli military and political figures for alleged war crimes and crimes against humanity that the African Union and the Arab league claim occurred during the Israeli military action against Hamas militants in Gaza in December 2008.

Leading human rights organizations such as Amnesty International,[21] and Human Rights Watch[22] and the report by Justice Richard Goldstone commissioned by the U.N. Human Rights Council[23] on the humanitarian law violations relating to Gaza have concluded that serious international crimes by both sides to the conflict did occur during the conflict. This has increased the sentiments of many in Arab countries, and indeed in African countries with large Muslim populations, that there is prosecutorial bias being demonstrated by the ICC. It is somewhat paradoxical that the potential for prosecution for war crimes by the Hamas militants in Gaza for firing rockets into Israel is often ignored by the same Arab and African critics of the ICC.

What is being ignored also by those who criticize the lack of action by the ICC regarding Israeli military actions in Gaza, is that Israel is not a State Party to the Rome Statute (although it did sign the Treaty) and that there is considerable controversy as to whether there is an entity called the Palestinian State that can seek to trigger the jurisdiction of the Court by lodging a declaration of submission to the Court's jurisdiction under Article 13(3) of the Rome Statute.

The ICC Statute makes several references to the word 'state' in terms of jurisdiction of the ICC, but does not define it. As discussed in Chapter 1, Article 13 of the ICC Statute lists three situations where the Court may exercise jurisdiction: first by a referral by a State Party; second when the situation is referred to it by the U.N. Security Council; and thirdly when the Prosecutor has initiated an investigation, *proprio motu,* on the basis of information received and he is satisfied that there are reasonable grounds to proceed with an investigation. This *proprio motu* investigation can only proceed after authorization by the Pre-Trial Chamber.

However, Article 12(3) of the ICC Statute states that '[i]f the acceptance by a State which is not a Party to this Statute is required under paragraph 2, that State may, by declaration lodged with the Registrar, accept the exercise of jurisdiction by the Court with respect to the crime in question. . .'. Under this provision, the Palestinian National Authority filed with the ICC Registrar a declaration accepting the jurisdiction of the ICC in the territory of Palestine. The Declaration, filed under the letterhead of the Office of the Minister of Justice, stated:[24]

Declaration recognizing the Jurisdiction of the International Criminal Court

In conformity with Article 12, paragraph 3 of the Statute of the International Criminal Court, the Government of Palestine hereby recognizes the jurisdiction of the Court for the purpose of identifying, prosecuting and judging the authors and accomplices of acts committed on the territory of Palestine since 1 July 2002.

As a consequence, the Government of Palestine will cooperate with the Court without delay or exception, in conformity with Chapter IX of the Statute.

This declaration, made for an indeterminate duration, will enter into force upon its signature.

Material supplementary to and supporting this declaration will be provided shortly in a separate communication.

Signed in The Hague, the Netherlands, 21 January 2009.
For the Government of Palestine
Minister of Justice s/Ali Khashan

It should be noted that the declaration was not limited to any allegations of particular crimes in connection with the Gaza military incursion by Israel, or indeed any crimes committed by militants firing rockets into Israel before or after the military actions in December of 2008. The jurisdiction of the ICC over all such crimes could date back to July 1, 2002 when the ICC became operative. The declaration did not specify the territory of Palestine or the nature of the acts mentioned.

The Prosecutor could potentially initiate a *proprio motu* investigation into the actions by the Palestinian militants and the Israeli militants in the Gaza Strip under Articles 13 and 15 of the ICC Statute. This could occur if there were evidence that the Hamas militants who fired rockets into Israel potentially triggering allegations of war crimes and crimes against humanity were also Jordanian nationals (as Jordan is a State Party to the ICC), or Israeli commanders who are alleged to have committed similar international crimes were also nationals of other States Parties to the Rome Statute. However, as discussed above, such exercise of jurisdiction would have to be authorized by the Pre-Trial Chamber of the ICC. There is no guarantee that the Chamber would authorize such an investigation, and finding such dual national perpetrators may be either impractical or narrow the scope of the investigation to an unacceptable level.

Given the uncertainty of whether Palestine constitutes a 'state' for the purposes of Article 12(3), a rigorous academic and legal debate has ensued between those who claim that it does and those who claim that it does not. The debate so far has turned round whether Palestine qualifies generally as a state under customary international law principles. The focus of what constitutes an independent state triggers technical arguments about these principles drawn from the 1933 Montevideo Convention[25] and more modern principles of what constitutes state sovereignty. As discussed extensively in the international law literature, the Montevideo Convention purportedly laid down the following minimum standards before an entity could be regarded as a sovereign state. First, it must have a permanent population, which is a settled one rather than a transitory population. Second, it must have a defined territory the size of which is not specified in the Convention, but probably some kind of *de minimis* territorial size is required, keeping in mind some of the tiniest territories, like Luxembourg, qualify. Third, it must have an established government that has effective control, which need not be democratic. Finally, it must have capacity to enter into diplomatic relations. The more modern principles that have, in the view of some, supplanted the criteria in the Montevideo Convention include the impact of recognition of a new state by other states and the important role of the right of self-determination.[26]

Opponents of whether Palestine can qualify as a state for the purposes of

Article 12(3) point to the absence of any discussion at the 1998 Diplomatic Conference that established the Rome Statute on whether Palestine could be regarded as a state. This position is further strengthened by the argument that Palestine was not treated as such at the Conference. Likewise, these opponents also claim that the Palestinian Authority was not recognized by the U.N. or by the ICC's own documents or activities leading up to its establishment and in the development of the Court's policies and procedures by the Assembly of States Parties. When the Palestinian Authority had been invited to discussions on the Court, it was as an 'entity' or 'other organization' invited to observe. Referring to customary international law principles on state sovereignty, including those enunciated in the Montevideo Convention, these opponents also claim that the Palestinian Authority fails to demonstrate the requisite effective governmental control over claimed territory. Finally they claim that the ultimate decision on Palestinian statehood should be reserved to larger diplomatic negotiations and the ICC should not interfere with a unilateral decision on Palestinian statehood.[27]

Supporters of the legitimacy of the Palestinian Article 12(3) declaration, and indeed the wider status of Palestine as a sovereign state in international law, argue that it has existed as a state in international law since the League of Nations Mandate and was confirmed by the 1988 Declaration of Palestinian Statehood by the Palestinian National Council, which was confirmed by subsequent U.N. General Assembly Resolutions and recognized by a majority of the world's states.[28]

The decision of the Prosecutor and the ICC as to whether the Article 12(3) declaration can allow the Court to exercise jurisdiction will be one of the most crucial decisions facing the institution in its first decade in existence. Whatever the decision of the Prosecutor, there will inevitably be claims that the Prosecutor and the ICC have succumbed to political pressures. What this author witnessed while at the Court was a deeply professional focus by the top legal experts and the Prosecutor at the ICC to reach a decision on the Palestinian declaration based on the applicable law and a determination to avoid external pressures to arrive at a particular conclusion.

3. AFTER GEORGE W. BUSH; INTEGRATING THE U.S. BACK INTO THE GLOBAL FIGHT AGAINST IMPUNITY

With the growing challenges of assuring Africa and the Arab world of its prosecutorial and judicial fairness, the greatest hope of securing the future and legitimacy of the ICC would be integrating the U.S. into full participation in the Rome Statute. By full participation, what is meant is not only contributing to the meetings of the ICC States Parties on policies and procedures in which the U.S. already participates, but also becoming a State Party and erasing the adversarial legacy of the George W. Bush Administration discussed in Chapter 1. The Prosecutor of the ICC, Luis Moreno Ocampo, is quoted as stating that the ICC would have a greater ability to enforce its arrest warrants and prevent genocide if it had the full backing of the U.S.[29]

With the election of President Barack Obama there is widespread hope that the new Administration will integrate the world's most powerful superpower back into the fold of full membership of the Rome Statute. The major speech that President Obama gave in Accra, Ghana, would give every indication that such integration is only a matter of time. This may not be completely realistic for reasons discussed below. The relevant portions of the speech dealt with the tragic and crude caricature of Africa being the continent of perpetual war. While accepting that tribal, ethnic and religious differences have fueled conflict, he urged that Africans should seek a common humanity and stand up to inhumanity in Africa's midst:

> [W]e must stand up to inhumanity in our midst. It is never justified, never justifiable to target innocents in the name of ideology. It is the death sentence of a society to force children to kill in wars. It is the ultimate mark of criminality and cowardice to condemn women to relentless and systemic rape. We must bear witness to the value of every child in Darfur and the dignity of every woman in the Congo. No faith or culture should condone the outrages against them. And all of us must strive for the peace and security necessary for progress.

Then, in words that should signal a clear support for the work of the ICC, he continued:

> America has a responsibility to work with you as a partner to advance this vision, not just with words, but with support that strengthens African capacity. When there's a genocide in Darfur or terrorists in Somalia, these are not simply African problems – they are global security challenges, and they demand a global response. And that's why we stand ready to partner through diplomacy and technical assistance and logistical support, and we will stand behind efforts to hold war criminals accountable. And let me be clear: Our Africa Command is focused not on establishing a foothold in the continent, but on confronting these common challenges to advance the security of America, Africa and the world.

> In Moscow, I spoke of the need for an international system where the universal rights of human beings are respected, and violations of those rights are opposed. And that must include a commitment to support those who resolve

conflicts peacefully, to sanction and stop those who don't, and to help those who have suffered.

Since Barack Obama assumed the Office of President of the U.S., there are positive and contrary trends in terms of his support for universal human rights and the global fight against impunity. In one of his first executive decisions, he signed an order for the closure of the U.S. prison on Guantanamo, Cuba, where the detention and treatment of prisoners has been decried as a violation of international law and the Geneva Conventions by most of America's own allies and also by the U.S. Supreme Court itself.[30]

President Obama has outlawed the use of torture by U.S. security agencies.[31] However, the President has resisted the pressure by many of his own supporters to instigate legal proceedings or even a truth commission to identify those most responsible for the practice of torture and other human rights abuses during the regime of the former Bush Administration.[32]

This early record on the fight against impunity both inside the U.S. and beyond its borders may signal a reticence on joining the ICC in a manner not unlike that shown to the Court by the Bill Clinton Administration.

The Clinton Administration signed on to the Rome Statute just before the time for adhering to it expired, but its officials warned that ratification would be unlikely due to the resistance of the U.S. Congress to give its consent to ratification. In all likelihood, there was great concern in the Congress, the U.S. Defense Department and in the Clinton Administration that membership of the ICC would trigger politically motivated prosecutions of U.S. military and civilian officials.[33]

It could be argued, on one hand, that this fear of politically motivated prosecutions seemed almost an exercise itself in politically motivated ignorance, as in the vast majority of possible scenarios the ICC would never be able to overcome the complementarity hurdle by asserting that the U.S. was unwilling or unable to genuinely carry out any relevant investigation or prosecution. Even the former U.S. Secretary of State Madeline Albright has asserted that '[a]s long as U.S. courts try cases of Americans alleged to be involved in wrongdoing, there's no reason U.S. citizens would ever end up in The Hague'.[34] On the other hand, the Obama Administration is showing reluctance to even start domestic investigations or legal proceedings or initiate some form of truth commission to investigate the involvement of high level officials in the sanctioning of torture in Guantanamo. Such investigations could go as high as former Secretary of Defense, Donald Rumsfeld, and Vice-President Dick Cheney. In such a situation it is not impossible to contemplate scenarios of the ICC starting investigations of high level U.S. officials that could appear to have been politically motivated, even though most likely there was no scintilla of such motivation. The most recent indication is that it is the U.S. Attorney General, Eric Holder, who may start such investigations despite any reluctance from the White House, which indicates that it is highly unlikely that the ICC would meet the complementarity threshold test in a situation involving high level officials.[35]

Given the stirring words of President Obama regarding the fight against impunity in his landmark speech in Accra, Ghana, such possible scenarios should not be an impenetrable barrier to the U.S. acceding to the Rome Statute, especially given the President's interest in combating impunity in the African Continent. Comfort in this possible change of heart by the U.S. towards the ICC is also coming from the appointment of Susan Rice as U.S. Ambassador to the U.N., who in her first appearance before the U.N. Security Council on January 29, 2009, sated that the Court 'looks to become an important and credible instrument for trying to hold accountable the senior leadership responsible for atrocities committed in the Congo, Uganda and Darfur'.[36]

Perhaps there are two other main reasons for the reticence of the U.S. to join the ICC under the Obama Administration which must be tackled and resolved. First, there is a view enunciated by leading U.S. international relations experts that American is more comfortable with being the lead nation in establishing international rules than becoming the subject of them.[37]

Even Harold Koh, confirmed in July of 2009 as Legal Counsel for the U.S. State Department and recognized internationally as the U.S. jurist most supportive of multilateralism, has described the possible ratification of the Rome Statute by the U.S. as 'complicated'. In a confirmation hearing before the U.S. Congress, Koh added that the U.S. could not reengage without fully protecting American interests.[38]

If there is too long a delay in examining how to fully protect American interests before attempting ratification of the Rome Statue, David Scheffer, the former U.S. war crimes Ambassador who was also instrumental in developing the Rome Statute, warns that the country will lose its leverage over the development of international criminal law in which all its major allies are actively participating as States Parties to the ICC.[39]

There is a more worrisome second reason for possible U.S. reticence in actively supporting and joining the ranks of States Parties to the Rome Statute. It involves the emerging policy of the Obama Administration towards Sudan and the regime of the indicted President Omar al-Bashir. Critics have suggested that the U.S. may be moving to a friendly relationship with the Khartoum regime as the main method of achieving a peaceful settlement in Darfur, which could be at the expense of supporting the arrest warrants against the President.

The Obama Administration's Special Envoy to Sudan, Scott Gration, is quoted as stating in a meeting on April 2, 2009 with the Sudanese government that '[t]he United States and Sudan want to be partners and so we are looking for opportunities to build a stronger bilateral relationship. I come here with my hands open and it will be up to the Sudanese government to determine how they want to continue with that relationship'.[40]

This desire for a 'friendly' relationship may be the prize that the U.S. is willing to pay for not fully engaging with the ICC, not only as regards the arrest warrants for al-Bashir and the two other indicted persons, but also in general support for the Court. This would be contrary to the strong opposition that Obama enunciated against the Khartoum government as a U.S. Senator and as a candidate for the Presidency.[41]

The influential chair of the U.S. Senate's Foreign Relations Committee, John Kerry, has suggested that Sudan could even be removed from the list of countries that support terrorism and lifting economic sanctions contingent on developments.[42] Those developments were unlikely to include an insistence on enforcing the arrest warrants against any of the Sudanese officials. The priority of the former George W. Bush Administration on developing a strong partnership with Sudan on counterterrorism at the expense of ignoring the ICC's arrest warrants may well be continuing with the Obama Administration under the leadership of Special Envoy Scott Gration.[43] There may well be a heavy price to pay for such a prioritization. The special relationship with the architects of the Darfur slaughter has included, both in the U.S. and Sudan, business and entertainment meetings between the CIA and Salah Gosh, the brutal Sudanese intelligence chief who has been instrumental in the commission of the serious crimes in Darfur.[44] The price for such appeasement is that sustainable peace for all of Sudan's peoples may well be sacrificed. As discussed throughout this text, there can be no sustainable peace without justice.

4. DOES THE COURT NEED A NEW FORM OF ENFORCEMENT MECHANISM FOR ITS DECISIONS TO GUARANTEE ITS CREDIBILITY INTO THE FUTURE? THE ROLE OF THE INTERNATIONAL MONETARY FUND AND EXTERNAL CREDITORS

In national criminal justice systems the courts rely on the police and security forces of the country for the enforcement of their decisions. The ICC is deeply disadvantaged by not having such forces to enforce its decisions, including the implementation of the arrest warrants handed down by the

Court. In the absence of such enforcement agencies is there a substitute for applying pressure to countries to respect and implement the decisions of the Court?

It is suggested that there could well be such a new form of enforcement mechanism that is situated in the world of global financial institutions and the power of the purse to bring accountability to those who are acting with impunity. In this regard, the case study that could be an example is Sudan and the critical need for the arrest warrants issued by the ICC to be implemented for the future credibility of the Court.

The conflict that had engulfed the south of Sudan in civil war before the fragile Comprehensive Peace Agreement (CPA) and that is threatening the survival of much of the population in Darfur is foundationally about a battle for power, resources and money across this tragic land. Associated with this economic reality is the existence of a government in Khartoum that does not seem genuinely interested in real peace negotiations and has demonstrated a xenophobic ideology towards the African peoples of Sudan. I have argued in all the chapters in this book that there is little hope that there can be a sustainable peace without accountability for the mass atrocities committed in conflict zones around the world, certainly in the south of Sudan and presently in Darfur. There has been a failure to focus on what could be the most powerful lever against the Khartoum government, namely to make the burgeoning debt of Sudan a lever for accountability for the most serious crimes known to humanity.

Sudan's massive and unsustainable external debt could be an important lever to bring Sudan back into the fold of nations that respect the global rule of law, but to make this happen will require exceptional effort from the international financial community in particular. The external debt level stands at $30.4 billion (U.S.) at the end of 2008, of which a substantial majority is in arrears.[45]

This is one of the highest *per capita* debts in the world, and the World Bank has confirmed that the country is in debt distress.[46] The debt is owed to commercial and bilateral creditors of the Paris Club and Arab creditors, as well as multilateral and regional banks and development agencies. There is also a huge Chinese dimension to the external debt. In 2004, the largest external debt payments at the height of the atrocities in Darfur were to China ($102 million) to repay loans for servicing oil refinery construction. China and India are also becoming long term creditors to the NCP government, with India giving $392 million (U.S.) in non-concessional loans and China giving $182 million (U.S.). There are also reports that over the last decade the Export-Import Bank of China has given more than $1 billion (U.S.) in concessional loans to Sudan to assist with the building of oil and other infrastructure which is crucial to the sustainability of the oil exports to China. China has thus become Sudan's biggest economic partner, accounting for 75 percent of its exports and a large part of its imports, much of it in the form of military equipment.[47]

The US Defense Department published online in May a report (but subsequently removed it) entitled 'Military Power of the People's Republic of China 2009'. The report concluded that Sudan is the second leading military client of China and that it received a significant portion of the nearly $7 billion worth of Chinese defence exports from 2003 through 2005, the peak years of the conflict in Darfur. The report also identified that the Chinese arms sales contracts were closely linked to the concession contracts given by the Khartoum government to the Chinese oil companies and the support the al-Bashir government enjoys in the international arena.

The Khartoum government is well aware that the delays in dealing with the external debt arrears problem are an obstacle to getting critical concessional external financing. Debt forgiveness could, in effect, be vital to the survival of the al-Bashir regime. Critical to Sudan dealing with the arrears of its external debt is its eligibility for the Heavily Indebted Poor Countries Initiative (HIPC) of the International Monetary Fund (IMF) and the World Bank. The HIPC involves coordinated action by the multilateral and regional financial institutions and governments to reduce the external debt of the selected countries. Debt reduction relief under the HIPC program has been given to some twenty-seven countries in Africa.

Sudan is listed as a 'pre-decision point' country that may be eligible for such critical assistance from the HIPC program. The normalization of relationships with international creditors and debt relief under the HIPC initiative could bring about economic stability and therefore greater political longevity to the government of President al-Bashir, if there are large injections of cash from the international community to the multilateral agencies for the benefit of Sudan, once the arrears are dealt with. The past record of the NCP, the governing party of the al-Bashir regime, demonstrates that it has used all its resources, including those from external sources, to keep power by permitting the fire sale of state and private assets by its supporters and buying out its opponents in a similar fashion. This will be explained in greater detail below.

International financial institutions, their member governments and other external creditors could use the external debt of the Khartoum regime as a massive 'financial carrot' strategy to exert effective pressure on the Khartoum government to live up to its legal obligations to hand over some or all of the individuals under arrest warrants from the ICC. Far from this happening, there seems to be an almost sympathetic attitude to the masterminds of the most serious international crimes in the Sudanese government.

4.1 The Analysis by the IMF of the Macroeconomic Record of the al-Bashir Regime

In the 2003 to 2004 period, at the height of the massacres by the Khartoum government and its Janjaweed proxies in Darfur, the Staff Monitored Program (SMP) of the IMF, while describing the important steps towards the implementation of the Comprehensive Peace Agreement (CPA) in the south of Sudan, seemed to follow the press releases of the Khartoum government regarding what was actually occurring in Darfur:[48]

> The government and the Sudan People's Liberation Army (SPLA) signed on May 26, 2004 agreements on the outstanding issues regarding the status of the capital and three areas bordering the south and the sharing of political power at the national level. Agreements on security and resource-sharing were signed earlier in September 2003 and January 2004, respectively. In the next few weeks, the parties will consolidate all the agreements into a single peace agreement and finalize the implementation modalities. Hostilities broke out in Darfur in western Sudan in 2003 because of tribal clashes and local insurrection. A ceasefire has recently been negotiated through Chad's intermediation, but the situation remains grave.

In this 2003–2004 period of the SMP review, Sudanese alleged international crimes could hardly be viewed as 'tribal clashes and local insurrection'. The characterization seemed to smack of surprising blindness regarding the primary role, in the Darfur carnage, of the Khartoum government, the economic and structural management of which the IMF was extolling. The IMF and Sudan's creditors also seemed to be ignoring that the oil revenues arising out of the macroeconomic success of the Khartoum government were partly being invested in military equipment from Russia and China that would be killing tens of thousands of innocent civilians in Darfur.

Since the start of the new millennium in 2000, Sudan has been quietly engaging with the international financial institutions to normalize relations, without having its international creditors and monitors, including the IMF, demand that it stop its actions amounting to serious international crimes in Darfur and continue the pressure on the Khartoum government to live up to its obligations under the CPA.

In 2002, Sudan began to normalize relations with the IMF, the World Bank, the OPEC Fund, the African Development Bank and the Arab Fund for Economic and Social Development. Sadly, despite its actions in the South and in Darfur, in recognition of its progress in certain structural reforms, the IMF restored Sudan's voting and related rights. Sudan continues to get high praise for its economic performance from the IMF. In the 2007–2008 SMP review of Sudan, the IMF report seemed to be more concerned about the cost of the peace agreements than the past or the ongoing international crimes in Darfur:[49]

> Sudan's economic outlook is favorable, but will hinge on the authorities' ability to correct past slippages, reestablish fiscal credibility, and restore the safety and soundness of the financial system. This will not be an easy task given the heavy commitments imposed by various peace agreements and an uncertain regional environment. The rise in world food prices poses a particular challenge to containing inflation, requiring cautious monetary and fiscal policy implementation.

In September of 2008, the staff of the IMF again reported that '[t]he third Sudan Consortium held in Oslo in May 2008 recognized that important commitments were met over the past year of CPA implementation, but the overall progress has been below expectations'. In keeping with the studied understatements of the IMF regarding Sudan, the report went on to state that

> The Darfur issue is far from resolved, despite the advent of the U.N.–African Union Mission in Darfur which took over the peacekeeping mission in early January 2008. After troops from the north and south clashed in the oil rich area of Abyei, relations between the two sides have improved following a June 2008 agreement to allow for international arbitration regarding the Abyei region. However, the charges formulated by the prosecutor to the International Criminal Court generated further tensions in July 2008. Under the CPA, local, legislative, and presidential elections are mandated to take place in 2009, followed by a referendum in Southern Sudan in 2011 to decide on unity or secession.[50]

The national elections have been delayed until February 2010 and are almost certain to be delayed by Khartoum, as some argue will likely be the case with the 2011 referendum.

This most recent analysis of the macroeconomic situation in Sudan seems to place more emphasis on arrears clearance than the past and ongoing international crimes in Darfur in deciding whether to give the ultimate economic gift to the indicted President of Sudan: admission to the HIPC category. Also seemingly ignored are credible reports that a major part of the oil revenues – some assert as high as 70 percent[51] – which could go to debt clearance ends up supporting and arming the Sudanese military and their Janjaweed allies in Darfur and elsewhere.

Nowhere in the analysis of the IMF is the understanding that the government that it has been praising for its economic and structural reforms has also brought the country to the point of the world's most serious humanitarian crisis and the brink of a break up first in the South, through well documented evidence of the undermining of the CPA, and then in Darfur, and even further afield in Chad and Uganda through the support given to the actions of the Lord's Resistance Army led by Joseph Kony, also under an arrest warrant from the ICC.

Nowhere in any of the IMF's analysis of Sudan is the discussion of how to use its power and influence to pressure the government to stop its actions and those of its proxies on the killing fields of Darfur. Instead, the IMF seems ready to consider the Khartoum government for the most generous debt relief initiative in the world, the HPIC, with the blessing of not only the Arab allies of Sudan, but the most powerful western governments that hold the reins of power in the IMF and other international financial institutions.

4.2 Using the Lever of Assistance with the External Sudanese Debt as a Carrot to Enforce the Global Rule of Law in Sudan

What should be advocated by those who seek a new form of enforcement of ICC decisions is not the imposition of any new sanctions on Sudan, but the offer of encouragement to those who want to bring Sudan into the community of nations that are willing to adhere to the rule of law and universally recognized human rights. The encouragement will be the promise of a new financial, political and social relationship between Sudan and its major external creditors and the international financial institutions that goes beyond anything that China or some of Sudan's regional allies can provide.

New forms of sanctions should not be encouraged as they would enhance what some commentators have termed the ongoing criminalization of Sudan's economy. What should be proposed is that the IMF and all external creditors put the fact of the indictments against the President and two other individuals on the table in any prospect of assisting with the external debt of Sudan. Such a strategy would use the enforcement potential of the absolutely critical financial carrots that Sudan needs as levers in the fight against impunity in Darfur and potentially other parts of the country as well as continuing the pressure for the Khartoum government to live up to its obligations under the CPA. This could also set a major precedent for other countries in similar situations.

The international community should pay attention to regional experts who claim that the understandable reaction that any form of financial pressure against Sudan will only hurt the poor does not really apply to the political economy of Sudan.

One regional commentator, Abd al-Wahab Abdalla, describes the

Sudanese economy in the following terms: '[d]ominated by a scramble for rents, and particularly those derived from the nexus of sovereign rents, forcible asset transfer, and the mining of natural resources, the Sudanese state has come to resemble a vortex sucking the life out of an eviscerated peasantry to generate hyper-profits and the dictatorship of a security establishment'.[52]

Another longstanding regional scholar, Dr. Fatima Babiker Mahmoud, describes how the economy was forced out of the hands of the formerly dominant mercantile capitalists from the riverain classes under successive colonial regimes.[53] The wealth of this mostly sectarian class was based on the rapid dispossession and pauperization of the agrarian smallholding class, followed by massive internal capital and human migration to the metropolis that started the process of hyper-urbanization. This grossly inequitable economic structure laid the ground for the rise of the National Islamic Front (NIF) which transformed into the present day governing National Congress Party (NCP), as discussed in Chapter 2.

What triggered the forced change of control of the economy from the mercantile capitalists was the huge foreign exchange flows by Islamic financial institutions and Diasporas remittances from the Gulf States following the 1970s oil boom. This led to the rise in power of the Muslim Brothers, who saw the opportunity to take the reins of the economy and indeed political power from the sectarian mercantilist class.[54]

Ominously for the people of Darfur, Abd al-Wahab Abdalla goes on to say that one of the main strategies of this new coalition was '[u]nder the pretext of a state of emergency, the militarization of capitalism decriminalized asset-stripping at the point of a gun'.[55]

What much of the IMF analysis fails to comprehend is that this coalition led to the bankruptcy of the state, including its systemic default to the international financial institutions and the external creditors.

When Sudan was listed as a terror supporting state by the United States while playing host to Osama Bin Laden, the stick of new economic sanctions had the counterproductive effect of bolstering the rent-seeking of the governing coalition through informal Islamic financial networks and markets and increased the power of the security apparatus.[56] Meanwhile the external bankruptcy of the state kept increasing, as evidenced by the rising unsustainable external debt of the country.

The influence of the Chinese investment in the oil sector has, in my view, only greatly enhanced this state led rent-seeking. Indeed the seeds of the destruction of this coalition may well be the competition from within their own ranks for what Abd al-Wahab Abdalla calls hyper-accumulation of assets and associated state power. This may explain the attempt to overthrow al-Bashir by Hassan al-Turabi who brought al-Bashir to power.

With al-Bashir successfully fending off the challenge, some of the former members of the coalition are dispersing across Sudan, some, including al-Turabi, forming opposition to al-Bashir even within Darfur.

Despite this oil sector revenue strengthening of the al-Bashir coalition that has not lessened significantly the social costs of dispossession and pauperization of large parts of the Sudanese population, the international community and the associated financial institutions have been willing to bail out the self-induced massive social dislocations and hyper-urbanization. In those urban centers, while some supporters of the present regime like de Waal observe 'social peace', others like Abd al-Wahab Abdalla see dangerous social and economic stratification that is based on a racialized hierarchy where the greatest prospects for integration and employment are limited to those linked to the ruling elites and coalition partners.

The al-Bashir governing coalition can buy time with the help of the foreign investment and rents in and from the oil sector, but the moment of truth will come for him, and it may be only a matter of time before a faction, perhaps even within the present ruling elites, realizes the instability of the present economic and power structure cannot continue. In this situation, bringing al-Bashir, Harun and Kushayb to the ICC as a global refusal to accept impunity could be regarded by more moderate elements of the ruling Sudanese elites as a potential catalyst for regaining the financial, social and economic stability that the Sudanese people so desperately need. Given the analysis above of the present Sudanese economy, what is desperately needed in Sudan is the emergence of a new governing elite which governs in the interests of all sectors of the Sudanese population.

4.3   The Important Role that the IMF and External Creditors could Play in the Fight against Impunity in Sudan

There have been sounds of silence from the most powerful governments and institutions of the world to the contempt shown by the Khartoum government to the global rule of law as interpreted by the ICC and backed by the U.N. Security Council in the case of the arrest warrants of Ahmad Harun, Ali Kushayb and President al-Bashir. This is now further exacerbated by the decision by the Arab League, and the African Union and the Organization of Islamic States to urge their members, even those which are States Parties to the Rome Statute, not to assist in the enforcement of the ICC arrest warrant against President al-Bashir. Recently, the indicted President has been testing how effective this support is by traveling to states that are not States Parties, like Libya, Egypt, Ethiopia and most recently Zimbabwe.

In this context, it is worth examining the wording of the U.N. Security Council Resolution 1593 (2005).[57] With this resolution, the Council, acting under its Chapter VII powers, when it considers there was a threat to international peace and security, decided to refer the situation in Darfur to the Chief Prosecutor of the ICC. In particular it is worth examining the extent of the imposition of legal obligations on both Sudan and member states of the Rome Statute. The main provision of Resolution 1593 that is relevant in this regard is paragraph 2 of the Resolution which states that the Security Council

> Decides that the Government of Sudan and all other parties to the conflict in Darfur shall cooperate fully with and provide any necessary assistance to the Court and the Prosecutor pursuant to this resolution and, *while recognizing that States not party to the Rome Statute have no obligation under the Statute, urges all States and concerned regional and other international organizations to cooperate fully.* (emphasis added)

Resolution 1593 (2005) of the U.N. Security Council raises interesting legal questions about whether its wording imposes legal obligations on member states and international organizations to which they belong. It seems clear from the wording of the Resolution, paragraph 2 in particular, that the Security Council imposed no obligations *under the Rome statute* for non-states parties. It does not exclude obligations on such non-states parties arising out of other international legal obligations, such as obligations imposed under the *ius cogens* rules of international law. Such rules include rules concerning the prevention and punishment of genocide and torture.[58]

This may not have been pointed out to states such as Ethiopia which may have interpreted Resolution 1593 as totally exonerating them from any duties related to the alleged international crimes in Darfur. It should also be noted that countries like Ethiopia are highly dependent on foreign aid and financial debt relief from countries that are states parties to the Rome Statute.

Turning to the obligations of the international financial institutions (IFIs), the IMF, as one of the Bretton Woods institutions created after the Second World War, claims that it is independent from the U.N. and cannot be regarded as a U.N. agency. It also claims that by its constituting document, the Articles of Agreement, the IMF cannot get involved in political matters as opposed to its macroeconomic oversight functions. This logic implies that such macroeconomic functions are devoid of any political functions, which, from the very reports of the IMF described above, clearly show that the domestic political and legal situation of countries are critical to the macroeconomic performance of the country.

It is also highly questionable whether specialized multilateral institutions like the IMF, the World Bank and the World Trade Organization can legitimately claim that they have a self-contained field of international law contained in their constitutive documents and do not have to adhere to the rules set down by the general international public order laid down since the end of the Second World War that include the U.N. Charter and the mandatory rules contained therein, such as adherence to binding resolutions of the U.N. Security Council that expressly do apply to them.

IFIs are created under international law rules, and so are part of the international legal order, including any obligations under *ius cogens* rules. This has been confirmed by the International Court of Justice (ICJ) in the advisory opinions in the *Reparations* case[59] and the *WHO/Egypt* case.[60] In the latter decision, the ICJ made the following ruling:

> International organizations are subjects of international law and, as such are bound by any obligations incumbent upon them under general rules of international law, under their constitutions or under international agreements to which they are parties.[61]

Thomas Buergenthal, the eminent jurist who was both President of the Inter-American Human Rights Court and presently a judge of the ICJ, has confirmed in his writings that the World Bank is bound by its obligations under the U.N. Charter and other human rights treaties.[62] An accepted principle, even by the most international organizations, is that a violation of an international law principle which the body is bound to follow can result in international responsibility and give rise to the obligation to provide reparations.

However, there could well be situations in which an IFI may claim that it has violated no principle of international law as it has been following only its self-contained body of international law under the Articles of Agreement. In this context, the International Law Association has asserted that the determination of whether there has been an international wrongful act by the organization should be done by applying the general rules of international law. How an international organization determines the legality of its own actions under its internal legal order cannot be determinative of the outcome.[63]

The response of the IFIs to this legal position has traditionally been that they can only operate under the mandate of their constitutive documents. In the case of both the IMF and the World Bank, their constitutive documents are contained in the Articles of Agreement from both institutions have expressly excluded political considerations including, in the view of many officials, the arena of human rights. What is ignored by this position is that in the evolution of the work of the IFIs, especially the World Bank, the mandate has been interpreted to include considerations of at least economic rights such as poverty alleviation, health, education and good governance.

What seem to have been interpreted as being excluded from the IFIs Articles of Agreement are civil and political rights. The confirmation by substantially the entire world's nations at the 1993 Vienna World Conference on Human Rights that civil and political rights and other rights are indivisible makes the exclusion unjustifiable.[64]

However, no IFI constitutive document, including that of the IMF, has expressly excluded rights that underlie the fight against impunity for the most serious international crimes, such as the basic right to life and security of the person.

Indeed, if there were to be such a prohibition in the IFIs Articles of Agreement, it could well be regarded as in violation of international human rights law, and in particular the body of rules comprising *ius cogens*. There could well be issues of state responsibility for member states of the IFIs if there were to be such an express exclusion of considerations of fundamental human rights that underpin the fight against impunity for the most serious of international crimes.

The European Bank for Reconstruction and Development in the preamble to its constitutive document stated the commitment to fundamental principles of multiparty democracy, the rule of law, respect for human rights and market economics. This could be taken as demonstrable proof that human rights are not incompatible with the main financial objectives of the IFIs, and indeed may be central to achieving the same goals.

The World Bank, or at least one of its former Legal Counsel, Roberto Danino, had come round to this view when, in a legal opinion, he stated that '. . . there are instances in which the Bank *may* take human rights into account and others in which it *should*. Indeed, there are some activities in which the Bank cannot *properly* undertake without considering human rights.'[65]

As regards the state responsibility of states which are the influential decision makers at the highest levels of the IFIs, there is an interesting legal argument to be made regarding the impact of decisions on human rights in any given situation. It could be cogently argued that such state responsibility is triggered when there is an absence of or virtual blindness to the necessity of mechanisms to protect fundamental human rights in the operations of the IFIs. Directors from the Group of Seven (G7) control more than 60 percent of votes at the Bank and Fund, while the U.S. Director of the IMF acting in concert with the U.S. Administration has veto power over any extraordinary vote that requires a supermajority vote of 60 percent or more. The power of the G7 countries comes from their respective quotas in the IMF based on the ability to provide financial resources to the Fund and its potential vulnerability to balance-of-payments challenges. The quota thereby not only governs how much the member can draw on the IMF resources, but also the member's voting power in the Fund's two governing bodies, the Board of Governors and the all powerful Executive Board.

The U.S. has nearly 17 percent of the voting power of the executive directors, enough to veto any change in the size of the Board and other important decisions, including changes to the quotas and amendments of the Articles of Agreement. Other than the G7 countries only Saudi Arabia, China and Russia have individual membership, while the rest of the 177 member countries are grouped into sixteen multi-country constituencies, each of which has an executive director who casts the votes of all countries in the constituency. It is unlikely that the U.S. would ever agree to change its veto power on the Executive Board, given the fact that a supermajority of 85 percent is needed to change quotas or amend the Articles of Agreement.

Therefore, the main countries that profess to champion universally accepted human rights and the fight against impunity have overwhelming control over one of the most important levers in the promotion of global justice and accountability. In this regard, it is instructive to note how a former U.S. Administration defended its decision before the U.S. Congress to back a $40 billion IMF loan and its own $3 billion emergency back up loan to Indonesia under the repressive regime of President Suharto during the Asian financial crisis. Two Treasury Department officials (which included in a former role the present Treasury Secretary under the Obama Administration, Timothy Geithner) made, inter alia, the following arguments: first, that among the pantheon of human rights violators the government of President Suharto did not rank among the worst of the worst; second, it had blocked the IMF from considering loans to Iran and Sudan and held up loans for Croatia while it was harboring war criminals.[66]

In the present situation in Sudan, the U.N. itself has asserted that Darfur represents the worst of the worst global humanitarian crises caused by the al-Bashir regime and that regime is harboring three alleged war criminals that include the President himself! The European Court of Human Rights has ruled that in situations regarding the responsibility of states for the acts of international organizations, under the doctrine of 'equivalence' the Court will examine whether there are adequate substantive guarantees for human rights protections offered and mechanisms controlling their observance that are equivalent to those which the European Convention of Human Rights provides, although there is a presumption of legality.[67]

It could be argued in a similar fashion that the states which control the decision making of the IMF have a similar state responsibility to ensure that it has adequate and effective mechanisms for the protection of human rights in dealing with regimes such as those of the al-Bashir government. Given that the majority of the key decision makers at the IMF are States Parties to the Rome Statute of the ICC, perhaps the standards in that treaty should be the guide as to what those mechanisms should be. It could also be argued that the IFIs cannot *properly* undertake their role in dealing with the macroeconomic situation of Sudan without considering the gross violations of human rights and the ICC arrest warrants. Both state and non-states parties *and* international financial institutions which are external creditors of the present Sudanese government are fully able to use the provisions of Resolution 1593 to urge the moderate elements in the Sudanese government to cooperate with the ICC as a precondition to assistance with the external debt of Sudan.

4.4 Who has the Power to Create the New Economic Enforcement Mechanisms for the ICC?

For the legal reasons outlined above, there is no doubt that the states which are members of and contributors to the IMF and the World Bank are bound by Security Council resolutions and relevant international treaties that member countries have signed and ratified. This is especially relevant to the external creditor nations and the influential members of the IMF that have signed and ratified the Rome Statute of the ICC.

Both the financial institutions and the States Parties which are key members of the IMF have a positive duty to promote the objectives of the Rome Statute, which include bringing pressure to bear on the Sudanese government to cooperate with the ICC. A source of the positive duty of member states of the ICC to bring pressure to bear to ensure serious crimes do not go unpunished is the ICC Statute itself, and several provisions that urge the full cooperation of member states, such as Article 86 which mandates a general duty to cooperate.[68]

In this regard, it is also instructive to note that while the U.S. has the greatest decision making power in the IMF, it could be argued that the power of the E.U., along with Australia, Canada and Japan together, is as great, if not even greater, given that three of the most powerful Executive Directors on the governing Executive Board are appointed by individual EU countries along with Japan, all of which are also States Parties to the ICC. In addition, four of the multi-country constituencies on the Executive Board are led by E.U. countries, namely the Netherlands, Italy, Belgium and Finland, which are also States Parties to the ICC along with Australia and Canada, which are also two of the strongest supporters of the ICC.

The IMF, the World Bank and the key countries that are States Parties that are dominant in those institutions can legitimately insist the Sudanese officials subject to the ICC's arrest warrants must be handed over to the Court if there is to be any possibility of assisting with the external debt of Sudan, and definitely if there is any remote chance of Sudan acceding to the immensely treasured HIPC status that could potentially wipe out the entire external debt. This could well be the most powerful lever that is available to deliver these officials to the Court.

The very existence of the government of President al-Bashir depends on his having the financial ability to keep all his actual and potential enemies satisfied and not engaged in unseating his fragile governing coalition. The IMF, the World Bank and their controlling member governments therefore have a powerful lever they can use to advance at least one part of the fight against impunity that has wrought havoc on the people of Sudan. The International Financial Institutions and the external creditors should be helping the people living under and victims of the al-Bashir regime, not those who have perpetrated the worst crimes known to humanity upon them. This is an area where the political will of the U.S., the members of the European Union and Japan can, using their acknowledged financial power, effect the desired change. The world will watch as to whether they choose to continue the macroeconomic dance of blindness with Khartoum or show some element of moral courage and help bring the indicted Sudanese officials to justice in The Hague. The hundreds of thousands of innocents who have lost their lives in Darfur and the 2.7 million who still live in fear and desperation in the refugee camps in Darfur and Chad demand no less.

5.   CONCLUSION

Europe witnessed the first major attempt to entrench certain rights of elite groups together with an emerging legal and judicial system with the establishment of the Magna Carta in 1215. Ancient Middle Eastern, Asian and other cultures also saw early in human civilization similar attempts to impose duties upon rulers and offer limits on how subjects can be treated under the law and long standing cultural and religious traditions.[69] Since then, history has revealed a struggle by humanity and societies around the world to progressively entrench fundamental rights for all members of society with more robust and more egalitarian guarantees of rights and accompanied by judicial systems that can combat the impunity of those who violate such rights.

It is often overlooked that most of these advances in the constitutionalization of rights occurred during times of social, economic or political upheaval. It was certainly true of the Magna Carta when the barons and other elites, faced with crippling demands for taxation, and King John, faced with a potential civil war, agreed to the entrenchment of enforceable rights. Parallels could easily be made with similar societal upheavals that led to the French Declaration of the Rights of Men and Citizens and the enactment of the U.S. Bill of Rights.

As the preceding chapters of this text have attempted to demonstrate, the ICC is the latest in this progression of history which reveals an unquenchable thirst by humanity to reconcile peace with justice. The Court is a product of the determination of civilized nations and human rights champions in global civil society that the 20th Century human rights horrors and the impunity of the perpetrators of those horrors that accompanied the social, economic and political upheavals of that century should not be repeated in the new Millennium.

But, it should never be forgotten that such historical progress cannot be speeded up. In fact, it can be agonizingly slow. The powerful legal regimes that protect human rights in Britain, Europe and the United States, along with many of the countries around the world that were the former colonies of these western nations, had their roots in what occurred in England in 1215. The evolution of the legal systems and constitutional systems of these countries that are designed to protect the fundamental rights of individuals spanned 800 years. Those centuries have included periods that, many times over, have mocked the commitment to fight impunity and protect the entrenched rights. The most well known of these periods in the modern era encompassed the centuries of the slave trade and colonization and the human rights horrors of the 20th Century with its two World Wars and the Holocaust.

The establishment of the Rome Statute and the coming into being of the International Criminal Court on July 1, 2002 can be regarded as a global culmination of the first steps that one society took in England in 1215. However, modern global society, with the tools of rapid human progress and the weapons of rapid human destruction, cannot wait for 800 years. Global society must also not be too impatient to see the record of uncontestable successes for the first permanent global criminal court that has been in existence for only seven years at the time of writing this text. The proof that the Court is a vital instrument of reconciling peace with justice and is not an adversary of peace will only come with accurate historical reflection after the first trials have finished and their consequences are fully played out. This text has in particular attempted to show that it is the facts of each situation before the Court that must be factored into not only the after-the-trials reflection, but also when the first cases are in their very earliest stages and where arrest warrants have yet to be implemented.

This is especially important in the cases before the Court regarding the situation in Darfur and in Northern Uganda: hence the focus on these cases in this text. The final two chapters of this text have also attempted to demonstrate that it if it is left only to the Court to be the sole combatant against impunity for the most serious crimes, it will fail.

There are worrying signs that key co-combatants in the fight against impunity are retreating from the battlefield. These include not only recalcitrant regional organizations such as the African Union and the Arab League, but even the powerful States Parties to the ICC and the U.S. which are on the U.N. Security Council and doing little to come to the aid of the Court in getting the arrest warrants issued by the Court enforced, especially those against the Sudanese officials. The Office of the Prosecutor in its evolving prosecutorial strategy is seeking to stop the retreat from the battlefield against impunity and obtain greater cooperation from the international community, including all States Parties.

Such cooperation must include eliminating non-essential contacts with those subject to arrest warrants issued by the Court and in bilateral and multilateral meetings proactively expressing support for enforcement of Court decisions. This cooperation should also include collaborative efforts, even with non-states parties, in the planning and execution of arrest warrants. In addition all States Parties to the ICC should contribute to the marginalization of fugitives who are the subjects of arrest warrants from the Court.[70] The Prosecutor's Office will also attempt to strengthen ties to regional and multilateral organizations by developing focal points within the OTP for a range of organizations that include the U.N., the European Union, the African Union, the ASEAN group of Asian countries, the Organization of American States, the Commonwealth Secretariat and the global police organization, INTERPOL. There is hope that such organizations will reciprocate with similar focal points for the ICC within their structures which may ultimately lead to specific cooperation agreements with the ICC.[71]

In a similar fashion there is also hope that the Court, and in particular the Prosecutor, will continue maximizing its impact in the promotion of international justice by increasing interaction with a wide range of external non-state actors, including other judicial and police/security organizations, both national and international, affected communities, policy institutes, student networks, the media, NGOs, experts (including those skilled in financial investigations) and academics. To increase the knowledge of these external actors and also dispel misleading perceptions of the work of the Prosecutor and the Court, internal policies and practices in a range of areas including selection of cases, gravity of crimes, interests of justice, focused investigations and prosecutions, positive complementarity, sexual/

gender crimes and participation and protection of victims will be disseminated widely to these groups.[72]

However, as discussed in this chapter, there are still potentially very powerful potential co-combatants that seem deliberately unconnected to the global fight against impunity, like the international financial institutions.

The Prosecutor hopes in the three years beginning in 2009 that, while improving the quality of prosecutions, the ICC will complete three trials and start a new one, while also handling any appeals from the decisions of the Trial Chambers. The Prosecutor also hopes to continue with seven investigations and conduct up to four new ones in current or new situations, while being ready to start another investigation at any time.

The Prosecutor has also given notice that he will conduct up to ten new preliminary examinations in current or new situations while continuing to press for cooperation with all states and relevant actors to help in the execution of the existing arrest warrants issued by the Court. Some human rights NGOs such as Human Rights Watch have urged the Prosecutor to issue periodic reports on the results of preliminary examinations and public monitoring.[73] Such reports could reveal what *prima facie* evidence the examinations may have uncovered. These public reports could be an added incentive for nations under examination to take effective action to combat impunity, while allowing the Prosecutor to more concretely focus the preliminary examination.

Finally, the Prosecutor has also argued that contributing to the fights against impunity also means focusing on the prevention of future crimes. This must involve not only the ICC, but also all relevant actors in States Parties and the rest of the world. Prevention strategies for serious international crimes in conflicts must be taken up wherever educational and training activities take place, including schools, colleges, universities and government and military training centres. The Court can assist in these prevention and education centres but the main burdens must rest elsewhere.

What has become clear is that the ICC is at the leading edge of a transformative era of global justice and international relations with the establishment of the Rome Statute. In this transformative era there will have to be new global perspectives and frameworks to manage the relationship of international and national security to the imperatives of global justice and the fight against impunity. Those perspectives and frameworks are still being worked out, but this book has suggested that the cornerstone will be what has been termed in Chapter 4 'proactive international complementarity'. This cornerstone requires all relevant actors to shoulder the burden of combating impunity and preventing future serious international crimes.

After this work goes to press, in June of 2010, the first Review on the Rome Statute takes place in Kampala, Uganda. The Review conference is a special meeting of the States Parties to review and consider amendments to the Rome Statute and will also address the inclusion of a provision on the crime of aggression and a review of the transition provision in Article 124. However, there are a number of States Parties and civil society groups such as the Coalition on the International Criminal Court that have urged the Review Conference to engage in a substantial stocktaking that will focus on the successes and challenges for the Court and identify room for improvement. But, as this final chapter of the book has emphasized, it is also the States Parties and indeed the rest of the international community that must take stock of whether they also have done their part to ensure a successful future for the Court. This includes the role of the U.N. Security Council in ensuring the execution of the arrest warrants issued by the Court.

History may be slow, but history is a harsh judge against those who abysmally failed to do their assigned part to ensure the progress of humankind through the global fight against impunity for the most serious crimes that shock the conscience of all mankind.

NOTES

1. Roland Abeng, 'ICC doing the job of failed African judiciary' *The East African* (2 May 2009) located at the following URL: http://www.theeastafrican.co.ke/news/-/2558/593228/-/rgkv6jz/-/index.html.
2. African Union Commission, Restricted Circulation, 'Concept note for the meeting of African States Parties to the Rome Statute of the International Criminal Court (ICC)', MinICC/Legal/3.
3. *Ibid.* at 9–10.
4. *Ibid.*
5. *Ibid.*
6. *Ibid.* at 10–16.
7. See the site of the Institute at the following url: http://www.iss.co.za/index.php?link_id=5&slink_id=7843&link_type=12&slink_type=12&tmpl_id=3.
8. *Ibid.*
9. See the attempt by the A.U. to justify its actions in a press release, 'Decision on the meeting of African states parties to the Rome Statute of the International Criminal Court (ICC)' (14 July 2009) at the following url: http://www.africa-union.org/root/au/Conferences/2009/july/Press%20Release%20-%20ICC.doc.
10. *Ibid.*
11. Statement by Luis Moreno-Ocampo to the U.N. Security Council, 5 June 2008 pursuant to U.N. Security Council Resolution 1593 (2005). The full statement can be located at the following url: http://www.icc-cpi.int/NR/rdonlyres/A5534B60-BE19-49D4-8FC7-8DD7FC139984/277790/ICCOTPST20080605ENG.pdf.
12. *Prosecutor v. Omar Hassan Ahmad Al Bashir*, ICC-02/05-01/09-3, Decision on the Prosecution's Application for a Warrant of Arrest against Omar Hassan Ahmad Al Bashir (4 March 2009) (International Criminal Court, Office of the Prosecutor). The

full decision can be found at the following site of the ICC: http://www.icc-cpi.int/NR/exeres/4C445705-1300-4D94-9502-E42067474468.htm.

13. *Ibid.*
14. *Case Concerning the Arrest Warrant of 11 April 2000 (Democratic Republic of the Congo v. Belgium)* [2002] I.C.J. Rep. 3 at paras 53–54.
15. See *Democratic Republic of the Congo v Belgium* at para 61: 'an incumbent or former Minister for Foreign Affairs may be subject to criminal proceedings before certain international criminal courts, where they have jurisdiction. Examples include the International Criminal Tribunal for the former Yugoslavia, and the International Criminal Tribunal for Rwanda, established pursuant to Security Council resolutions under Chapter VII of the United Nations Charter, and the future International Criminal Court created by the 1998 Rome Convention. The latter's Statute expressly provides, in Article 27, paragraph 2, that "[i]mmunities or special procedural rules which may attach to the official capacity of a person, whether under national or international law, shall not bar the Court from exercising its jurisdiction over such a person".'
16. The analysis in this area has been greatly helped by an outstanding unpublished paper by Rod Rastan, Legal Advisor to the ICC, entitled 'The Emerging Jurisprudence of the International Criminal Court – Legal Issues arising from the First Case-law' Paper prepared for Symposium on the New Development of International Criminal Law, 25–26 April 2009, Beijing China.
17. *Ibid.*; *see* art.7 Nuremberg Charter; art.6 Tokyo Charter; art.7(2); *Affirmation of the Principles of International Law recognized by the Charter of the Nurnberg Tribunal*, General Assembly Resolution (11 December 1946) A/RES/95(I).
18. Rastan, *supra* note 16. Rastan argues that this interpretation is in line with the *travaux préparatoires* of consultations on the Rules of Procedure and Evidence at a 1999 Preparatory Commission session between States Parties on the relationship between Article 27 and Article 98(1); see also Bruce Broomhall, *International Justice and the International Criminal Court: Between Sovereignty and the Rule of Law* (Oxford University Press, 2003) at 144; Robert Cryer, Darryl Robinson, Håkan Friman and Elizabeth Wilmshurst, eds., *An Introduction to International Criminal Law* (Cambridge University Press, 2007) at 441.
19. *Ibid.*
20. *Ibid.*
21. 'Israel/Gaza: Operation "Cast Lead": 22 days of death and destruction' *Amnesty International* (2 July 2009) Index Number: MDE 15/015/2009 The full report is available at the Amnesty website at the following url: http://www.amnesty.org/en/news-and-updates/report/impunity-war-crimes-gaza-southern-israel-recipe-further-civilian-suffering-20090702.
22. See 'Rain of Fire' *Human Rights Watch* (25 March 2009) available at the Human Rights Watch website at the following url: http://www.hrw.org/en/node/81726/section/2, which claimed the indiscriminate use of white phosphorus munitions against civilians in densely populated areas in Gaza could amount to a war crime. Subsequently HRW accused the Hamas militants also of war crimes for firing rockets at civilian targets in Israel: see the report entitled 'Gaza/Israel: Hamas Rocket Attacks on Civilians Unlawful' *Human Rights Watch* (6 August 2009) which can be found at the url: http://www.hrw.org/node/84925. See also the Human Rights Watch report on the 'White Flag Killings of 11 Palestinian Civilians' (13 August 2009) located at the following url: http://www.hrw.org/en/reports/2009/08/13/white-flag-deaths-0.
23. Report of the United Nations Fact Finding Mission on the Gaza Conflict, Human Rights in Palestine and other Occupied Arab Territories, A/HRC/12/48, 15 September 2009. The full report can be located at the following url: http://www2.ohchr.org/english/bodies/hrcouncil/specialsession/9/docs/UNFFMGC_Report.pdf.

The Goldstone Report has recommended that the Human Rights Council ask that the report should be brought to the U.N. Security Council by the U.N. Secretary

General seeking a Security Council resolution that Israel take all appropriate steps, within a period of three months, to launch appropriate investigations that are independent and in conformity with international standards. Failure to do so should lead to the U.N. Security Council referring the matter to the prosecutor of the ICC.

24. The Palestinian Declaration can be found at the website of the ICC at the following url: www.icc-cpi.int/NR/rdonlyres/74EEE201-0FED-4481-95D4C8071087102C/279777/20 090122PalestinianDeclaration2.pdf.

25. Montevideo Convention on the Rights and Duties of States, 1933, 165 I.N.T.S. 19. The treaty was ratified by 19 Latin American states and the U.S. Landmark analysis of this Convention which laid down some of the customary international law principles for the existence of sovereign states can be found in A. Cassese, *International Law*, 2nd ed. (Oxford University Press, 2005); James Crawford, *The Creation of States in International Law* (Clarendon Press, 1979).

26. For a discussion of some of these modern principles see David Raic, *Statehood and the Law of Self-Determination* (Kluwer Law International, 2002).

27. Memorandum submitted to the Prosecutor of the ICC by the following U.S. academics: Ruth Wedgewood, Marshall Breger, George P. Fletcher, Richard H. Steinberg, Paul B. Stephen III.

28. See John Quigley, 'The Palestinian Declaration to the International Criminal Court: The Statehood Issue' (2009) 35 *Rutgers Law Record*, The Legal Implications of Operation Cast Lead, The Internet Journal of Rutgers School of Law, Newark located at the following url: http://www.lawrecord.com/files/35-rutgers-l-rec-1.pdf.

29. As reported by Bloomberg.com reporter Indira A.R. Lakshmanan in an article entitled 'Obama War-Crime Verdict May Echo Bush Objection to Global Court' (5 May 2009) located at the following url: http://www.bloomberg.com/apps/news?pid=20601103&sid =axBVQVbQJIbM.

30. In *Hamdan v. Rumsfeld*, 548 U.S. 557 (2006) the U.S. Supreme Court held that the military commissions established by the Bush Administration to prosecute detainees at Guantanamo violated both the Uniform Code of Military Justice of the U.S. and the 1949 Geneva Conventions, specifically Common Article 3.

31. See 'US: Steps to end Torture Sets a New Course' *Human Rights Watch* (22 January 2009) located at the following url: http://www.hrw.org/en/news/2009/01/22/us-steps-end-torture-set-new-course.

32. See *Time Magazine* Report by B. Gosh and M. Scherer, 'Obama Still Opposed to Truth Commission' *Time Magazine* (21 May 2009). The full article can be located at the following url: http://www.time.com/time/nation/article/0,8599,1900035,00.html.

33. See B.S. Brown, 'Unilateralism, Multilateralism and the International Criminal Court' in Stewart Patrick & Shepard Forman (eds.) *Multilateralism and US Foreign Policy: Ambivalent* (Lynne Rienner, 2002) 323 at 331.

34. Lakshmanan, *supra* note 29.

35. See the Report by D. Klaidman, 'Independent's Day: Obama doesn't want to look back, but Attorney General Eric Holder may probe Bush-era torture anyway' *Newsweek* (11 July 2009). The full article is located at the following url: http://www.newsweek.com/id/206300.

36. Lakshmanan, *supra* note 29.

37. *Ibid*. In this article on Bloomberg.com, Stewart Patrick, Director of the International Institutions and global governance program at the Council of Foreign Relations is quoted as stating: 'There is a tension in U.S. foreign policy that's pretty longstanding: The U.S. is far more comfortable as the maker of international rules than as subject to them.'

38. Lakshmanan, *supra* note 29.

39. *Ibid*.

40. Quoted in the online Africa news portal Africa.com article by Marina Litivinsky, 'Sudan: Darfur Activists Deplore Closer Ties With Khartoum' *allAfrica.com* (1 May 2009) located at the following url: http://allafrica.com/stories/200905010435.html.

41. See the Enough Project interview of the two main Presidential Candidates, John McCain and Barack Obama, by John Norris, Executive Director of the Enough Action Fund; Jerry Fowler, President of the Save Darfur Coalition; and Mark Hanis, Executive Director, Genocide Intervention Network entitled 'McCain and Obama Speak out on Darfur and More – Summary.' The full interview is located at the following url: http://www.enoughproject.org/files/Obama_McCain_questionnaire.pdf (accessed 15 June 2009).
42. Litivinsky, *supra* note 40.
43. *Ibid.*
44. See the Sudan Tribune Report of 28 May 2009 entitled 'US Senators lay down markers for better relations with Sudan' located at the following url: http://www.sudantribune.com/spip.php?article31308.
45. CIA, The World Factbook, 2008, located at the following url: https://www.cia.gov/library/publications/the-world-factbook/geos/su.html#Econ (accessed 12 July 2009).
46. World Bank, 'Sudan: Joint Bank – Fund debt sustainability analysis' (August 2007).
47. For details of the critical role China plays in the economic and military spheres in Sudan see 'Investing in Tragedy, China's Money, Arms and Politics in Sudan' *Human Rights First* (March 2008), available at the following url: http://www.humanrightsfirst.info/pdf/080311-cah-investing-in-tragedy-report.pdf.
48. See the IMF website for report entitled 'Sudan: Report on the Final Review of the 2003 Staff-Monitored Program and the 2004 Staff-Monitored Program' (June 2005), IMF Country Report No. 05/187 located at the following url: http://www.imf.org/external/pubs/ft/scr/2005/cr05187.pdf.
49. See the IMF website for report entitled 'Sudan: First Review of Performance Under the 2007–08 Staff-Monitored Program' (June 2008), IMF Country Report No. 08/174 located at the following url: http://www.imf.org/external/pubs/ft/scr/2008/cr08174.pdf.
50. See report prepared by the Staffs of IDA and IMF, Danny Leipziger and Mark Allen, 'Heavily Indebted Poor Countries (HIPC) Initiative and Multilateral Debt Relief Initiative (MDRI) – Status of Implementation' (12 September 2008).
51. *Human Rights First, supra* note 47 at ii of the Executive Summary.
52. See the first part of a three part article by Abd al-Wahab Abdalla entitled 'Sudan at the Crossroads' (9 June 2009) which can be found at the U.S. Social Science Research Council website at the following url: http://www.ssrc.org/blogs/darfur/2009/06/09/sudan-at-the-crossroads-1/.

   It should be noted that al-Wahab Abdalla is not a supporter of the ICC or its indictments against the Sudanese officials because he is convinced that other similar characters would replace him and, once they have the cover of an important international power, would continue the same actions as the al-Bashir regime. In the view of this author, it makes his own analysis even more credible as the thesis of this paper is that the pressures of international organizations like the IFIs and external creditors, are needed to ensure what al-Wahab Abdalla calls 'democratic sovereignty' is restored in Sudan for the benefit of all its peoples.
53. Fatima Babiker Mahmoud, *The Sudanese Bourgeoisie* (Zed Press, 1984).
54. Abd al-Wahab Abdalla, *supra* note 52.
55. *Ibid.*
56. I am using the definition of rent-seeking first suggested by economist Gordon Tullock as the situation where governing elites, organizations or even individuals use their power and resources to obtain an economic gain from others or an entire country without reciprocating any benefits back to society through wealth creation.
57. See the full text at the U.N. website at the following url: http://www.un.org/News/Press/docs/2005/sc8351.doc.htm.
58. For a detailed discussion of the scope of the *ius cogens* rules of international law and citations to other leading authorities see P. Malanczuk & M.B. Akehurst, *Äkehurst's Modern Introduction to International Law,* 7th ed. (Routledge, 1997) at 57–60.
59. Reparation for Injuries Suffered in the Service of the United Nations, Advisory

Opinion, [1949] I.C.J. Rep. 174. Confirmed by Certain Expenses of the United Nations, Advisory Opinion, [1962] I.C.J. Rep. 151.

60. Interpretation of the Agreement of 25 March 1951 between the WHO and Egypt, Advisory Opinion, [1980] I.C.J. Rep. 73 at 88.

61. *Ibid.* at 89–90.

62. Thomas Buergenthal, 'The World Bank and Human Rights' in E. Brown Weiss, A. Rigo Sureda & L. Boisson de Chazournes (eds), *The World Bank, International Financial Institutions and the Development of International Law* (1999).

63. 'Report of the Seventy-First Conference, Berlin', Final Report of the International Law Association Committee on Accountability of International Organizations, Aug. 16–21, 2004, 27.

64. See the Report of the Conference and the Vienna Declaration on Human Rights on the website of the U.N. High Commissioner for Human Rights at the following url: http://www.unhchr.ch/huridocda/huridoca.nsf/(Symbol)/A.CONF.157.24+(PART+I).En?OpenDocument.

65. Roberto Dañino, *Legal Opinion on Human Rights and the Work of the World Bank* (27 January 2006) at para. 18.

66. See David E. Sanger, 'IMF Loans to Rights Violators Are Attacked in Congress' *New York Times* (22 April 1998) also located at the *Times* website at the following url: http://www.nytimes.com/1998/04/22/world/imf-loans-to-rights-violators-are-attacked-in-congress.html.

67. *Bosphorus Airways v. Ireland* no. 45036/98, [2005] E.C.H.R. 440 at paras. 155–156.

68. Article 86 states: 'States Parties shall, in accordance with the provisions of the Statute, cooperate fully with the Court in its investigation and prosecution of crimes within the jurisdiction of the Court'. Other provisions of the Statute that also mandate full cooperation on all aspects of the ICC's mandate and operations include Article 93.

69. See M.R. Ishay, *The History of Human Rights, From Ancient Times to the Globalization Era* (University of California Press, 2008). The author details the civilizational evolution of the idea of rights attaching to individuals from the Hammurabi Codes in Mesopotamia, circa 1790 BC, to rights in the era of globalization. Some assert that the first declaration of human rights by a ruler was that of Cyrus, the King of Babylon, who in 539 BC after allowing the return of the Jews to Jerusalem ordered that he would allow no oppression of them or other peoples in his kingdom and would penalize those who disobeyed. See M. & M.B. Woods, *Seven Wonders of the Ancient Middle East* (Lerner Publishing Group, 2008) at 28. There are also many who argue that the first Bill of Rights was encompassed in the Edicts of Ashoka, the ruler of the Maurya Empire in Ancient India, who after a brutal conquest of Kalinga around 265 BC felt remorse and adopted Edicts around India that created an official regime of non-violence and protection of human rights based on the view that all belong to one human family and all are entitled to freedom, tolerance and equality. See N.A Nikam & R. McKeon. *Edicts of Asoka* (University of Chicago Press, 1958, reprinted 1978).

70. The Office of the Prosecutor, Prosecutorial Strategy, 2009–2012 obtained by the author.

71. *Ibid.*

72. *Ibid.*

73. Statement made by Ken Roth, Executive Director, Human Rights Watch, at the Consultative Conference on International Criminal Justice, September 9–11, 2009 at the U.N. Headquarters.

Index